THE METAPHYSIC

Aristotelian Society Series

Volume 1
COLIN MCGINN
Wittgenstein on Meaning:
An Interpretation and Evaluation

Volume 2
BARRY TAYLOR
Modes of Occurrence:
Verbs, Adverbs and Events

Volume 3
KIT FINE
Reasoning with Arbitrary Objects

Volume 4
CHRISTOPHER PEACOCKE
Thoughts:
An Essay on Content

Volume 5
DAVID E. COOPER
Metaphor

Volume 6
DAVID WIGGINS
Needs, Values, Truth:
Essays in the Philosophy of Value
Second Edition

Volume 7
JONATHAN WESTPHAL
Colour:
Some Philosophical Problems from
    Wittgenstein
Second Edition

Volume 8
ANTHONY SAVILE
Aesthetic Reconstructions:
The Seminal Writings of Lessing, Kant
    and Schiller

Volume 9
GRAEME FORBES
Languages of Possibility:
An Essay in Philosophical Logic

Volume 10
E. J. LOWE
Kinds of Being:
A Study of Individuation, Identity and
    the Logic of Sortal Terms

Volume 11
I. MCFETRIDGE
Logical Necessity★

Volume 12
JIM HOPKINS AND ANTHONY SAVILE (Editors)
Psychoanalysis, Mind, and Art:
Perspectives on Richard Wollheim

Volume 13
TIM MAUDLIN
Quantum Non-Locality and Relativity:
Metaphysical Intimations of Modern Physics

Volume 14
JOHN MARTIN FISCHER
The Metaphysics of Free Will:
An Essay on Control

Volume 15
JOHN BACON
Relations particularized

Aristotelian Society Monographs Committee:
Martin Davies (Monographs Editor); Thomas
Baldwin; Jennifer Hornsby; Mark Sainsbury;
Anthony Savile

★ This volume is not published by Blackwell.
Copies may be purchased by contacting:
    Majid Amini
    Aristotelian Society
    Birkbeck College
    Dept. of Philosophy
    Malet Street
    London, WC1E 7HX
    Tel: 0171–255 1724

John Martin Fischer

The Metaphysics of Free Will

An Essay on Control

Aristotelian Society Series

Volume 14

BLACKWELL
Oxford UK & Cambridge USA

First published 1994
First published in paperback 1995

Blackwell Publishers Inc.
238 Main Street
Cambridge, Massachusetts 02142
USA

Blackwell Publishers Ltd
108 Cowley Road
Oxford OX4 1JF, UK

Library of Congress Cataloging-in-Publication Data

Fischer, John Martin, 1952–
The metaphysics of free will: an essay on control / John Martin
Fischer.
p.   cm. — (Aristotelian Society series; v. 14)
Includes bibliographical references and index.
ISBN 1–55786–155–2 (hbk) — 1–55786–857–3 (pbk)
1. Free will and determinism.   2. Responsibility.   3. Agent
(Philosophy)   I. Title.   II. Series.
BJ1461.F49   1994   123'.5—dc20   93–51073   CIP

British Library Cataloguing in Publication Data

A CIP catalogue record for this book is available from the British Library.

Typeset in 10½ on 12½ pt Plantin
by Best-set Typesetter Ltd, Hong Kong
Printed in Great Britain by Hartnolls Ltd, Bodmin

This book is printed on acid-free paper

For Tina

"*Under the trees of England I meditated on this lost and perhaps mythical labyrinth. I imagined it untouched and perfect on the secret summit of some mountain; I imagined it drowned under rice paddies or beneath the sea; I imagined it infinite, made not only of eight-sided pavilions and of twisting paths but also of rivers, provinces and kingdoms. I thought of a maze of mazes, of a sinuous, ever growing maze which would take in both past and future and would somehow involve the stars.*"

Jorge Luis Borges, *The Garden of Forking Paths*

Contents

Acknowledgments

Some of the ideas in this book were developed when I was a graduate student at Cornell University. I was especially helped by Carl Ginet, Sydney Shoemaker, T. H. Irwin, and Robert Stalnaker. I am very grateful for their continued encouragement and philosophical help in the years since I left Cornell. At Yale University I had many extremely valuable discussions about the issues treated in this book with Harry Frankfurt, Phillip Bricker, and Anthony Brueckner.

Carl Ginet, Nelson Pike, Anthony Brueckner, and Tim O'Connor have read a preliminary manuscript (or parts of it). I am very grateful for their careful, detailed, generous, and incisive comments.

Paul Hoffman read various versions of the manuscript, offered many penetrating insights, and helped me immeasurably in the process of revision. His close reading of the manuscript, and our conversations about it, have resulted in many improvements.

Over the past seven years I have had the pleasure of working with Mark Ravizza. I have learned more than I can ever say from our countless conversations. He has been very kind in allowing me to borrow some of our joint work and present it as my own in this book. His suggestions about the manuscript have been invaluable.

Andy Coats provided conscientious and very helpful technical assistance.

The ideas presented in this book have evolved over the past decade. I have the temerity to include a bibliography of my published work on free will and moral responsibility. I thank the publishers for their permission to reprint parts of the entries prefixed by asterisks (pieces on which I rely heavily here): "Power Over the Past," *Pacific Philosophical Quarterly* 65 (1984), pp. 335–50; "Power Necessity," *Philosophical Topics* 14 (1986), pp. 77–91; "Responsiveness and Moral Responsibility," in Ferdinand Schoeman, ed., *Responsibility, Character, and the Emotions:*

New Essays on Moral Psychology (Cambridge: Cambridge University Press, 1987), pp. 81–106; and "When the Will is Free" (with Mark Ravizza), in James E. Tomberlin, ed., *Philosophical Perspectives VI: Ethics* (Atascadero, Ca.: Ridgeview Publishing Co., 1992), pp. 423–51.

The article cited on p. 21, "Lyle Menendez Admits Lies, Insists He Killed in Fear" by Alan Abrahamson, is copyright 1993, *Los Angeles Times*. Reprinted by permission.

Finally, I want to thank my family for (sort of) allowing me to write this book: Tina, Aja Marie, Ariel Marton, and the one on the way. I tried various times to write this book when I was single; but it was only in the context of the impossible demands of family life that I actually managed to finish it! They gave me just enough room to do this lonely thing, and the love to sustain me in my efforts.

Riverside, California
September, 1993

The "one on the way" turned out to be Zoe Sigrid.

Riverside, California
May, 1994

1

The Issues

Each murder was a fluke – at least that's what I told myself. I knew that I was a "good" person, that I tried to help people, and certainly I didn't want to hurt anybody . . . Even now, I know that I have done it and know that I could do it again, but I can't imagine myself actually doing it, or even wanting to do it . . .

For a long time I looked for excuses . . . But the end result was the same, each murder was a fluke. I made myself believe that there was an excuse and that it would never happen again. And the contradiction that it did happen again, and again, was ignored because it didn't fit in with my perception of myself.

I couldn't acknowledge the monster that was inside . . . Sometimes I feel that I am slipping away and I'm afraid of losing control. If you are in control you can handle anything but if you lose control you are nothing.[1]

Michael Ross (the "mild-mannered" Cornell
graduate who has been sentenced to death for
raping and murdering four Connecticut teenagers)

1 Introduction: What's at stake

One of the most basic and important distinctions is between persons and non-persons. This is a distinction we rely upon, if not explicitly, then certainly implicitly. Although typically the distinction and its character-ization are not matters for conscious thought, our behavior reveals our commitment to it every day.

The notion of personhood is in part normative. One ingredient in our concept of personhood might be expressed by the claim that a person has a stringent right to life. Alternatively, one could make the point by saying that it is prima facie seriously wrong to kill a person. (Of course, other considerations may conspire to create a situation in which, all things considered, it is permissible to kill a person; on this picture, rights and the associated moral claims are not construed as absolute.)

Simply put, we (almost all of us) do not believe it is seriously wrong painlessly to kill a rodent or a stray cat (for whom an owner cannot be found), whereas it is certainly prima facie seriously wrong painlessly to kill a normal adult human being or an orphan. Whereas it is not morally wrong (on the face of it) to dismantle one's adding machine, it is obviously morally outrageous to dissect one's roommate. Further, we normally think it is a particularly bad thing – perhaps a tragedy – when a normal adult human being or a child dies, whereas we do not consider it bad in the same way when a fish or a puppy dies. Our practices presuppose a basic distinction between entities with a stringent right to continued existence and those which lack this right, even if it is dauntingly complex to elaborate the basis for the distinction.

Also, persons (in contrast to non-persons) are appropriate candidates for a range of distinctive attitudes, and they can be participants in associated activities. I might kick my television set if it is not working during a crucial episode of "Murphy Brown," but this frustration could hardly be called resentment or indignation. Further, I might say I'm grateful for the many years of service given by my Hoover vacuum cleaner, but this feeling is fundamentally different from the kind of gratitude I feel toward a friend who remembers my birthday with a telephone call. Persons are appropriate candidates for such attitudes as love, respect, gratitude, resentment, indignation, and hatred. In his path-breaking essay, Peter Strawson dubbed these the "reactive attitudes."[2]

The reactive attitudes are essential ingredients of our lives as we lead them. Imagine, if you can, a world without love, gratitude, indignation, and resentment. It would be a colorless and cold world, and certainly radically different from ours. Further, the relationships and practices built upon the reactive attitudes are central features of our lives. Friendship, for example, seems to be intimately bound up with the network of reactive attitudes. And the institution of punishment is interlaced with the attitudes of moral blame and the expression of moral condemnation. I shall call rational (or appropriate) accessibility to the reactive attitudes and the attendant practices of moral reward and punishment, "moral responsibility."[3]

There are then at least two key normative ingredients in the notion of personhood: having a stringent right to continued existence, and being an appropriate candidate for the reactive attitudes and certain associated practices (such as moral reward and punishment). I do not have any sort of argument that we could not give up these elements and still lead lives that are recognizably human and even appealing in certain respects.[4] I have no interest here in making this sort of argument. It suffices for my purposes to point to the indisputable fact that these elements are significant features of our lives as we lead them. Even if we cannot articulate its basis, the distinction between persons and non-persons is fundamentally important, and it is encoded in the fabric of our personal lives, relationships, and social institutions.

But this is not a book on personhood. It is a book on free will. This having been said, it is nevertheless true that there is an important connection between personhood and free will. It is generally thought that a person must possess (among other things) a certain sort of *control*. Whatever particular explication (if any) of the distinction between persons and non-persons is ultimately tenable, it is plausible that it will contain the claim that a person has a certain kind of freedom or control over his behavior. More specifically, it is generally thought that this freedom or control is what grounds the second normative ingredient: rational or appropriate accessibility to the reactive attitudes and the activities – such as reward and punishment – bound up with them. (Thus, for the purposes of my discussion here, the second normative ingredient in the concept of personhood is most relevant.)

The notion of control is the principal subject of this book. I shall be developing the thoughts that there are importantly different kinds of control and that distinguishing between them is crucial to understanding the cluster of issues pertaining to free will and moral responsibility (and thus to a central element of personhood). I wish to begin by sketching one notion of control – a notion that links control to alternative possibilities – and its supposed connection to moral responsibility and personhood. Then I shall explain why there is some reason to worry about whether we do in fact have the sort of control which requires alternative possibilities. A good portion of the book will explore this question of whether we can be confident that we have this sort of control.

2 Control, alternative possibilities, and moral responsibility

The Argentine fabulist, Borges, put it crisply: the future is a garden of forking paths.[5] And this is an extremely natural picture. We tend to think of the future as a branching, tree-like structure with many nodes at which there are various paths into the future. Perhaps there are points at which we have no alternatives to our actual course of action. And maybe some individuals rarely or never have such alternatives. But we naturally think that there are many times when we (most of us) have various paths genuinely open to us. That is, we think of ourselves as frequently having alternative possibilities.

When we take one path rather than another in a situation in which the other path is genuinely available to us, we say that we have a certain kind of *control* over our behavior. In this kind of circumstance, a person has the sort of control which involves alternative possibilities: he follows one path, and yet he *can* ("is able to," "has it in his power to") follow another path.[6]

Not only is it natural to suppose that we sometimes have this sort of control, it is widely thought that this sort of control is required for moral responsibility (and thus personhood). To illustrate the prevalent traditional assumption of an association of moral responsibility with the sort of control that involves alternative possibilities – the "forking-paths" model of the future of a person – let us look at a couple of articulations of this idea. In his essay, "The Interest in Liberty on the Scales," Joel Feinberg says:

> We can think of life as a kind of maze of railroad tracks connected and disjoined, here and there, by switches. Wherever there is an unlocked switch which can be pulled one way or the other, there is an 'open option;' wherever the switch is locked in one position the option is 'closed.' As we chug along our various tracks in the maze, other persons are busily locking and unlocking, opening and closing switches, thereby enlarging and restricting our various possibilities of movement. Some of these switchmen are part of a team of legislators, policemen, and judges; they claim *authority* for their switch positionings. Other switchmen operate illicitly at night, often undoing what was authoritatively arranged in the daylight. This model, of course, is simpler than the real world where the 'tracks' and 'switches' are not so clearly marked; but it does give us a sense for how some closed options can be more restrictive of liberty than others. When a switchman closes and locks a switch, he forces us to continue straight on, or stop, or back up. What we cannot do is move onto a different track heading off in a different direction from the one we are on.
>
> . . . The 'open option' theory of liberty is to be preferred, I think, to its main rival, the theory of liberty as the absence of barriers to one's actual desires, whatever they should happen to be. Suppose that Martin Chuzzlewit finds himself on a trunk line with all of its switches closed and

locked, and with other 'trains' moving in the same direction on the same track at his rear, so that he has no choice at all but to continue moving straight ahead to destination D. On the 'open option' theory of liberty, this is the clearest example of a total lack of liberty: all of his options are closed, there are not alternative possibilities, he is forced to move to D. But now let us suppose that getting to D is Chuzzlewit's highest ambition in life and his most intensely felt desire. In that case, he is sure to get the thing in life he wants most. Does that affect the way the situation should be described in respect to liberty? According to the theory that one is at liberty to the extent that one can do what one wants, a theory held by the ancient Stoics and Epicureans and many modern writers too, Chuzzlewit enjoys perfect liberty in this situation because he can do what he wants, even though he can do nothing else. But since this theory blurs the distinction between liberty and compulsion, and in this one extreme hypothetical case actually identifies the two, it does not recommend itself to common sense. . . . If Chuzzlewit is allowed no alternative to D, it follows that he is forced willy-nilly to go to D.

What then is the basis of our interest in liberty? Why should it matter that we have few 'open-options' if we have everything else we want and our other interests are flourishing? Our welfare interest in having a tolerable bare minimum of liberty is perhaps the easiest to account for of the various kind of interests persons have in liberty. If human beings had no alternative possibilities at all, if all their actions at all times were the *only* actions permitted them, they might yet be contented provided their desires for alternative possibilities were all thoroughly repressed or extinguished, and they might even achieve things of value, provided that they were wisely programmed to do so. But they could take no credit or blame for any of their achievements, and they could no more be responsible for their lives, in prospect or retrospect, than are robots, or the trains in our fertile metaphor that must run on 'predestined grooves.' They could have dignity neither in their own eyes nor in the eyes of their fellows, and both esteem for others and self-esteem would dwindle. . . . The self-monitoring and self-critical capacities, so essential to human nature, might as well dry up and wither; they would no longer have any function. The contentment with which all of this might still be consistent would not be a recognizably human happiness.[7]

In this extended passage, Feinberg gives voice to a powerful and prevalent picture of the relationship between moral responsibility and the sort of control which involves alternative possibilities. Simply put, the view is that moral responsibility *requires* liberty in the sense of the existence of genuine alternative possibilities. Without such freedom, it is alleged, there is no responsibility, no dignity, and ultimately, no personhood.[8]

Richard Swinburne articulates the "forking-paths" model in his discussion of moral responsibility within a theological context:

> ... an agent would not be morally responsible at all (he would never be praiseworthy or blameworthy) if he was caused necessarily, predetermined, to try to do what he did, by his brain state, and that in turn by some prior state, until we come to causes outside the agent's body and ultimately to causes long before his birth. For in that case in a crucial sense the agent could not have done other than he did do . . . [9]

Swinburne worries that causal determination would rule out moral responsibility; this is a worry to which I shall turn in the next section. The basis for Swinburne's worry that determination would rule out responsibility is that it would rule out *alternative possibilities*. Indeed, much of Swinburne's account of the interconnected web of theological and moral notions such as merit, guilt, atonement, forgiveness, and redemption depends upon the forking-paths model.

3 Threats to personhood: The transfer version of the argument

Our ordinary practices evince a commitment to the distinction between persons and non-persons. And this commitment seems to be invulnerable to certain sorts of discoveries about the nature of the world. That is, it seems incredible that we would give up the distinction (or the behavior that flows from it), if we discovered that a certain sort of scientific theory were true. Suppose, for example, that a consortium of well-respected scientists announce that they have developed a remarkable new theory which implies that all events can in principle be fully explained by previous events and the laws of nature. That is, they claim that, although they cannot at present make all the predictions about the future, their theory implies that the world is *not* fundamentally indeterministic as many scientists had previously thought; rather, if one knows enough about the past states of the world and the laws of nature, one can confidently predict all the states of the world in the future.

Such an announcement would evoke considerable interest and, no doubt, skepticism. But what if the scientists' result, having been subject to critical scrutiny, were corroborated? What if we had good reason to suppose the universe to be deterministic? Under these circumstances, I do *not* believe we would have *any* inclination to give up the reactive attitudes, or to *assimilate* all entities with regard to the attitudes and activities constitutive of personhood. (That is, I do not think we would have any such inclination, apart from considerations arising from some sort of theoretical or philosophical argument: our strong intuitive reaction would be to preserve the fundamental features of ourselves as persons.) How could such a scientific discovery cause us to change (or attempt to change) our basic attitudes and behavior in this way?

Of course, empirical discoveries can cause us to change our behavior in important ways. For example, the discovery of a link between tobacco and various health problems can cause us to stop (or at least to attempt to stop) smoking. But I am suggesting that it is jarring and implausible to suppose that an empirical discovery *of the sort envisaged* should result in radical changes (of the kind imagined) in the ways we think about ourselves and others. Why should a new scientific discovery about the form of the laws of nature cause us to stop thinking of ourselves or certain others as persons – as subject to love, hatred, respect, indignation, and so forth? How could such a discovery impel us to treat rodents and robots in the same way as human beings? Our sense of ourselves as persons is relatively firm and impervious to most imaginable scientific discoveries.

Let me make my point here a bit more explicit. I am *not* making primarily a "psychological claim." That is, I am not saying that it is somehow psychologically impossible for us to abandon our view of ourselves as persons (in light of an empirical discovery of the sort described above). Rather, I am making a *normative* point. I am saying that, upon due reflection, it just does not seem appropriate or plausible to think that we should abandon our view of ourselves as persons, if it turned out that the consortium of scientists were correct.

Although I am not sure how precisely to articulate the basis of this point, it does seem to be strong. And, of course, I am not here claiming that the normative point is obviously correct; I am merely pointing out that it has a rather strong intuitive basis. Our relationships with our family and friends are extraordinarily significant to us. And the differences in our behavior toward human beings and (most) mere animals (rodents, for example) are dramatic; indeed, these differences help to frame and constitute our lives as persons. It is very hard to see how the discovery of the consortium of scientists should move us to give up these features of our lives.

The commitment to personhood, then, is deep and natural. But a strong challenge to its appropriateness can be generated by employing ingredients which are *also* extremely compelling and intuitive. This challenge suggests that if it did indeed turn out that the scientists' claim were true and thus that causal determinism obtains, then we would *not* have the kind of control ordinarily thought necessary for moral responsibility – we would not, despite the appearances, have freedom to do otherwise. Thus, despite the very strong natural commitment to personhood and the associated resistance to giving it up on the basis (say) of a theoretical discovery of the sort announced by the consortium of scientists, perhaps there is reason for anxiety.

I will now lay out a version of this challenge to our strong natural conviction.[10] This version of the challenge employs an ingredient which I shall call the "Principle of the Transfer of Powerlessness," or the "Transfer Principle" (or "Transfer"). It is a very attractive and reasonable principle, which I shall investigate at length in chapters two and three. Here I shall simply set out the principle and show how it can be employed to generate the conclusion that if causal determinism obtains, no one has the kind of control which involves alternative possibilities.

I shall say that when a proposition p obtains and a person S does not have it in his power so to act that p would not obtain, p is "power necessary" relative to S.[11] Power necessity is that kind of necessity which implies that a person does not have control over whether or not a proposition obtains. When a proposition is power necessary relative to a person, he has "no choice" about whether the proposition obtains. The abbreviation, "$N_{S,t}$ (p)", will be used to stand for: it is power necessary for S at t that p – that is, p obtains and S is not free at t to perform any action such that if S were to perform it, p would not obtain.

Consider now the following rule of inference involving the power necessity operator:

If: (a) $N_{S,t}$ (p)
and (b) $N_{S,t}$ (If p, then q),
then: (c) $N_{S,t}$ (q).

Call this the "Principle of the Transfer of Powerlessness." Roughly, it says that if a person is powerless over one thing, and powerless over that thing's leading to another, then the person is powerless over the second thing. More carefully, the principle says that if p obtains and a person S cannot so act that p would be false, and S cannot so act that it would be false that if p then q, then S cannot so act that q would be false.

The principle is plausible. Suppose, for example, that a meteorite hits my house today, and that I am powerless to prevent this. Imagine, further, that the meteorite is big enough to destroy my roof, so that it is true that if it hits my house, it destroys my roof (and, again, I am powerless to alter this truth). It seems that it follows that the meteorite destroys my roof, and I am powerless to prevent the destruction of my roof. Rather than going into a detailed discussion of the principle here, let us simply acknowledge its apparent appeal, and move on to the other ingredients in the challenge to the appropriateness of personhood. (I shall consider the Transfer Principle in detail in chapters two and three.)

The second ingredient is again a very appealing, natural idea – one is tempted to say an assumption of common sense. It captures the intuitive idea that the past is currently "fixed" and "out of our control." The idea is that we do not now have any "control over" or "choice about" certain facts about the past. For example, neither I nor anyone else now has any choice about or control over the fact that Bill Clinton defeated George Bush in the 1992 presidential election. One way (admittedly, a preliminary way which will be refined later in the book) of putting the idea is this: no person can act in such a way that some fact about the past would not have been a fact. Put differently, the principle says that if a person's performing a certain action would require some actual fact about the past *not* to have been a fact, then the person *cannot* perform the act. This might be dubbed the "Principle of the Fixity of the Past."

Similar to the idea of the fixity of the past is the idea that the natural laws are also "fixed" and "out of our control." For example, neither I nor anyone else has any choice about or control over the speed of light. Intuitively, then, no person can act in such a way that some natural law would not be a law. In different words, the "Principle of the Fixity of the Laws" says that if a person's performing a certain action would require that some actual natural law *not* be a law, then the person *cannot* perform the act.

Another ingredient is the account of causal determinism:

> Causal determinism is the thesis that, for any given time, a complete statement of the facts about that time, together with a complete statement of the laws of nature, entails every truth as to what happens after that time.[12]

Note that the imaginary discovery of the consortium of scientists discussed above was the putative discovery of the truth of causal determinism. Note also that it is not part of the thesis of causal determinism that any human agent actually *know* the relevant statements about times and the laws of nature; the thesis of causal determinism merely posits the *existence* of such statements (which presumably are *in principle* possible to know).

Now the challenge to the idea that we have freedom to do otherwise can be set out very simply. Suppose that the consortium of scientists is in fact correct and causal determinism obtains. Imagine also that you do something quite ordinary (like mowing the lawn) at a certain time: you do X at $t2$. It follows from the truth of causal determinism that conditions obtaining in the past (say, $t1$), together with the laws of nature, imply that you do X at $t2$. And since you have no control over the past, and you have no control over the laws of nature, it follows (given the Transfer Principle) that you have no control over your behavior – you are not in fact free at $t2$ to refrain from doing X.

Put slightly more rigorously, the argument can be stated as follows. Given that causal determinism obtains, there is some statement of the condition of the world at $t1$, b, which, together with the laws of nature, entails that you do X at $t2$. Since you have no control over the past,

(1) $N_{you,t2}(b)$.

And since you have no control over the laws of nature,

(2) $N_{you,t2}$ (If b at $t1$, then you do X at $t2$).

And from the Transfer Principle it follows that

(3) $N_{you,t2}$ (You do X at $t2$).

This version of the challenge to control, moral responsibility, and personhood employs certain ingredients, including the Transfer Principle, the Principle of the Fixity of the Past, and the Principle of the Fixity of the Laws. The argument issues in a very startling conclusion: since we don't know that the thesis of causal determinism is false, we don't know whether we have the sort of control that is traditionally associated with moral responsibility. That is, for all we know, we do not have the relevant sort of control, and thus we are *not* persons.[13] The unsettling and disturbing nature of the conclusion is highlighted in this slightly ironic but nevertheless forceful passage from Don Delillo's novel, *White Noise*:

They can trace everything you say, do and feel to the number of molecules in a certain region. . . . What happens to good and evil in this system? Passion, envy and hate? Do they become a tangle of neurons? Are you telling me that a whole tradition of human failings is now at an end, that cowardice, sadism, molestation are meaningless terms? Are we being asked to regard these things nostalgically? What about murderous rage? A murderer used to have a certain fearsome size to him. His crime was large. What happens when we reduce it to cells and molecules?[14]

I wish to emphasize that, like various other philosophical challenges to our conventional wisdom, the argument is interesting at least in part because the ingredients are so plausible. That is, the ideas embodied in the Transfer Principle, the Principle of the Fixity of the Past, and the Principle of the Fixity of the Laws are widely held, natural, intuitive ideas. This is what helps to make the challenge to personhood so fascinating: we naturally believe we are persons, and yet we can naturally be led to question this belief.

The situation here is similar to the challenge to our intuitive belief that we know various things about the empirical world. It is natural to believe that we can have this sort of knowledge. And yet we can naturally be led to question this belief. That is, ingredients that capture widely held and intuitive ideas can be employed to call into question our common-sense view that we can have knowledge of the empirical world. I shall discuss the parallels between epistemological skepticism and skepticism about personhood more carefully in chapter two. But the point here is that the two sorts of skepticism are similar to the extent that they both challenge deep and widely-held views by employing ingredients that are intuitive and natural. Thus, these kinds of skeptical arguments issue in a sort of internal tension or "cognitive dissonance," and they challenge us to scrutinize our beliefs more finely.

We do not know for certain that the thesis of causal determinism is false. Similarly, I would think that we cannot be absolutely certain that God does not exist. And it is interesting to see that a challenge to personhood which is structurally similar to the challenge from causal determinism can be developed, given the existence of God. I shall now lay out this challenge.

"God" is to be construed as a proper name, rather than a "title-term." Further, I assume that "God" names a person who has the divine attributes (such as eternality, omniscience, moral perfection, and so forth) *essentially*. For my purposes here, it is enough to assume that among the divine attributes are (at least) eternality and omniscience. Of course, these do not exhaust the divine attributes, but they are the only properties needed to generate the challenge.

God's eternality is here understood in the sense of "sempiternality": He has always existed, exists now, and will always exist. That is, God is assumed to be within the same temporal framework as humans, and He is assumed to exist at all times (given that He exists at all). Further, God is essentially eternal insofar as He must be sempiternal, if He exists: He is sempiternal in all possible worlds in which He exists.

God is taken to be essentially omniscient. A person is omniscient only if he believes all and only true propositions. It will be useful here to assume that propositions can be true (or false) *at times*.[15] Now it can be said of a temporal being that he is omniscient only if: for any time t and proposition p, he believes that p at t if and only if p is true at t. Further, a person is essentially omniscient insofar as it is necessarily true that, if he exists, then he is omniscient – that is, he is omniscient in every possible world in which he exists.

Now, given these sketchy but not unreasonable assumptions about God, together with the ingredients adumbrated above – the Transfer Principle and the Principle of the Fixity of the Past – the challenge to personhood from God's existence can be developed. Suppose again that you simply perform some ordinary act X at $t2$. Assume, further, that God exists and has the properties sketched above. Because you perform X at $t2$, it appears to follow that it was true at some prior time $t1$ that you would do X at $t2$. (Of course, this assumes both that propositions can be true at times and, more specifically, that "future contingent propositions," such as that a particular person will do X at $t2$, can be true at prior times.) It follows from God's eternality and omniscience (as articulated above) that He believed at $t1$ that you would do X at $t2$. Now, since God's belief at $t1$ is a condition that obtained in the past relative to $t2$, it follows from the Principle of the Fixity of the Past that you cannot at $t2$ act in such a way that God would not have believed at $t1$ that you would do X at $t2$. That is,

(4) $N_{you,t2}$ (God believed at $t1$ that you would do X at $t2$).

Further, in virtue of God's essential omniscience, we have:

(5) $N_{you,t2}$ (If God believed at $t1$ that you would do X at $t2$, then you do X at $t2$).

Now it follows from the Principle of the Transfer of Powerlessness that

(6) $N_{you,t2}$ (You do X at $t2$).

That is, the conclusion of the argument is that you do X at $t2$ and that you *cannot* refrain from doing X at $t2$. Thus, we have an argument (which is quite similar to the argument from causal determinism) that God's foreknowledge is incompatible with human freedom to do otherwise.

Of course, I do not ask anyone to suppose that God does in fact exist, just as I do not simply assume that causal determinism obtains. Rather, I invite you to suppose that we cannot be *certain* that God (as envisaged above) does not exist or that causal determinism does not obtain. And given this, we are in a puzzling situation. We naturally hold that we have control over our behavior, are morally responsible agents, and persons; and we do not think these views depend on discoveries about the form of natural laws or the existence of God. (Indeed, some have argued that God's existence is *necessary* for moral responsibility and personhood; what would be implausible is to suppose that a discovery that God does in fact exist should force us to abandon our view of ourselves as persons.) But there are potent arguments employing intuitive ideas that can lead us to question whether we have the relevant sort of control and thus are morally responsible agents and persons. These arguments seem to establish a connection between the existence of God (or the truth of causal determinism) and the lack of control – the basis of responsibility and personhood. Again, it is not as though common sense is being assaulted from some external vantage point. Rather, there is an internal tension within common sense. This is what gives skepticism about control its impetus and force.

Return for a moment to the natural picture of the future as a garden of forking paths. The challenges from God's existence and causal determinism call this very appealing picture into question. They suggest that, for all we know, our future might look very different from Borges' pleasant garden. Indeed, they raise the possibility described above by Feinberg:

> Suppose that Martin Chuzzlewit finds himself on a trunk line with all of its switches closed and locked, and with other 'trains' moving in the same direction on the same track at his rear, so that he has no choice at all but to continue moving straight ahead to destination D. On the 'open option' theory of liberty, this is the clearest example of a total lack of liberty: all of his options are closed, there are not alternative possibilities, he is forced to move to D.

The challenges from causal determinism and God's existence call into question the forking-paths picture. Perhaps, for all we know, we are like

Chuzzlewit in the scenario in which all the switches are closed and locked: we must proceed straight ahead, and all the branching "tracks" are mere illusions. Carl Ginet has presented a nice (albeit distressing) story which illustrates this possibility:

> In those rides that amusement parks sometimes provide, in which one sits in a car that follows a track through a darkened room of illuminated objects, the car sometimes has a steering wheel. If one turns the wheel in the directions suggested by the environment – directions in which the car is actually going – one can easily get the feeling that one *is* steering the car – even though one knows all along that he is not. A child might think he actually was steering the car . . .
>
> [We can make] our ride example more fanciful. Suppose that the path that the car takes is controlled by some person other than the rider, who also controls (through, say, instruments attached to the rider's brain) what delusions or illusions of steering the rider will have, and suppose that this controller sees to it that the path he makes the rider think he is choosing is always the same as the path he (the controller) makes the car take. In this case, even though it is true that, if the rider had had the impression of choosing a different path the car would have taken a correspondingly different path, it is still the case that the rider's choice-impression does not determine what path the car takes, that the rider has no choice of any sort as to what path it will take, and, hence, that he does not effectively choose its path.[16]

We have, then, competing models of the future. On the one hand, we have the extremely deeply entrenched and attractive forking-paths model. On the other, there is the possibility raised by the remarks of Feinberg and Ginet: the alternatives are illusory and there is just one path into the future. If causal determinism is true or God exists, it seems that we are in a situation like that of Chuzzlewit (whose options are all cut off) or the rider on Ginet's diabolical amusement park ride.

4 Control, bugbears, and bogeymen

Let us think a bit more about Ginet's example of the weird amusement park ride. What is so disturbing about it is that it presents in a graphic way the possibility that we are deluded into thinking we have genuine alternatives, and yet at some level our behavior is produced by a process quite "external" to us and beyond our control – the mechanism that causes the car to take the path it actually takes. Although we believe we are determining the direction of the car, making it the case that it will go one way rather than another, in fact this is accomplished by a process involving gears, pulleys, wheels, and so forth whose operation is quite out of our control.

Now it might be thought that the reason we find the example so disturbing is at least in part that we would be controlled by *someone else*. And this is indisputably something which is to some degree disturbing. But I would claim that the basic distress at lacking control does *not* depend on the fact that someone else is controlling one. Imagine, for example, that there is nobody who is controlling the instruments which induce brain processes and also determine the path of the car. Rather, as the car approaches the points at which a decision is to be made, some purely mechanical randomizing device is activated which causes the car to proceed along a certain path (and also causes the appropriate brain processes to occur). Other than lacking an agent who is in control, the example is precisely as before, and I think one should find it equally disturbing. At least it is true that removal of the other agent does nothing to assuage the worry that one is not in control of the movements of the car and that one's sense of the existence of genuinely open alternatives is a pathetic illusion. After all, it is the operation of the gears, pulleys, wheels, and so forth (having been triggered by the randomizing device) which causes the car to move as it does, and this is entirely out of one's control.

Although the other *agent* may make the example a bit simpler and more "realistic," it is in no way necessary to the point of the example. Clearly, there are at least two ways in which one might lack control: *someone or something else* may be controlling one, or there may be *no* locus of control. Typically, when it is tempting to say that someone is "out of control," it is *not* because someone else is controlling him, but rather because there is no locus of control. And, in general, it is *not* essential to lacking control that one be controlled by someone else.

I believe this point can help us to see why a criticism by Daniel Dennett of the challenge (say) from causal determinism is misleading. Dennett says:

Contrary to the familiar vision . . . *determinism does not in itself 'erode control'*. . . . Moreover, *the past does not control us*. It no more controls us than the people at NASA can control the space ships that have wandered out of reach in space. It is not that there are no causal links between the Earth and those craft. There are; reflected sunlight from Earth still reaches them, for instance. But causal links are not enough for control. There must also be feedback to inform the controller. There are no feedback signals from the present to the past for the past to exploit. Moreover there is nothing in the past to foresee and plan for our particular acts, even if it is true that Mother Nature – gambling on our general needs and predicaments – did, in effect, design us to fend quite well for ourselves.[17]

Certainly, neither the past nor the laws controls us (given the truth of causal determinism) in the way in which another agent or thing may control us. Perhaps this does indeed show that we are not controlled by the past or laws. But it would not follow that the truth of causal determinism does not entail that we *lack control*, for it is not the case that the *only* way in which we can lack control is in virtue of being controlled by someone or something else.[18]

Dennett argues that many of the thought-experiments employed by philosophers in discussing aspects of the free will problem are misleading precisely because they conjure up the worry that we are being controlled by someone else – someone mysterious, sinister, and frightening. Dennett says:

> Why do people find the free will problem gripping? In part, surely because it touches deep and central questions about our situation in the universe, about 'the human condition,' as one portentously says. But also, I will argue, because philosophers have conjured up a host of truly frightening bugbears ['A sort of hobgolin . . . supposed to devour naughty children; hence, generally, any imaginary being invoked by nurses to frighten children.' (*Shorter Oxford English Dictionary*)] and then subliminally suggested, quite illicitly, that the question of free will is whether any of these bugbears actually exist.
> . . . it is my view that these metaphors have done most of the work behind the scenes in propelling the free will problem, and that they do not in the slightest deserve the respect and influence they typically enjoy.[19]

Dennett goes on to characterize a class of bugbears he calls "bogeymen":

> The first of the bugbears are quite literally bogey*men* – bogeypersons if you insist – for they are all conceived as *agents* who vie with us for control of our bodies, who compete against us, who have interests antithetical to or at least independent of our own. These fearsome fellows are often used by philosophers as reverse cheerleaders (gloomleaders, you might call them) ushered onto the stage whenever anxiety flags . . .[20]

The first such bogeyman discussed by Dennett is the "Invisible Jailer." He then gets to a character close to my heart: the "Nefarious Neurosurgeon":

How would you like to have someone strap you down and insert electrodes in your brain, and then control your every thought and deed by pushing buttons on the 'master' console? Consider, for instance, the entirely typical invocation of this chap by Fischer ["Responsibility and Control," 1982, p. 26]; the ominous Dr. Black, who arranges things in poor Jones' brain so that Black can 'control Jones' activities. Jones, meanwhile, knows nothing of this.' First, we may ask – as we always should – why is this other, rival *agent* introduced? Why bring Dr. Black into it? Couldn't the example get off the ground just as well, for instance, if Jones had a brain tumor that produced odd results? What makes Fischer's version more dreadful is that Jones' control of his own activities has been usurped by another controller, Dr. Black. A tumor might cause this or that in someone's brain, and it would be terrible indeed to have a debilitating brain tumor, but it would take an awfully smart tumor to *control* someone's brain.

Variations on the Nefarious Neurosurgeon are the Hideous Hypnotist and the Peremptory Puppeteer . . .

I cannot prove that none of the bogeymen in this rogues' gallery really exist, any more than I can prove that the Devil, or Santa Claus, doesn't exist. But I am prepared to put on a sober face and assure anyone who needs assuring that there is absolutely no evidence to suggest that any of these horrible agents exists. But of course if any of them did, woe on us! A closet with a ghost in it (except for lacking the ghost) is nothing to fear, so we arrive at what may turn out to be a useful rule of thumb: whenever you spy a bogey*man* in a philosophical example, check to see if this scary agent, who is surely fictitious, is really doing all the work.[21]

Let me first say a few words about Dennett's analysis of the Nefarious Neurosurgeon case. Then I have something to say about the role of the relevant thought-experiments in general in the debates about free will. First, recall Ginet's amusement park ride example. It is framed in terms of another agent who controls the rider. But I argued that this element of the story is *not* essential to the point: one would equally lack control if there were a randomizing device, and not another agent, which was producing the operations of the mechanism that steers the car. And so also with the Nefarious Neurosurgeon. It is perhaps heuristically useful to posit an agent such as a neurosurgeon to make the story a bit more realistic (although of course we are dealing with a rather fanciful example in any case). And I admit that the addition of this agent may make the example slightly more gripping and disturbing, especially upon initial consideration. But I contend that, once the agent is removed and one reflects upon the example, one will *still* conclude that the person lacks control in an important sense. Indeed, Dennett provides a nice way of seeing this: "Couldn't the example get off the ground just as well, for instance, if Jones had a brain tumor that produced odd results?" Of course, the answer is, "Yes!" If the brain tumor caused Jones' behavior in a way analogous to the stimulation of the brain envisaged in the original version of the case, then certainly Jones would lack control to exactly the same degree as in the original case. Thus, the insertion of the neurosurgeon can be seen as a heuristic device or rhetorical ploy, but it is not essential to the point of the example.

Again, it is important to remember that there are at least two ways in which it can be true that one lacks control: someone or something else may be controlling one, or there may be *no* locus of control. Dennett appears again to be assuming that the *only* way in which one can lack control is in virtue of being controlled by someone or something else: "A tumor might cause this or that in someone's brain, and it would be terrible indeed to have a debilitating brain tumor, but it would take an awfully smart tumor to *control* someone's brain." Of course, even if the tumor does not control one's brain, its existence can render it true that one does not control one's behavior.

My main point here is that there is no relevant difference (as regards the agent's having control) between a context in which *someone else* is controlling him and a context in which there simply is *no* locus of control. The key insight is that one's control can be diminished equally effectively, even where there is no agent to undermine it.

It is difficult to know how seriously to take some of Dennett's remarks about the various free will thought-experiments. For example, he says, "I am . . . speaking with deliberate disrespect (and a smidgen of carica-ture in this first chapter) when I speak of these bugbears. . . . my point is to heighten sensitivity to them, and to undercut their traditional emi-nence with my pejorative characterizations."[22] But even so it is worth spending some time thinking about the role of the thought-experiments in the discussions of free will. Dennett is certainly correct to warn us against certain sorts of abuses and misuses of the thought-experiments. If they are used simply or primarily to scare us and to generate anxieties which distract us from focusing on the underlying philosophical issues, this is clearly an abuse of the thought-experiments. Specifically, if the examples cause us to worry primarily about being controlled or manipulated by someone else, this will distract us from the important meta-physical issues.

Similarly, the following strategy involves a clear misuse of the examples. One starts with an example, such as the Nefarious Neuro-surgeon, Hideous Hypnotist, or Peremptory Puppeteer. One points out that in these cases the relevant agent lacks control, even though this fact is not phenomenologically accessible to him – his lack of alternatives does not manifest itself in explicit coercion. One then points out that if causal determinism were to obtain (or God were to exist), we would be in a relevantly similar situation, i.e., we would lack control even though this fact would not be phenomenologically accessible to us. One then concludes that if causal determinism were to obtain (or God were to exist), we would not be morally responsible agents – we would be just like puppets and individuals subject to manipulation or hypnosis. As Dennett puts it, "The more or less traditional philosophical practice is to move briskly through the analogies to a conclusion . . ."[23]

I agree with Dennett that here, as elsewhere in philosophy, one should not move briskly in drawing conclusions from thought-exper-iments. I think it is a mistake hastily to conclude that if (say) causal determinism were to obtain, we would be *relevantly similar* to the pup-pets and individuals subject to hypnosis or manipulation. It must be conceded that we would indeed be similar *in certain respects*. More specifically, it seems that in both the thought-experiments and the cases of causal determinism and God's existence, factors entirely "external" to the agent and out of his control obtain and constitute sufficient con-ditions for the agent's actual behavior. In this respect the thought-experiments are similar to our situations (given causal determinism or God's existence). And yet there may be important differences between the thought-experiments and the cases of causal determinism or God's existence in the *way in which* the behavior is produced. Thus, although there are certain similarities, it remains an open question whether the thought-experiments are *relevantly similar* to the contexts of causal deter-minism or God's existence.

Thus, it is a mistake to proceed briskly here. But it does *not* follow that the thought-experiments have no useful place in our thinking about free will. In my view, the thought-experiments, aside from their heuristic and pedagogical utility, constitute an *invitation* and a *challenge*. They invite us carefully to scrutinize the relationship between the fanciful cases and the situations of causal determinism and God's existence. And they challenge us to say what precisely the *differences* are, given that there are some salient similarities. Surely *this* use of the thought-experiments is not objectionable. On this approach, the thought-experiments are not the *end* of theorizing, but an *impetus* for it (although obviously not the only one).

Consider now the full range of Dennett's "Bogeymen": the Invisible Jailer, the Nefarious Neurosurgeon, the Hideous Hypnotist, the Peremptory Puppeteer, the Cosmic Child Whose Dolls We Are, and the Malevolent Mindreader. Notice that they all have the feature identified above: there is in each of these examples some factor quite external to the relevant agent which is sufficient for the agent's behavior. There is even a more specific similarity to the situations of causal determinism and God's existence: in all of the cases, it seems that an application of the Principle of Transfer of Powerlessness naturally explains the relevant agent's lack of control.

Let us focus on the example of the Nefarious Neurosurgeon. Here Dr Black has his mechanism set up in such a way that Jones has no control over its operation. And Jones has no control over the fact that, if Black operates the mechanism in a certain way, Jones will behave in such and such a manner. Thus, it seems to follow from the Transfer Principle that Jones cannot do otherwise. And precisely the same result issues from the version of the thought-experiment in which Dr Black is replaced by a tumor. And a similar sort of analysis applies to *all* the thought-experiments in the range of Bogeyman cases.

Thus, we can think of this range of cases as an invitation and a challenge. They invite us to see structural similarities between a certain set of cases (in which we are clearly not morally responsible for what we do) and our actual situations, given the assumptions of causal determinism or God's existence. Further, they challenge us to say precisely what the difference is between these two groups of situations. Alternatively, one could put the challenge as follows. Given that in the range of thought-experiments an application of the Transfer Principle yields the result that the respective agents lack control in the sense that involves alternative possibilities, why shouldn't an application of the Transfer Principle yield a similar result in the cases of causal determinism and God's existence? And if so, how can we be morally responsible if causal determinism obtains or God exists, given that we are *not* morally responsible in the thought-experiments?

In the introductory chapter of his book, Dennett says, "In the following chapters, I maintain that the free will problem *is* the family of anxieties briefly sketched in this chapter."[24] By this I believe Dennett means that once the worries about being controlled by another agent –

a neurosurgeon, puppeteer, hypnotist, mind-reader, and so forth – are put to the side, we will see that there is no important residuum. I disagree. As I argued above, deep worries remain about our control, even if we eliminate the elements of the thought-experiments which produce the specific anxieties in question. If moral responsibility and personhood require control of the sort that involves alternative possibilities, then how *precisely* are we different from the agents in the thought-experiments?

5 Conclusion

It is an absolutely fundamental presupposition of common sense that we are persons and thus that we can be held accountable for at least some of our behavior. And it is also a basic tenet that this accountability is grounded in *control*. Without control, Michael Ross (that "mild-mannered Cornell graduate") claimed, "you are nothing." Consider also this gripping interaction between Lyle Menendez (accused – along with his brother – of murdering his rich Beverly Hills parents) and the prosecutor:

> 'I loved my mother,' Lyle Menendez testified Tuesday.
> 'When you put the shotgun up to her left cheek and pulled the trigger, did you love your mother?' Bozanich asked him.
> 'Yes,' he said.
> 'Was that an act of love, Mr. Menendez?'
> 'It was confusion. Fear.'
> Bozanich asked if he was afraid of his mother when he reloaded and fired the final shot to her face. 'Something I saw or something that I heard freaked me out even more,' he said. 'I was afraid.'
> 'You were afraid she was going to live, weren't you?' Bozanich asked.
> 'It was a kind of caving in kind of fear,' he said. 'I was not really in control.'
>
> Alan Abrahamson, *Los Angeles Times*[25]

We assume that we are accountable for our behavior – when indeed we are accountable – in virtue of our possession of control of this behavior. And yet I have sketched an argument-structure which calls into question the presupposition of our control over our behavior. Crucial to this pattern of argumentation is the Principle of the Transfer of Powerlessness. Also, I pointed out that the Principle appears to underlie our judgments about a range of hypothetical scenarios. In the next chapter I wish to think about this principle more carefully. If we are to take seriously the worries about our control and personhood, the arguments so lightly sketched in this chapter need to be articulated and evaluated more carefully.

2

The Transfer Principle: Its Plausibility

1 Introduction

In chapter one I employed the Principle of the Transfer of Powerlessness to generate a challenge to some of our deepest intuitive commitments – our view of ourselves as in control of our behavior and morally responsible for it, indeed, our view of ourselves as persons. Because these are such basic commitments, it is especially important to scrutinize the Transfer Principle (and the other elements of the challenge) with some care.

It must be stated at the outset that the Transfer Principle is extremely attractive. Think of it this way. One starts with a modal property (power necessity) which attaches to something (relative to an agent and time). The principle states that if the thing has the property, and there is an appropriate connection between the first thing and a second thing, then the second thing has the property. That is to say, given an appropriate link, the modal property is projected or transferred from the first thing to the second. (The Transfer Principle is a mechanism of projection, kind of like a slingshot. And the relevant connection or "linkage" may be provided by such phenomena as natural laws or God's knowledge.) This provides some measure of intuitive motivation for the principle, as well as suggesting some reasons why the principle may fail of application. For example, if the putative link is not of the appropriate sort, then although one starts with the modal property attaching to the one thing, it cannot be transferred to the other. And if there is no modal property attaching to the first thing, then there is simply nothing to be transferred.

Schematically, the Transfer Principle is:

If: (a) $N_{S,t}(p)$
and (b) $N_{S,t}(\text{If } p, \text{ then } q)$,
then (c) $N_{S,t}(q)$.

I have been interpreting the necessity operator as expressing power necessity. If one interprets it more strongly as some sort of logical necessity (in the broad sense), the principle becomes clearly valid: logical necessity is obviously closed under entailment.

Later in this chapter I shall consider various other interpretations of the necessity operator. But let us now go back to the power interpretation. Recall that if the link in question is not sufficiently strong, then the modal property of power necessity cannot be transferred from the first thing to the second. This would be the case, for example, if we envisaged a context in which the laws of nature were not deterministic. And if there is no modal property attaching to the first thing, then there is nothing to be transferred. This would be the case, for example, if we simply posited that at $t1$ it is true that at $t2$ you will do X, and then attempted to begin our argument with the claim that it is out of one's control at $t2$ that it was true at $t1$ that you would do X at $t2$. This is the general form of the argument for *fatalism*. It proceeds to the conclusion of lack of control without any special assumptions about causal determinism or God's existence. Later in the book (in chapter six), I shall explore in detail the reason why facts about the past such as "At $t1$ it was true that you would do X at $t2$" are not typically thought to fall within the scope of the Principle of the Fixity of the Past. Now it suffices to say that intuitively this fact is *not* the sort of fact to which the necessity of the past attaches. Thus, the argument for fatalism fails: there is no power necessity with which to begin, and thus nothing to transfer.[1]

As I have suggested in chapter one, the Transfer Principle is frequently employed in the skeptical argument for the incompatibility of causal determinism (and God's existence) and our possession of control of our actions. It is thus a useful starting point for a detailed discussion of this argument. In this chapter I shall consider certain (although certainly not all) interesting arguments which appear to call the Transfer Principle into question. The first argument is presented by Anthony Kenny, and the second by Michael Slote. I shall be defending the Transfer Principle against the worries generated by these arguments. Although the arguments of Kenny and Slote are highly suggestive and help us to gain greater insight into the Transfer Principle and its modality (power necessity), they do not give us good reason to reject the principle.

Of course, there may be *other* reasons to reject the Transfer Principle (apart from the arguments of Kenny and Slote). Further, I do not propose to *establish* it, nor do I see how one could do this. These ruminations will leave Transfer intact, but in a somewhat precarious position. It is not straightforwardly refuted (at least in certain salient ways); but it also is not easily given a firm foundation. Thus, in the next chapter, chapter three, I will explore the *role* of the Transfer Principle in our thinking about control. Among the issues I discuss there is whether, despite its prominent place in many formulations of the argument for incompatibilism, the Transfer Principle is really necessary in order to make the skeptical argument. Given its *status* as described in this chapter, it will be worthwhile to consider its *role* in our reasoning about control.

2 Kenny's critique

On a number of occasions, Anthony Kenny has presented a critique of versions of the argument for the incompatibility of causal determinism (and God's existence) and freedom to do otherwise.[2] These versions of the argument appear to depend on some sort of "transfer-like" principle, and Kenny's argument is directed against this sort of principle. Although his critical remarks are not directed against the Transfer Principle as I have specifically formulated it, a consideration of Kenny's critique will help us to gain a better understanding of Transfer.

To understand Kenny's critique, it will be useful first to set out Kenny's way of framing the incompatibilist's challenge to control.[3] Begin by again supposing that God exists and that you perform some ordinary act X at $t2$. It follows from God's essential omniscience and eternality (as understood above) that God believed at $t1$ that you would do X at $t2$. So if you can at $t2$ refrain from doing X at $t2$, one of the following possibilities obtains:

(1) You can bring it about that God held a false belief at $t1$, or
(2) You can bring it about that God held a different belief from the one He actually held at $t1$, or
(3) You can bring it about that God didn't exist at $t1$.

But the incompatibilist points out that no one can bring about a logical falsehood, so (1) is ruled out. And (2) and (3) appear to be ruled out in virtue of the Principle of the Fixity of the Past. Thus, it seems that you cannot at $t2$ refrain from doing X. Note that this formulation of the incompatibilist's challenge (specifically, the challenge from God's existence) is slightly different from the version presented in chapter one (employing the Principle of Transfer of Powerlessness).

Kenny has a parallel understanding of the challenge from causal determinism. Again imagine that you do X at $t2$, but this time imagine also that causal determinism obtains. Further, let us say that b is a statement of the total state of the world at $t1$. If you can at $t2$ refrain from doing X at $t2$, then one of the following two possibilities obtains:

(A) You can at $t2$ bring it about that b was false, or
(B) You can at $t2$ violate a law of nature.

But (A) is ruled out by the Principle of the Fixity of the Past, and (B) is ruled out by the Principle of the Fixity of the Laws.

In order to see the structure of Kenny's argumentation, consider the following transfer-like principle, which I shall call "Transfer*":

S can (cannot) do X.
In the circumstances, doing X is (would be) doing Y.
Therefore, S can (cannot) do Y.

It should be evident that the incompatibilists' arguments, as formulated by Kenny, depend on Transfer*. For example, in the first argument a *reductio ad absurdum* is generated by going from "You can refrain from doing X at $t2$" and "Refraining from doing X at $t2$ would be (for instance) bringing it about that God has a false belief at $t1$" to "You can bring it about that God has a false belief at $t1$." (Of course, refraining is here being construed as a kind of doing, in a broad sense of "doing".) Similarly, the second version of the argument appears to rest on Transfer*. The argument moves (as part of the *reductio*) from the suppositions that you can refrain from doing X at $t2$, and refraining from doing X at $t2$ would be (say) violating a natural law, to the claim that you can violate a natural law.

Kenny then proceeds to attack Transfer*. He gives various examples which are intended to exhibit its unacceptability; I shall focus on Example One, which I find the most interesting:

> *Example One.* I may be able to hit the dartboard; on this particular occasion, I may hit the dartboard by hitting the center of the bull; but it by no means follows that I am capable of hitting the center of the bull.[4]

Kenny elaborates, "Any particular exercise of power and skill will have other descriptions besides the one which occurs in the specification of the power; and the possession of the power specified in no way involves the possession of the power to perform acts answering to those other descriptions."[5] According to Kenny, this example impugns Transfer★. And if Transfer★ is invalid, then so apparently is the incompatibilist's argument (both with respect to causal determinism and also God's existence).

I shall call the strategy which denies Transfer★ and thus incompatibilism, "Scotism."[6] Although I believe it is worthwhile to pursue (briefly) here, I do not believe that Kenny's Scotism succeeds. It will be useful to begin my critical discussion of this strategy by distinguishing two versions of Transfer★ (which differ only with respect to whether they pertain to ability or inability):

I S can do X.
    In the circumstances, doing X is (would be) doing Y.
    Therefore, S can do Y.
II S cannot do X.
    In the circumstances, doing X is (would be) doing Y.
    Therefore, S cannot do Y.

I shall argue that Kenny's putative counterexample to Transfer★ I is not convincing. I shall focus primarily on Transfer★ I, since this is the principle employed in Kenny's reconstruction of the incompatibilist's argument; I will however have a few things to say about Transfer★ II as well.

Begin with Transfer★ I, and recall Example One. Here it is claimed that I can hit the dartboard; that, in the circumstances, hitting the dartboard is hitting the bull's-eye; and that I cannot hit the bull's-eye. As Kenny presents the example, what makes true the identity claim, "in the circumstances, hitting the dartboard is hitting the bull's-eye," is that I actually throw the dart and hit the bull's-eye.

There is some tendency to think that from the fact that I *do* hit the bull's-eye, it follows that I *can* do so. But against this one might insist that it was after all a matter of considerable *luck* that I hit the bull's-eye on this occasion; thus, whereas it is conceded that I can hit the dartboard, nevertheless one might insist that I *cannot* hit the bull. So arguably Kenny is right about the example: it seems to be a case in which I can do X, doing X is on this occasion doing Y, and nevertheless I cannot do Y.

But all this can be granted without conceding that Kenny's Scotistic strategy is successful. Kenny is in effect making a point about how "can" works (or about the "logic" of "can"). That is, he is saying that it does not follow from the truth of "S can perform some particular act X" and the fact that the particular act X is truly describable as a *D-type* act that S can D. So, more specifically, Kenny's claim is that it does not follow from the truth of "S can perform some particular act of hitting the dartboard" and the fact that this particular act of hitting the dartboard is truly describable as hitting the bull's-eye, that S can hit the bull's-eye. As a point about the "logic" of "can," I am willing to grant (for the sake of argument) that Kenny is correct. But it does not matter, because the incompatibilist can accommodate this truth about "can," if indeed it is a truth.

As I pointed out above, Kenny construes the incompatibilist as arguing in the following way. The incompatibilist's argument moves (as part of a *reductio*) from the suppositions that you can refrain from doing X at *t2*, and refraining from doing X at *t2* would be (say) violating a natural law, to the claim that you can violate a natural law. It then points out that you *cannot violate a natural law*. But the incompatibilist could equally well argue from the suppositions that you can refrain from doing X at *t2*, and refraining from doing X at *t2* would be truly describable as violating a natural law, to the claim that you can perform some particular act which would be truly describable as a violation of a law of nature. And this is bad enough, according to the incompatibilist. Surely, if it is objectionable to suppose that some human agent can violate a natural law, it is equally objectionable to suppose that some human agent can perform an action which is truly describable as a violation of a natural law. This suggests the following sort of revision (or perhaps reading) of Transfer★ I:

> S can do X.
> In the circumstances, the particular act X is (would be) truly describable as D.
> Therefore, S can perform some particular act which is truly describable as D.[7]

This version of the Transfer★ I, together with the appropriate version of the assumption of the fixity of the natural laws, is sufficient for the incompatibilist's purposes. Thus, even if Kenny is correct about the logic of "can," he has not given us reason to reject the incompatibilist's argument.

I have argued that Transfer★ I, *understood as I have suggested*, is not obviously invalid. And this (as opposed to Transfer★ II) is the principle employed in Kenny's reconstruction of the incompatibilist's argument.

Note that Transfer★ II, in contrast to Transfer★ I, is readily seen to be invalid. Recall Transfer★ II:

S cannot do X.
In the circumstances, doing X is (would be) doing Y.
Therefore, S cannot do Y.

There are many contexts in which doing X is just one of various possible ways of doing Y, and although one cannot do X, one can do something else which would constitute doing Y.

Suppose, for instance, that Sam is attending a lecture by a famous and prestigious philosopher in a rather small room. If Sam were to get up and dance a jig, he would horribly embarrass the chair of the department. Sam is however unable to do so, since he has recently broken his leg and is temporarily in a very cumbersome cast. But Sam could presumably embarrass the chair in various ways, including suddenly shouting obscenities at the speaker. Thus, although Sam cannot dance a jig, and his dancing a jig would be his embarrassing the chair, he nevertheless *can* embarrass the chair.[8]

Thus, inability does not transfer in the way suggested by Transfer★ II. But of course this does not in itself threaten the incompatibilist, since the incompatibilist's argument does *not* employ Transfer★ II. And as far as I can see, it is impossible to generate counterexamples to the Transfer Principle (introduced in chapter one and employed in the argument for incompatibilism presented there) along the lines of the counterexamples to Transfer★ II.[9] Thus, Kenny's examples do not cast doubt on the incompatibilist's argument, and Scotism is not a promising approach to defending the conventional wisdom (that we are in control of our behavior and can be held morally responsible).

3 Slote's critique

Thus far, we have not found reason to jettison Transfer, a salient ingredient in the powerful skeptical challenge to our common-sense view that we have the sort of control that underwrites moral responsibility. Michael Slote, however, has developed an interesting strategy for casting doubt on Transfer.[10] Slote's approach is first to point out that there are various types of necessity – epistemic, deontic, and "causal–

alethic" – for which the relevant modal principle fails (i.e., for which the analogue to Transfer with the appropriate interpretation of the modal operator fails). Slote suggests that the failures can be explained in virtue of the "selectivity" of the pertinent forms of necessity. Finally, Slote assimilates power necessity to the forms of necessity for which the modal principle fails, and he suggests a kind of selectivity which allegedly applies to power necessity.

In the discussion of Slote's critique, I shall explore a number of analogies between power necessity and various other modalities. Of course, the heart of this book concerns power necessity, and thus the other modalities are investigated with an eye to gaining a better understanding of power necessity. Throughout the rest of the book I shall be especially concerned to develop the analogy between power necessity and epistemic necessity (knowledge). Although the analogies between power necessity and the various other normative and non-normative modalities are all interesting, the analogy between power necessity and epistemic necessity is particularly rich and illuminating.

3.1 Knowledge and power

Closure and selectivity Slote claims, "It is generally agreed that '*A* knows that *p*' and '*A* knows that (*p* ⊃ *q*)' do not entail '*A* knows that *q*' . . . People may fail to make inferences they are entitled to make."[11] Thus, if Slote is correct, epistemic necessity provides an interpretation of the modal operators on which the analogue to Transfer is invalid. And if power necessity either has an "epistemic component" or simply can be assimilated to epistemic necessity in some relevant respect, then Transfer could plausibly be denied.

Daniel Dennett refers to Slote's article as a "pioneering article."[12] Dennett claims that power necessity is epistemic in a way which allows for the invalidity of Transfer. In a second piece, Slote says, ". . . although the notion of (not) being able to do otherwise at issue in the free-will controversy is not simply an epistemic modality, it may in unsuspected ways contain epistemic elements suffcient to unhinge [it from Transfer]."[13] Given what Slote takes to be the evident failure of the analogues of Transfer for epistemic and deontic necessity, Slote calls into question the incompatibilist's tenacious adherence to Transfer. For Slote it is more sensible to abandon Transfer than to give up our view of ourselves as persons or to embrace some sort of indeterministic picture of control.

The "Slote/Dennett" strategy for attacking Transfer places considerable weight on the analogy with the epistemic version of the principle. It will be useful to begin by asking why it might be thought that the epistemic version of the principle fails. Slote's claim is that "it is generally agreed" that the epistemic version is invalid. But it is not clear that this is so, and even if one's ultimate view is that the epistemic version is to be rejected, it is crucial to see why.

A way in which one could be led to reject the epistemic version of the principle would be to fail to distinguish it from a related principle. It is important to distinguish between the Principle of Closure of Knowledge Under *Known* Implication and the Principle of Closure of Knowledge Under Implication. And whereas it is relatively uncontroversial that knowledge is not closed under implication, it is more controversial (and certainly more difficult to establish) that knowledge is not closed under *known* implication. And it is only the Principle of Closure of Knowledge Under Known Implication (and not Closure of Knowledge Under Implication) that is structurally parallel to Transfer.

To help to see the relationships among these principles, recall first the structure of Transfer:

If: (a) $N_{S,t}$ (p)
and (b) $N_{S,t}$ (If p, then q),
then (c) $N_{S,t}$ (q).

Now it is evident that only the Principle of the Closure of Knowledge Under *Known* Implication is structurally parallel to Transfer. Replacing "N" (power necessity) with "K" (knowledge), the Principle of the Closure of Knowledge Under Known Implication is as follows:

If: (a) $K_{S,t}$ (p)
and (b) $K_{S,t}$ (If p, then q),
then (c) $K_{S,t}$ (q).

In contrast, the second premise of the Principle of Closure of Knowledge Under Implication is merely:

(b) (If p, then q).

To proceed. It should be obvious that knowledge is not closed under mere implication. Suppose that A knows that p. And imagine also that p logically implies q (but that A does not know this). It does not seem to follow that A knows that q. Thus, knowledge is not closed under implication. Slote's statement, "People may fail to make inferences they are entitled to make," is ambiguous. On one reading, it (quite plausibly) denies closure of knowledge under implication. But of course one should not conflate this principle and the Principle of Closure of Knowledge Under *Known* Implication. And it would only be a failure of the latter that could be employed to support the alleged inadequacy of Transfer.

Another possible route to a rejection of the Principle of Closure of Knowledge Under Known Implication would be to claim that closure of knowledge under implication is a *necessary condition* of it (and to deny closure of knowledge under implication). If closure under known implication required closure under implication, then (of course) the failure of closure under implication would entail the failure of closure under known implication.

Although Slote does not explicitly adopt this strategy, his remarks strongly suggest it. Slote *does* make the parallel claim about the parallel modality, power necessity; that is, he suggests that closure under logical implication is a necessary condition for the power version of the main modal principle:

> Anyone who assumes the validity of arguing from 'Np' and 'N($p \supset q$)' to 'Nq' would seem to be tacitly assuming that the necessity expressed in the operator 'N' is both agglomerative (closed with respect to conjunction introduction) and closed under logical implication, so that one can, *e.g.*, validly move from 'Np' and 'N($p \supset q$)' to 'N(p & p $\supset q$)' and from the latter to 'Nq'.[14]

But it seems pretty clear that closure of knowledge under known implication does *not* require closure of knowledge under implication. And what is in any case true is that this putative connection cannot be established in the way suggested. If epistemic necessity were closed under logical implication and agglomerative, then (as Slote points out) one could *derive* closure under known implication. But of course this shows that closure under implication and agglomerativity are *sufficient* for closure under known implication, *not* that they are necessary. It seems to me that one can hold that knowledge is closed under known implication while admitting the falsity of either closure under implication or agglomerativity (or both). It is possible that closure under known implication is a valid principle which cannot be derived from more basic principles.[15] So the failure of closure under implication does not in itself establish a failure of closure under known implication.

Let us now briefly consider a third kind of attempt to establish the inadequacy of the Principle of Closure of Knowledge Under Known Implication. Fred Dretske has presented a number of examples which, he claims, suggest that the Principle of Closure of Knowledge Under Known Implication is invalid.[16] Consider Dretske's famous "zebra example":

(1) *A* knows that there is a zebra in front of him.
(2) *A* knows that if it is a zebra in front of him, it is not a cleverly disguised mule.
But (3) *A* does not know that it is not a cleverly disguised mule in front of him.

Dretske's claim is that (1) and (2) can be true in a situation in which (3) is also true. If so, then knowledge would not be closed under known implication. Consider also the following "Dretske-type" examples, which are similar to examples presented by Jonathan Vogel:

(1) I know that my car is now parked in Lot 5.
(2) I know that if my car is now parked in Lot 5, it has not been stolen and driven away in the last five minutes.
But (3) I do not know that my car has not been stolen and driven away in the last five minutes.

And:

(1) I know that Bill Clinton is now President of the US.
(2) I know that if Bill Clinton is now President of the US, then Clinton has not been assassinated in the last five minutes.
But (3) I do not know that Clinton has not been assassinated in the last five minutes.[17]

But the Dretske-type pattern of intuitions about these cases is highly controversial. If the (3)-claims are really true in the examples, then why is it plausible to think that the (1)-claims can also be true? One's reasons for accepting the (3)-claims might impel one to *reject* the (1)-claims. Alternatively, one's reasons for accepting the (1)-claims might cause one to *reject* the (3)-claims. Indeed, it is controversial (and most definitely not a matter of "general agreement") whether any Dretske-type example strongly supports the compatibility of claims such as (1), (2), and (3) and thus the rejection of the Principle of Closure of Knowledge Under Known Implication.[18]

Dretske himself does not rely solely upon examples to support his conclusion that the Closure Principle is invalid. Like Slote, Dretske suggests that there is an analogy between the modality under discussion (epistemic) and other modalities for which it is true that closure fails. And Dretske suggests a general theory which would explain the failure of closure in the epistemic case. It will be useful to sketch this theory in bare bones.

Consider what is involved in the claim that A knows that there is a zebra in front of him. Dretske suggests that this claim is supported by the idea that A can distinguish the situation from a range of *relevant alternatives*. On the relevant alternatives approach, knowledge consists in (or at least implies) a certain sort of discriminatory capacity – the capacity to distinguish the actual situation from a range of relevant alternative scenarios. And this approach allows for the possibility (although strictly speaking it does not entail) that not all logically possible alternatives are *relevant*.[19] Dretske points out that the possibility that the animal in front of A is a cleverly disguised mule may not be a relevant alternative, and thus it may not be necessary for A to rule this possibility out, in order to know that there is a zebra in front of him. But since this possibility is clearly a relevant alternative to the claim that it is not a cleverly disguised mule in front of A, A does not know that it is not a cleverly disguised mule in front of him. As one moves from Dretske's (1) through (3), the range of relevant alternatives shifts.

Of course, this is just the most minimal sketch of the relevant-alternatives approach. Also, there are other theoretical approaches (which are perhaps not properly described as relevant alternatives approaches) that appear to vindicate Dretske's pattern of intuitions about the cases and thus support the denial of the Principle of Closure Under Known Implication.[20] I cannot discuss these approaches in detail here. Rather, I simply want to point out that it seems to be difficult to establish such a theoretical approach in light of the existence of intuitions highlighted by the skeptic.[21] So, for example, how could one *argue* that A knows that there is a zebra in front of him? The skeptic will press the point that since A does not know that it is not a cleverly disguised mule, it does not seem that he really knows that there is a zebra in front of him. The skeptic's point here is that given this sort of intuition, the possibility that it is a cleverly disguised mule in front of A is indeed a relevant alternative.[22] This dialectical context can quickly come to a dead-end, with both sides clinging to their intuitions without being able to argue for them in a non-question-begging way. In particular, it is hard to see how the proponent of the claim that A does indeed know that there is a zebra in front of him can argue for this position without straightforwardly denying the Principle of Closure of Knowledge Under Known Implication (given the assumption that A does not know that it is not a cleverly disguised mule). And it is equally hard to see how the opponent of this claim can argue against it without simply asserting the Principle. Thus, appeals to theory here do not appear to be any more promising than appeals to intuitions about particular examples: invoking a particular theory to support the intuitions seems dialectically inappropriate insofar as the theories seem straightforwardly to beg the question at issue.

I believe however that there is a final strategy which is more promising for casting doubt on the Principle of Closure of Knowledge Under Known Implication. The Principle seems to fail in certain situations in which one's beliefs are not "fully integrated." Suppose that one knows (and thus believes) that p, and that one knows (and thus believes) that p implies q. But imagine that one has not "put these two beliefs together," and thus that one doesn't believe that q. Since knowledge requires belief, it seems that one doesn't here know that q. The apparent failure of closure under known implication here results from a kind of epistemic "carelessness" or lack of integration – it results from the failure of closure of *belief* under known (and believed) implication.

I think that there can indeed be cases of epistemic fragmentation of the sort just described. This gives a second reading to Slote's claim, "People may fail to make inferences they are entitled to make." (Recall that on the first reading Slote is simply pointing to the falsity of the Principle of Closure of Knowledge Under Implication.) Thus, whereas various strategies are not uncontroversially successful, the final approach seems to me to succeed in showing the Principle of Closure of Knowledge Under Known Implication to be problematic. It is important (for the discussion below of particularity and selectivity) to notice that in a case where a person believes that p and that p implies q but does not believe that q, he fails to make a *particular* inference; he *has reason* to believe that q but he doesn't *actually* believe that q. If the analogy between the Principle of Closure of Knowledge Under Known Implication and the Transfer Principle is to be useful, Slote will need to show that the kind of factor which produces the failure in the epistemic case *also* produces the failure in the power case, or that an analogous factor has this effect in the power case. Slote must point to some interesting similarity between the kind of factor which produces the failure of the modal principle for the various other modalities (such as epistemic modality) and for power necessity.

Digression: closure and skepticism   Before I consider whether Slote can succeed in this project, I wish to digress to say a few words about the role of the Principle of Closure of Knowledge Under Known Implication. I suggested in chapter one that skepticism about knowledge about the empirical world is in certain interesting respects similar to skepticism about the sort of control that grounds our moral responsibility and personhood. It can now be seen that they are in a specific and important respect similar: they make use of analogous modal principles. That is, the Principle of Closure of Knowledge Under Known Implication is sometimes used by the skeptic about our knowledge of the external world. Suppose I know some "mundane" proposition about the empirical world, *p*. Surely also I know (or can easily be brought to know) that if *p*, then there is no evil genius deceiving me into falsely believing that *p*. And if the Closure Principle holds, then it follows that I know that there is no evil genius deceiving me into falsely believing that *p*. But the skeptic insists that I *don't* know this latter proposition (i.e., I can't "rule out" the skeptical "counterpossibility" to *p* in which I am being deceived), so the skeptic concludes that I don't know that *p*.

The above argument is a kind of *reductio ad absurdum*. It starts with the supposition that I know some ordinary empirical proposition, *p*. It then proceeds to establish (given the Closure Principle) that I know that there is no evil genius deceiving me into falsely believing that *p*. But this contradicts what the skeptic thinks is obvious – that we *don't* know *this*. The two sorts of skeptical arguments – about knowledge and power – can be seen to employ structurally similar modal principles.

Now if epistemic fragmentation or carelessness of the sort described above shows the Principle of Closure of Knowledge Under Known Implication to be invalid, then the epistemic skeptic's argument, as stated, fails. But it is clear that the skeptic can revise the Principle fairly straightforwardly in light of such problems. A revision such as the following might be appropriate:

> If a person knows that *p* and knows that *p* implies *q* and he concludes that *q* as a result of his beliefs that *p* and that *p* implies *q*, then he knows that *q*.

Such a version of (or variant on) the Principle of Closure of Knowledge Under Known Implication is obviously not impugned by the strategy which involves lack of epistemic integration. Further, it can be employed to get the strong and interesting skeptical result that any agent who makes certain extremely reasonable (and trivial) inferences from beliefs he holds does not know any mundane proposition about the empirical world p.

My purpose here is certainly not to raise a banner for epistemic skepticism. Rather, my point is simply that the strategy which impugns the Principle of Closure of Knowledge Under Known Implication and which appears to serve *Slote's* purposes will not impugn a related principle (the revised version) which is just as useful to the skeptic about our knowledge of the external world. Thus, someone who wishes to refute the sort of closure principle which could be invoked by an epistemic skeptic must dig deeper and work harder.

3.2 Relationality, selectivity, and particularity

I have granted that the problem of fragmentation shows that the Principle of Closure of Knowledge Under Known Implication (unrevised to accommodate this problem) is invalid. Slote argues that there are also non-epistemic modalities which offer exceptions to the relevant analogues to Transfer. If there were some feature which explained the failures of the principles for these modalities, and if this feature were also possessed by power necessity, then it would be plausible to suppose that power necessity is not governed by Transfer.

One example of a kind of necessity which Slote claims is not governed by the appropriate modal principle is deontic necessity of the sort imposed by an obligation.[23] An obligation, let us agree, arises from a *particular* voluntary undertaking (for example, a promise to a particular person). Imagine that I have promised to Jones that I will go to the party, and that I have promised to Smith that if I go to the party, I'll bring champagne. So

(4) I have an obligation to go to the party.

And

(5) I have an obligation to bring champagne, if I go to the party.

But it seems that

(6) I do not have an obligation to bring champagne.

After all, I have not made a promise to anyone to bring champagne; to whom would I owe this putative obligation?[24]

As Slote points out, the sort of deontic necessity involved in obligation is a kind of "relational necessity." But he says

> relationality alone cannot explain why a given form of deontic or moral necessity fails the principle of agglomeration. Timothy Smiley has, for example, suggested that the moral 'ought' may express relative necessity, so that 'ought p' is true if and only if 'p' follows logically from some ideal moral code, i.e., is necessary in relation to (the fulfillment of) such a code. But such relational necessity is agglomerative: if 'p' and 'q' both follow classically from a code, so does their conjunction. On the other hand, some forms of relational necessity can arise only in certain narrowly circumscribed ways; and when restrictions on the way a given kind of necessity can come into being unhinge it from agglomerativity (or closure or our main principle), we may say that such necessity is *selective*. Thus if obligation is nonagglomerative, that is, as we have seen, because of limitations on the way (relational) obligations can arise; it is because obligations to do specific things typically derive from *undertakings* (to individuals) *to do those very things*. So obligation is not only relational, but selective. And both of these factors enter into the 'logic' of the notion.[25]

Let us look at another of Slote's purportedly "selective" kinds of necessity: non-accidentality.[26] Suppose that Jules is sent to the bank by his superior, so that

It is not accidental that Jules is at the bank now.

Note that Jules' being at the bank entails that he is alive, and if what is logically necessary is non-accidental, then

It is not accidental that if Jules is at the bank now, then he is alive now.

But imagine that the only reason Jules is alive now is that five minutes ago he made an unintentional and fortuitous swerve which prevented him from being flattened by a truck. So

It is accidental that Jules is alive now.

Non-accidentality seems to involve being called for by a specific plan; this factor produces "selectivity." A plan may call for X, X may require Y, but the plan may not call for Y – a plan need not call for all that it presupposes.[27] The selectivity of non-accidentality issues in the failure of the relevant modal principle for this sort of necessity.

In general, then, selectivity is alleged to issue from kinds of "particularity" – particular acts or undertakings or plans. And this explanation of selectivity appears to fit with our previous account of the selectivity of epistemic necessity. Even if an agent *has reason* to believe a proposition *q*, he may not *actually infer* that *q*. The failure of agents to perform the particular acts of "putting their beliefs together" explains the selectivity of epistemic necessity, and it appears to be relevantly similar to the sort of factor which explains the selectivity of such modalities as obligation and non-accidentality.

Having produced examples of kinds of necessity for which the relevant modal principle fails, Slote now claims that power necessity is *also* such a kind of necessity. Slote says:

> When we say of any past event that we can *now* do nothing about it, I think we are saying that our *present* desires, abilities, beliefs, characters, etc., are no part of the explanation of it. And, more generally, the particular kind of factor in relation to which unavoidability exists at any given time, the factor 'selected' by such necessity, is simply, some factor (or set of factors) that brings about the unavoidable thing *without making use of (an explanatory chain that includes) the desires, etc., the agent has around that time.*[28]

Slote's argument against Transfer can now be developed straightforwardly. If *p* is a statement saying that some past event occurs, then since *p* is about an event whose occurrence is *not* explained by my present motivational states,

(7) It is now unavoidable that *p*.

Now Slote says, "And appropriate laws of nature have the same sort of necessity because whatever it is that makes them be as they are (certain deeper laws, the basic structure of the universe or what have you) is surely something that does not involve our present abilities and desires."[29] So, where *q* says that some action of mine now occurs (and $p \supset q$ is entailed by the laws of nature),

(8) It is now unavoidable that $p \supset q$.

But since the explanation of my present action *does* (according to Slote) refer to my present desires, beliefs, etc.,

(9) It is now *not* unavoidable that q.

If the factor cited by Slote is indeed what produces power necessity, then he can apparently explain why power necessity is not governed by Transfer.

3.3 Criticism

It seems to me that Slote's explanation of the "selectivity" of power necessity is, as it stands, unacceptable. Consider again Slote's claim, "When we say of any past event that we can *now* do nothing about it, I think we are saying that our *present* desires, abilities, beliefs, characters, etc., are no part of the explanation of it." But why assume that there is just *one* explanation of an event? Surely, there can be various different explanations of an event, and similarly, there can be various different explanations of (or factors that bring about) an "unavoidable thing" such as a proposition. (Presumably, a factor explains or brings about the *truth* of a proposition.) Given that there can be more than one explanation of the truth of a proposition, it is important to distinguish two senses of unavoidability:

(A) It is now unavoidable for an agent that r if and only if there exists an explanation of r which does not refer to the agent's present motivational states.

(B) It is now unavoidable for an agent that r if and only if there exists no explanation of r which refers to the agent's present motivational states.

Having distinguished these two senses of unavoidability, let us examine Slote's claims that (7), (8), and (9) are all true. First, consider the claims, adopting sense (A). I shall grant that (7) and (8) are true. The problem is that (9) seems to be false, on sense (A). To establish that (9) is true, on (A), it is *not* sufficient to point out that there exists some explanation of my action which does refer to my present motivational states. What must be shown is that there exists *no* explanation of my action which does *not* so refer. But Slote has never argued for this claim; he has only suggested that there exists some explanation of my action which does refer to my present motivational states.

Under causal determinism, there surely will be at least one explanation of my present action which does not refer to my present motivational states. As argued above, if causal determinism obtains, then there exists a proposition describing the state of the universe prior to my birth, which, together with the natural laws, entails that q obtains. So there is at least one pertinent kind of explanation of my present action, and (9) is false, on sense (A).

Now, let us consider sense (B) of unavoidability. I contend that (B) is clearly an unacceptable explication of the intuitive notion of unavoidability. There are at least the three following problems with (B). First, it seems to imply that it cannot be said that any *action* is unavoidable. If r says that I perform a certain action, then presumably there exists at least one explanation of r which refers to my practical reasoning or my motivational states; otherwise, it would be hard to see how r could describe an *action* rather than a mere event. But now on (B) r would not be considered unavoidable. Thus, in this respect (B) is not sufficiently strong: it does not deem unavoidable certain things we intuitively think are unavoidable.

Also, note that there are some actions which are unavoidable in virtue of the fact that an individual's motivational states are distorted in certain ways. Suppose, for example, that someone kills another because of some sort of psychotic episode or because he is in a blind rage. The actions may intuitively be unavoidable, and yet certainly an explanation will refer to the (deficient) motivational states, and thus (B) will not deem them unavoidable. Perhaps these actions are unavoidable precisely because there are explanations of them which do refer to the motivational states and which show that the agent's powers of reason or at least control have been obliterated or diminished by these states.

Finally, it seems to me that if there is a certain sort of explanation of r which does not refer to my present states, this suffices to render r unavoidable for me, even if there also exists an explanation of r which does refer to my present motivational states. Suppose, for instance, that wind conditions (and the condition of my boat) are such that the only way I can sail is westward. But imagine that I do not know this – I believe I could go eastward, if I wanted – and that I freely choose to go westward. There *is* an explanation of my sailing westward which refers to my present motivational states, and yet my sailing westward is intuitively unavoidable: it would occur, no matter what my motivational states were. It is possible that one "freely" (or at least voluntarily) perform an action which is nonetheless unavoidable, and this possibility (to be discussed at length later in the book) points to the unacceptability of (B). Thus, (B) can again be seen to be too weak.

The structure of my objection to Slote (thus far) is as follows. Slote unjustifiably refers to "the" explanation of an event (or truth of a proposition, and so forth). But there can be different explanations of an event or of the truth of a proposition. Given the fact of multiple explanations, one can try to reformulate Slote's suggestion in various ways. On sense (A) of unavoidability, (7) and (8) can be granted, but (9) is evidently false. And sense (B) is an unacceptable account of unavoidability. The plausible account fails to render Slote's trio of propositions true, and the account which has some chance of doing this is implausible. Perhaps Slote did not distinguish these two senses sufficiently carefully. Perhaps he was thinking of (A) when focusing on unavoidability and (B) when focusing on the argument's three propositions. Insofar as Slote has not offered a plausible account which renders his three claims true, he has not successfully explained the purported failure of Transfer.

In useful and generous personal correspondence, Slote has suggested a third interpretation of unavoidability which he believes merits attention:

(C) It is now unavoidable for an agent that r if and only if the "best" explanation of r does not refer to the agent's present motivational states.

On (C), it could be argued that (7), (8), and (9) are all true. But it is clear that everything hangs on the notion of the "best" (or perhaps "most adequate") explanation. And these notions would need considerable development, if the approach is to have substantive content.

Further, just as Slote's original formulation is shown to be problematic by the *multiplicity* of explanation, the new formulation seems to underestimate the *relativity* of explanation. That is, explanation is relative to contexts and purposes, and thus it is unclear that there can be any non-relative notion of the best explanation. And it is also unclear how the account can accommodate the relativity of explanation.

Finally, it seems to me that the sailing example discussed above points to the possible inadequacy (or at least incompleteness) of the third suggestion. When I sail westward voluntarily, I take it that the "best" explanation (relative to a range of contexts and purposes) of my sailing westward *does* refer to my motivational states: I sail westward because I really want to do so. Yet it is *unavoidable* that I sail westward. What makes it true that I can't avoid sailing westward may play no role in my sailing westward and thus may be irrelevant to the (best) explanation of my sailing westward. Thus, I do not believe Slote's third interpretation of unavoidability is promising.

To drive home the general problem with Slote's approach, recall that Slote claims that the selectivity of certain kinds of necessity is generated by *particular* undertakings or events (promises, plans, irresistible impulses, etc.). The selectivity is not supposed to come from mere relationality (as in Smiley's account of "ought").[30] But notice that the notion of explanation is crucially ambiguous: one can *offer* a particular explanation to a person, and there can *exist* an (adequate) explanation. The first notion involves a particular act of explaining (and perhaps a particular act of accepting the explanation), but of course it is not plausible to connect power necessity with this sort of actual particular activity. (An action does not become unavoidable simply because someone – perhaps mistakenly – accepts an explanation of it which makes no reference to the agent's present motivational states. Nor does an action fail to be unavoidable simply because no one has engaged in the activity of explaining it to anyone.) Power necessity rather derives (on the approach which embraces Slote's (A)) from the *existence* of an adequate explanation of a certain sort, and this kind of factor would not seem to produce selectivity, but mere relationality. So power necessity (on Slote's (A)) would appear to be more properly assimilated to the deontic necessity expressed by "ought" than the necessity expressed by "obligation". But if so, then it is not surprising that power necessity (on (A)) has not been shown to be selective.

We are now in a good position to see why Slote has not exhibited a suitable parallel between the failure of the epistemic analogue of Transfer (the Principle of Closure of Knowledge Under Known Implication) and the alleged failure of Transfer itself. The failure in the epistemic case was explained by an agent's failure to perform a particular act of epistemic integration. He didn't actually form a belief he had reason to form. But the failure to *form* a belief is similar to the failure to *offer* or *accept* an explanation. And whereas these factors are plausibly taken to be selectivity-generating, the failure to *offer* or *accept* an explanation is *not* plausibly connected to power necessity (or its absence). "Particularity" of a certain sort may generate "selectivity" of epistemic necessity, but it has *not* been shown that such particularity is involved in power necessity.

Knowledge is "epistemic necessity." It comes from belief *plus* something (which I shall call the "necessitating component" – justification, reliability, tracking, etc.). The failure of the epistemic modal principle discussed above (the Principle of Closure of Knowledge Under Known Implication) comes from the belief component, rather than the necessitating component. It is for this reason a relatively "superficial" way in which the principle fails. Most of the discussions of the alleged failure of Closure of Knowledge Under Known Implication have focused on putative failures of closure for the *necessitating* component of knowledge. Only such a failure will be useful to an anti-skeptic. I conjecture that only a failure of closure in the necessitating component of knowledge could help us to understand (by analogy) how power necessity could fail to abide by the main modal principle.

3.4 Summary

Slote and Dennett suggest that, if power necessity is partly epistemic, then since epistemic necessity doesn't obey the analogue of Transfer, power necessity also might not obey Transfer. Further, Slote claims (a) that there are certain non-epistemic kinds of necessity for which the relevant modal principles fail, and (b) that there exists a kind of factor which explains the failure in both the epistemic case and the other cases and which is analogous to some factor which explains the failure of Transfer.

I have challenged (b). First, I identified the specific reason why the epistemic version of the principle is invalid, if indeed it is invalid. This involves a certain kind of "particularity" which plausibly generates selectivity. But I argued that this sort of factor is not obviously present in the case of power necessity. Thus, the relatively clear cases of epistemic (and non-epistemic) failure of the modal principle seem to be crucially different from the case of power necessity. The multiplicity and relativity of explanation render Slote's approach seriously flawed, as it stands; at best it is an intriguing gesture toward a full account.

It may be, as it is often said, that knowledge is power. But it has yet to be established that epistemic necessity is relevantly similar to power necessity: it has not been established that the failure of the relevant epistemic principle based on epistemic fragmentation has an analogue in the context of power necessity and Transfer. Slote's article may indeed be a pioneering effort; but I suppose the Donner Party were pioneers as well!

4 Conclusion

In this chapter I have looked closely at two attempts (by Kenny and Slote) to cast doubt on Transfer. I have argued that Transfer cannot be impugned *in these ways*. Indeed, if we are to secure "elbow room" by denying Transfer, I am afraid this will require some Elbow Grease.

The possibility of showing Transfer to be invalid is left open by the fact that neither I nor (as far as I know) anyone else has been able to *prove* it. The situation here is analogous to the situation with regard to Closure of Knowledge Under Known Implication. In both cases it does not appear to be possible to start with "simpler, more basic" ingredients and *derive* the principles as conclusions of uncontroversially sound arguments. Thus, although I have argued that the Transfer Principle cannot be disproved in certain ways, it is not evident to me that it can be proved.[31]

3

The Transfer Principle: Its Role

1 Introduction

In the previous chapter I evaluated various strategies for calling Transfer into question. I argued that these strategies are not successful. But I also conceded that my reflections still leave Transfer's status in doubt. It cannot be easily disproved, nor can I see how it could be established. In this chapter I shall look carefully at the *role* of Transfer. In chapter one I pointed out that Transfer can be employed to generate worrisome challenges to the conventional wisdom that we are in fact in control of our behavior. There I suggested that the challenges employ various ingredients, including the assumptions of causal determinism or God's existence. In this chapter I wish to begin by considering a fascinating argument that Transfer *in itself* (i.e., apart from any special assumptions about causal determinism or God's existence) would generate the conclusion that we (across a wide range of cases) lack the kind of control that involves alternative possibilities. On this view, Transfer is in itself *sufficient* to generate the result that we lack control (in a very significant array of circumstances). In the first section I shall critically evaluate the argument; I shall be defending the view that the Transfer Principle does *not* in itself suffice for the jarring claim that (in many contexts) we lack the sort of control that involves alternative possibilities and grounds moral responsibility. The appearance generated by the argument of the first chapter – that Transfer must be *combined* with the other ingredients in order to generate the worrisome conclusion – can be defended.

Having argued that Transfer is not sufficient for the skeptical result, in the following section I go on to consider the view that Transfer is also not *necessary* for it. This is an extremely important project, precisely because of the uncertain status of Transfer – its failure to be susceptible to decisive proof.[1] If it should turn out that Transfer is not even necessary in order to generate the skeptical result, then it would have become clear that Transfer is considerably less central to the logic of arguments about control than many have supposed. Further, our focus of attention should then shift to the ingredients which *are* in fact needed to generate the skeptical challenge.

1.1 Restrictivism

In his article "When is the Will Free?"[2] Peter van Inwagen argues that any proponent of Transfer must *eo ipso* hold that we lack control (in the sense that requires alternative possibilities) in a *wide* variety of contexts in which we ordinarily think we have this sort of control. I shall use the term "restrictivism" to refer to van Inwagen's view that "one has precious little free will, that rarely, if ever, is anyone able to do otherwise than he in fact does."[3] Van Inwagen's argument is then that any proponent of Transfer must embrace restrictivism and thus that Transfer in itself (i.e., apart from any "substantive" assumption such as causal determinism or God's existence) is sufficient to generate something quite like the skeptical result that we lack control.

The structure of van Inwagen's argument is as follows. He considers three cases, in which he argues that the relevant agent is alleged not to be able to do other than he actually does. The first is one of duty unopposed by inclination; in such a case van Inwagen claims that "no one is able to perform an act he considers morally reprehensible."[4] The second case is one of unopposed inclination; in such a case, "no one is able to do anything that he wants very much *not* to do and has no countervailing desire to do it."[5] The third case is one in which we act without reflection or deliberation; van Inwagen claims that "if we regard an act as the one obvious thing or the only sensible thing to do, we cannot do anything but that thing."[6] Given these points, van Inwagen concludes that the only times an agent *is* free to do otherwise are times in which the agent is confronted with conflicting alternatives such that, even after reflection, it is not obvious to him what to do. Such conflict situations, van Inwagen tells us, occur *rarely* and can be divided into three general categories: (1) "Buridan's Ass" cases,[7] (2) cases in which duty or general policy conflicts with inclination or momentary desire, and (3) cases in which one must choose between incommensurable values.[8]

1.2 Unfree to ignore the obvious

In order to establish restrictivism, van Inwagen presents a series of three arguments (pertaining to the three cases just described). In the first, he argues that no one is able to act in a manner that he considers morally indefensible. The argument runs as follows:

(1) N_I (I regard A as indefensible).
(2) N_I (I regard A as indefensible $\supset$ I am not going to do A).

Hence (via Transfer),

(3) N_I (I am not going to do A).[9]

The intuitive idea behind the argument is that at this moment I don't have any choice about the fact that I now consider some action A indefensible, and I also don't have any choice about its being the case that if I regard an action as morally indefensible then I am not going to do it; these two premises being true, it follows that at this moment I'm not going to do A and I don't have any choice about this. In short, it is power necessary for me that I am not going to do A. Generalizing the results of this argument van Inwagen concludes that "no one is able to perform an act he considers morally reprehensible."[10]

Van Inwagen then extends the type of reasoning used in this argument about morally indefensible actions to the two other cases: cases of unopposed inclination in which we want very much to do one thing and have no opposing desires, and cases of unreflective action in which we know what the obvious thing to do is after little if any deliberation. In the case of unopposed inclination, we are asked to consider an example in which a person, Nightingale, is anxiously awaiting a phone call which he very much desires to receive. Nightingale has a very strong desire to answer the phone, and no countervailing desires not to do so. The question is: Can Nightingale refrain from answering the phone? The restrictivist reasons that he cannot, and in support of this conclusion he offers the same argument form used above. Skipping the formalization, the rough idea behind the argument is as follows. At this moment Nightingale does not have any choice about the fact that he very much desires to answer the phone. He also has no choice about its being the case that if he very much desires to answer the phone (and he has no countervailing desire to refrain from doing so), then he is going to answer the phone. These two premises being true, it follows that at this moment Nightingale is going to answer the phone and he doesn't have any choice about this. Van Inwagen concludes that "no one is able to do anything that he wants very much *not* to do and has no countervailing desire to do it."[11]

In the last argument, which is supposed to cover the broadest range of actions, the restrictivist turns to actions which "with little or no deliberation . . . just seem – or would seem if we reflected on them at all – to be the obvious thing to do in the circumstances."[12] Again we are asked to consider a situation in which a phone rings and a person immediately answers it without giving the matter a second thought. Following the same style of reasoning as in the Nightingale example, the argument claims that the agent is not free to refrain from answering the phone. The argument runs as before. At the moment the phone rings, the person has no choice about the fact that he has no reason not to answer the phone immediately or to deliberate about answering it. Furthermore, he has no choice about its being the case that if he hasn't any reason not to answer the phone, then he is going to answer it. From these two premisses it follows that at the moment the phone rings, the agent is going to answer it and he has no choice about this. Van Inwagen says:

> There are . . . few occasions in life in which – at least after a little reflection and perhaps some investigation into the facts – it isn't absolutely clear what to do. And if the above arguments are correct, then an incompatibilist should believe that on such occasions the agent cannot do anything other than the thing that seems to him to be clearly the only sensible thing to do.[13]

1.3 Critique of van Inwagen

I do not think van Inwagen's arguments are successful. To challenge these arguments, I want to take issue with the second premiss in each. The most detailed defense of premiss (2) is offered in the first argument; here van Inwagen maintains that the second premiss is true because the following conditional is a necessary truth and no one has a choice about a necessary truth.

(C1) If X regards A as an indefensible act, given the totality of relevant information available to him, and if he has no way of getting further relevant information, and if he lacks any positive desire to do A, and if he sees no objection to *not* doing A (again, given the totality of relevant information available to him), then X is not going to do A.[14]

Van Inwagen claims that the restrictivist's three arguments are similar, and thus I assume that van Inwagen imagines that there are conditionals parallel to (C1) which support the parallel premisses of the latter two arguments. Here, I will begin by discussing the latter two arguments – pertaining to unopposed inclination and unreflective action. I will deny the claim that the relevant conditionals successfully support the second premisses of these arguments. I shall focus my remarks on the argument concerning unopposed inclination; this argument appears to be the stronger of the latter two restrictivist arguments, and the considerations adduced against it can readily be applied to the third argument. Then I will turn to van Inwagen's first argument – concerning indefensible actions. Although I am departing from van Inwagen's order of presentation, the criticism can be developed more naturally in this fashion.

In his second argument, the restrictivist argues that in cases of unopposed inclination the agent cannot do other than what he actually does (despite the intuitive impression that he can so act). The argument has the same form as the argument concerning indefensible actions sketched above, but now the second premiss (upon which I shall concentrate) is:

(2) N_X (X has an unopposed inclination to do $A \supset X$ is going to do A).

And parallel to the conditional which allegedly supports the second premiss of the argument about indefensibility, we have:

(C2) If X very much desires to do some act A given the totality of relevant information available to him, and if he has no way of getting further relevant information, and if he lacks any positive desire to perform any act other than A, and if he sees no objection to doing A and refraining from doing anything else (again, given the totality of relevant information available to him), then X is not going to do anything other than A.

Now, the only way in which (C2) can support premiss two of the argument is if (C2) is *power necessary* for the relevant agent. That is, (C2) must be true and X must have no choice about whether (C2) is true.

The problem with the argument can be made clear as follows. (C2) admits of two interpretations. On one interpretation, (C2) is plausibly thought to be true and power necessary, but it does not support the second premiss of the argument. And on the other interpretation the second premiss is supported but (C2) is not plausible. Thus, there is *no* interpretation of (C2) that gives us reason to accept the second premiss of the argument for restrictivism.

Let us first consider the interpretation according to which (C2) is plausibly taken to be true and power necessary. This interpretation is motivated by the basic idea (presented above) that action requires some sort of "pro-attitude" – say, a desire. It might be argued (as I suggested above) that actions are distinguished from mere events in virtue of being preceded (in a suitable way) by special sorts of events: "volitions." Further, it might be claimed that a volition must be based (in a suitable way) on at least *some* desire. If these claims were true, it would follow that it would be impossible for an agent to perform an *action* without having some desire to do so. Presumably, the necessity of desire for action could be posited even by a theorist who does not believe in volitions. In any case, it is a plausible conceptual claim that it is impossible for an agent to perform an action without having some desire to perform the action in question.[15]

The key point is that the alleged conceptual truth cannot support premiss two of the argument. Note that the alleged conceptual truth can be regimented as follows:

(C2*) It is not possible that the following state of affairs obtain: that X performs an act other than A without having any desire to perform such an act.

And note further that (C2*) does *not* imply

(2) N_X (X has an unopposed desire to do $A \supset X$ is going to do A).

As long as there is no *obstacle* to the agent's having the desire to do other than A during the relevant temporal interval, I believe that (2) can be false compatibly with the truth of (C2*). (2) would be false if, despite the fact that X has an unopposed desire to do A, he *could* refrain from doing A; and, given that (during the relevant temporal period) X *can* acquire this sort of desire, I believe that it is reasonable to suppose that X can do other than A. (I will argue for this below.)

Now let us interpret (C2) such that it does entail (2):

(C2**) If X does not desire to do other than A, X cannot do other than A.

I concede that (C2**) supports (2), but at the price of plausibility. This is because, even if an agent does not actually desire to do other than A, he might well have the ability (during the relevant temporal interval) to generate such a desire, and to act on this desire. And it is extremely implausible to suppose that agents quite generally lack the *power* to generate the relevant sorts of desires.

To elaborate. Just about anybody can summon up the worry that he is not free to do otherwise. That is, one can worry that, despite the pervasive intuitive feeling that frequently we have genuine freedom to do various things, we do not in fact have such freedom. (Indeed, anyone who thinks about the restrictivist's argument certainly has reason to worry that he might not be free to do otherwise in many contexts.) This worry can then generate *some* reason (perhaps, a desire) to do otherwise simply to prove that one can do so.[16] Thus, barring special circumstances – to which the restrictivist does not allude in his arguments – even an agent who actually does not have any desire to do other than A can have the power to generate such a desire (during the relevant temporal interval). And insofar as: (1) the agent *can* generate the desire to do other than A, (2) the agent can try to act on this desire, and (3) if he were to try to act on this desire, he would succeed, then I believe that the agent *can* (during the relevant temporal interval) do other than A.[17] The leading idea here is that there is no reason to suppose that agents *generally* lack the power to generate (in some way or another) reasons to do otherwise, the power to try to act on those reasons, or the power to succeed in so acting.

Consider van Inwagen's own example in which Nightingale wants very much to answer the phone as soon as it rings. If Nightingale can call to mind the doubt that he is able to do otherwise in such situations, this very doubt can give him a reason to pause before picking up the receiver. (Perhaps he simply does not answer the phone on the first ring, but waits until it rings five times; this suffices, he might feel, to prove he was free to do otherwise.) In this scenario, Nightingale's worry has transformed a normally routine phone call into a situation in which Nightingale must decide between two conflicting desires: a desire to answer the phone as soon as it rings, and a desire to prove to himself that he doesn't have to answer it as soon as it rings. I claim that insofar as: (1) the agent can generate a desire of the second sort, (2) he can try to act on this desire, and (3) if the agent were to try to act on this sort of desire, he would succeed, then the agent *can* (during the relevant temporal period) refrain from answering the phone, even though he actually lacks any desire to do other than answer the phone.[18]

I believe that the above considerations show that, even if an agent actually lacks any desire to perform a given act, he *can* perform that action, insofar as certain conditions are met. These conditions involve the ability to generate certain reasons and to translate these reasons into action. Further, I suggested that it is extremely plausible to suppose that (absent special assumptions about causal determinism or particular psychological or physical impairments) these conditions are frequently met.[19] Thus, I believe that (C2**) is not in general true. I have argued, then, that whereas (C2*) is plausible, it does not imply (2); and whereas (C2**) implies (2), it is not plausible. Thus, I see no reason to accept the second premiss of van Inwagen's argument for restrictivism.

In order more clearly to highlight my position, it is useful to consider the complaint that I have simply missed van Inwagen's point.[20] Van Inwagen's claim is that if in some possible world, $w1$, Nightingale has a strong, unopposed inclination to answer the phone as soon as it rings, then Nightingale is going to answer the phone as soon as it rings and he is not able in $w1$ to do otherwise. But – the objector continues – all your reconstruction of the example shows is that if in some other possible world, $w2$, Nightingale's motivational set is changed so that he has two conflicting inclinations, then Nightingale in $w2$ is able to refrain from answering the phone as soon as it rings. Nightingale's ability in $w2$, however, is a function of his having opposing inclinations, and in itself this doesn't show that Nightingale in $w1$, without the opposing inclinations, is able to do otherwise. The issue, then, is not what Nightingale can do in $w2$ with a different motivational set, but rather what Nightingale can do in $w1$ given that his motivational set is just as van Inwagen stipulates.

I reply that, as long as Nightingale is genuinely *able* (during the relevant temporal interval) in $w1$ to generate a desire not to answer the phone, then he is *able* in $w1$ not to answer the phone. Insofar as $w2$ is *genuinely accessible* to Nightingale, then $w2$ is relevant to what Nightingale *can* do in $w1$. It is only if $w2$ is not so accessible that it is irrelevant to Nightingale's abilities in $w1$. In general, so long as some world $w2$ is in the appropriate sense accessible to $w1$, then $w2$ is relevant to the modal properties of individuals in $w1$. As a simple example, imagine that I am not wearing a red shirt in the actual world, but I (or my counterpart) is wearing a red shirt in another possible world w^* which is genuinely accessible to the actual world. Presumably, w^* is relevant to the modal properties I possess in the actual world; more specifically, in virtue of facts about w^* it is true that in the actual world I have the property of possibly wearing a red shirt. Of course, it is undeniable that in the actual world I am not wearing a red shirt, and that w^* is not the actual world. But equally clearly it does not follow that facts about w^* are not relevant to the modal properties I actually possess. And so also with power attributions.

1.4 Free to act indefensibly, free to act crazily

Thus far I have argued against the restrictivist's argument that in cases of unopposed inclination the agent is not free to do otherwise. I believe that the same considerations apply, *mutatis mutandis*, to the argument concerning unreflective actions. Thus, I believe that I have pointed to a way of salvaging the intuition that, even if Transfer were valid, individuals are often free to do otherwise in contexts of unopposed desire and unreflective action. Now let me turn to van Inwagen's parallel argument concerning indefensible actions.

Having developed the criticism of the argument pertaining to unopposed desire, it is now relatively simple to explain what is wrong with the argument concerning indefensible actions. In fact, the objection to the argument concerning indefensible actions is precisely the same as the objection to the argument concerning unopposed desires.

Recall that van Inwagen adduces (C1) in support of premiss (2) of the argument:

(C1) If X regards A as an indefensible act, given the totality of relevant information available to him, and if he has no way of getting further relevant information, and if he lacks any positive desire to do A, and if he sees no objection to *not* doing A (again, given the totality of relevant information available to him), then X is not going to do A.[21]

Given that van Inwagen adduces (C1) in support of (2), it is clear that he is interpreting the second premiss of the argument in the following way:

(2) N_X (X regards A as an indefensible act and X lacks any desire to do $A \supset X$ does not do A).

To proceed as above. (C1) can be interpreted so as to claim that the following state of affairs is not possible: that X regards A as indefensible, has no desire to perform A, and performs A. But (C1), so interpreted, does not imply (2). Alternatively, (C1) could be interpreted so as to claim that if X regards A as indefensible and X lacks any desire to do A, then X cannot do A. But, so interpreted, (C1) is false, insofar as X can (in the relevant temporal interval) generate the desire in question. Thus, as above, van Inwagen has offered no good reason to accept the second premise of his argument.

In the context of unopposed desire discussed above, it is not supposed that the agent believes that the act in question is *indefensible*. Might this belief constitute an obstacle to generating a reason (or desire of the sort discussed above) to perform the act? That is, is the context of indefensible acts relevantly different from the contexts of unopposed desire and unreflective action?

The examples adduced by van Inwagen in support of (C1) suggest that morally indefensible actions *do* have some special status such that one literally is unable to bring oneself to desire to do (and thus to do) them.[22] To make this point, van Inwagen begins with an example presented by Daniel Dennett in which Dennett makes the claim that he is unable to torture innocent victims for small sums of money.[23] Van Inwagen accurately observes that the point of the example is not so much that Dennett would not be able to torture these innocents if he so chose, but rather that, given Dennett's character, he simply is *unable to make such a choice* (and, presumably, unable to generate the relevant desire). Van Inwagen wishes to extend this line of reasoning to show that he also could not slander a colleague to prevent that colleague's appointment to Chair of the Tenure Committee, and similarly that none of us could do anything that he considers indefensible.

Now, I certainly grant that there may be *some* actions – call them "unwillable" actions – which a particular agent literally cannot bring himself to choose to do (and to do); and some (although not necessarily all) of these unwillable actions may be ones that are (believed to be) morally indefensible.[24] Indeed, Dennett's example of torturing innocents seems to be just such a case. I wish to emphasize, however, that it does not follow from an action's being morally indefensible that it is *unwillable*. That is, I suggest that the Dennett/van Inwagen point here gains plausibility from their focusing on a proper subset of the relevant cases: those morally indefensible actions which are *also* unwillable. But an indefensible action is not *eo ipso* unwillable. Thus, I wish to block the move from the specific case of one's not being able to torture innocents to the general claim that "no one is able to perform an act he considers morally reprehensible."[25]

I believe that there *can* be cases in which an agent believes that an act is morally indefensible and nevertheless has a desire to perform it (of the sort mentioned above) and indeed successfully acts on this desire. And it is in general plausible to suppose that agents have the *power* to generate this sort of desire. In order to support the claim that the context of indefensible action is not relevantly different from the other two contexts, I present the following examples in which an individual believes that the act in question is indefensible but nevertheless has a desire to perform it and does indeed perform it.

Consider first Augustine's famous account of the theft of pears in his boyhood. Shortly before this passage, Augustine is wondering about the reason for his stealing pears for which he had no desire, and after acknowledging the view that all action must be for the sake of some apparent good, he dismisses this explanation in his own case:

> . . . now that I ask what pleasure I had in that theft, I find that it had no beauty to attract me. . . . It did not even have the shadowy, deceptive beauty which makes vice attractive.[26]

> Let my heart now tell you what prompted me to do wrong for no purpose, and why it was only my own love of mischief that made me do it. The evil in me was foul, but I loved it. I loved my own perdition and my own faults, not the things for which I committed wrong, but the wrong itself.[27]

Augustine's reflections are disturbing precisely because they exemplify one man's ability not only to do something he takes to be morally indefensible, but to be drawn to the action precisely because it is so indefensible. This is not to say that Augustine did not see the robbery as having some desirable consequences. He himself admits that he would not have committed the crime had it not been for his companions and the "thrill of having partners in sin."[28] However, simply because Augustine wanted something from his thieving, this does not show that he saw the thieving as good, or that he believed it conformed to an overall system of values he was willing to defend. A person might see the pilfering of pears as wholly indefensible and still desire to do it, if for no other reason than to assert one's ability to act against moral value. Indeed Augustine's comments suggest that he saw his attraction to evil as being intimately connected to this desire for a perverse sort of freedom and power – a freedom to ignore the Good:

> What was it, then, that pleased me in that act of theft? Which of my Lord's powers did I imitate in a perverse and wicked way? Since I had no

real power to break his law, was it that I enjoyed at least the pretence of doing so, like a prisoner who creates for himself the illusion of liberty by doing something wrong, when he has no fear of punishment, under a feeble hallucination of power? Here was a slave who ran away from his master and chased a shadow instead! What an abomination! What a parody of life! What abysmal death! Could I enjoy doing wrong for no other reason than that it was wrong? . . . I loved nothing in it except the thieving, though I cannot truly speak of that as a 'thing' that I could love, and I was only the more miserable because of it.[29]

A different type of rebellion, but one which expresses a related yearning to flout moral prohibitions, is found in the story of a character quite distinct from St Augustine: Dostoevsky's Raskolnikov. Recall that at the outset of the story, Raskolnikov is contemplating killing and robbing the old pawnbroker, Alena Ivanovna, and as he does so, he is keenly aware of the evil at hand. He knows such acts are morally reprehensible and he is repulsed by his own musings:

'Oh God, how repulsive! Can I possibly, can I possibly . . . no, that's nonsense, it's ridiculous!' he broke off decisively. 'How could such a horrible idea [i.e., to rob and murder Ivanovna] enter my mind? What vileness my heart seems capable of! The point is, that it is vile, filthy, horrible, horrible!'[30]

In spite of this moral aversion, Raskolnikov nonetheless finds that he is able to do the indefensible: he takes a borrowed axe to the head of not only Alena Ivanovna but her sister as well. Later, as he thinks back on the murder and robbery, Raskolnikov dismisses the only reasonable motive for the crime:

'If you really knew what you were doing,' he ponders, 'if you really had a definite and constant objective, how is it that you have never even looked into the purse, and have no idea what you gained, or for what you underwent all those torments and consciously performed such base, vile, and ignoble actions?'[31]

Raskolnikov knows that he did not kill the old woman, as a more typical criminal might have, for her money. And later, as he confesses to Sonya, the deeper motivation behind the crime comes out:

'I realized then, Sonya,' he went on enthusiastically, 'that power is given only to the man who dares stoop and take it. There is only one thing needed, only one – to dare. . . . I wanted to *have the courage*, and I killed . . . I only wanted to dare, Sonya, that was the only reason!'

. . . 'what I needed to find out then, and find out as soon as possible, was whether I was a louse like everybody else or a man, whether I was capable of stepping over the barriers or not. Dared I stoop and take the power or not?'

. . . 'Listen: when I went to the old woman's that time, it was only to *test myself* . . . Understand that![32]

Raskolnikov's remarks are of interest because they give an example of a man who knows that robbery and murder are morally indefensible, is not driven to perform these acts in the pursuit of some good which can be separated from the crime itself, and nonetheless does rob and murder two people. Indeed, what is most important about Raskolnikov for my purposes, is that, given a straightforward reading, he seems drawn to murder the aging pawnbroker, precisely to see if he *can* do it. He wants to discover if he has the power to ignore moral prohibitions – he wants to know if he is free to do the morally indefensible.

What is striking about the crimes of both Augustine and Raskolnikov is that, unlike a more mundane robbery in which the wrongdoing is merely a means to material gain, the motive behind their crimes is inextricably bound up with a desire to do wrong and to flout moral constraints. This is not to say that the motivations of Augustine and Raskolnikov can be assimilated in every respect. Whereas Augustine seeks the freedom to do evil in order to rebel against the Good, Raskolnikov seeks this freedom to show that he is beyond good and evil. But the crucial point for this discussion is that both men claim to do what the restrictive incompatibilist says they cannot – freely perform an act that is perceived by the agent to be morally indefensible.

I have argued, then, that the context of indefensibility is not relevantly different from the context of (say) unopposed desire: an agent can generate a certain sort of desire to perform an action even though he believes that the action is morally indefensible. Thus, my critique of van Inwagen's argument about contexts of unopposed desire (and unreflective action) can be extended to apply to his argument about contexts of indefensible actions. Thus, the critique applies to *all* of van Inwagen's alleged contexts in which we lack freedom. I conclude that van Inwagen has not established his (rather surprising) contention that Transfer in itself is sufficient to generate the result that we rarely if ever have control over our actions.[33]

2 The Wolf/Dennett slide

Before leaving the question of whether we are free to act indefensibly, I want to consider a final worry about such freedom which is suggested by two interesting examples recently formulated by Susan Wolf. Wolf asks us to consider what it would mean for an agent to have the ability to act against everything he believes in and cares about:

> It would mean, for example, that if the agent's son were inside a burning building, the agent could just stand there and watch the house go up in flames. Or that the agent, though he thinks his neighbor a fine and agreeable fellow, could just get up one day, ring the doorbell, and punch him in the nose. One might think that such pieces of behavior should not be classified as actions at all – that they are rather more like spasms that the agent cannot control. If they are actions they are very bizarre, and an agent who performed them would have to be insane. *Indeed, one might think he would have to be insane if he had even the ability to perform them.* For the rationality of an agent who could perform such irrational actions as these must hang by a dangerously thin thread.[34]

Before directly discussing these examples, a word of qualification is in order. Wolf originally presents these examples to illustrate what it would mean for an agent's actions not to be determined by any interests whatsoever. One of the points she is making, if I have understood her properly, is that a person whose actions weren't determined by *any* interests could hardly be said to be acting at all. Rather, his behavior, since it did not reflect any interests or intention, would seem more like spasms or the bizarre movements of an insane person. Understood in this fashion Wolf's claim is certainly unobjectionable; indeed, this insight seems merely to reflect the (alleged) conceptual truth discussed above that all behavior, if it is to be considered action at all, must reflect some pro-attitude.

My interest in Wolf's examples comes from another more substantive claim which is also suggested by her examples and subsequent comments; this is the suggestion that anyone who even had the *ability* to perform indefensible acts (like allowing her children to burn, or punching her neighbor in the nose for no good reason) would have to be insane. This claim is not the trivial one that anyone whose bodily movements did not reflect her interests would be insane; rather, it is the more interesting and substantive claim that anyone who even had the ability to act against all seemingly good interests would be insane. A similar sentiment is found in the following statement by Daniel Dennett: "But in other cases, like Luther's, when I say I cannot do otherwise I mean I cannot because I see so clearly what the situation is and because my rational control faculty is *not* impaired. It is too obvious what to do; reason dictates it; I would have to be mad to do otherwise, and since I happen not to be mad, I cannot do otherwise."[35] Both Wolf and Dennett seem inclined to slide from the claim that "doing *A* would be crazy" to a stronger claim that "anyone who had the ability to do *A* would be crazy." If this "Wolf/Dennett slide" were correct, then, since most of us are not crazy, it would seem to follow that most of us are not able to act in a crazy, indefensible manner – a conclusion which the restrictive incompatibilist would welcome.

I think the conclusion reached via the Wolf/Dennett slide is false. What reason is there to think that the mere *ability* to act crazily should call one's rationality into question? After all, with respect to other vices, it is customary to accept a distinction between having an ability and exercising it. For example, having the ability to eat and drink to excess does not imply that one is intemperate; nor does having the ability to flee from the battlefield, a coward make. Indeed, this distinction seems applicable to a wide range of character traits – having the ability to be generous does not make one generous, having the ability to be dishonest does not make one a liar, and so forth. The point here is simply that someone's having the *power* to act in a certain way does not entail that he is the type of person who *will* act that way. And given this general fact, why should we expect the case to be otherwise with indefensible actions like punching one's neighbor for no good reason?[36] Why should simply having the ability to act crazily render one crazy? Why should there be this sort of asymmetry between the "ability to act crazily" and other dispositional notions?

An example might be helpful here. A traditional view has it that if we have a free will at all, we must have a perfect, God-like free will. The idea behind the view is that whereas there can be impediments to action – i.e., one can be unable to act in accordance with one's will – there cannot be any impediments to willing.[37] I raise this view not to defend it, but rather to assume, for the purposes of this example, that it is true. (If one prefers science fiction and fantasy to tradition, then simply imagine that you happen upon a magical ring, and after placing it on your finger, you discover that it has bestowed upon you the infinitely free will described by the traditional view above: a will that enables you to choose or not choose any option you desire irrespective of your morals or best interests.) Now one thing should be clear: simply because the range of your choices has been increased (thanks to the ring), your ability to listen to reason has not been decreased. Having this freedom does not somehow mute the voice of conscience, or leave you with no way to know which course of action is the most rational; it merely gives you the ability to pick a less optimal path if you so will. Like the motorist who reaches a junction from which she can take either a scenic parkway heading directly toward her destination or a one-lane dirt road that crawls through acres of sanitary landfill in the wrong direction, you more than likely will pick the most reasonable alternative. But surely we won't judge the motorist to be crazy simply because she is at a junction where she can choose a route which is not in her interests, and neither should we judge you crazy simply because you have the power to choose against your interests.

"Still" – one might complain – "being at a crossroads scarcely shows that one is free to turn as she pleases. After all, no sane motorist ever *will* take the dirt road, and similarly no sane person ever *will* knowingly act against her interests. Indeed having the freedom to act this way would appear to be less a blessing than a curse; for why would anyone ever want the ability to behave in such a contrary fashion? In short it would seem that the power to act both irrationally and immorally, if we have it at all, is hardly as much of an ability, as it is a *dis*ability – a character flaw which needs to be overcome."[38]

Two points are raised by this worry. One is easily dealt with; the other broaches a broader issue which I can only touch upon in the context of this discussion. As to the first point – that a sane motorist will never actually choose the dirt road, and a sane person will never actually act against her best interests – I can agree that in most cases this is true.[39] Nevertheless, as we saw above, the fact that someone never *will* act against her interests does not entail that she *cannot* do so. For surely there is nothing incoherent about a person having a power which she never exercises. Having given this response, however, I am led immediately to the second, more complicated worry: Why would a sane person ever want to have a power that she will never exercise, especially a power to act against all of her morals and best interests?[40]

But, lamentably, to ask whether we would *want* to have something is, of course, not the same as asking whether we *have* it, for it might turn out that we have the freedom to act indefensibly even though this is hardly a freedom we would *like* to have (or would wish to exercise).[41] Hence, this worry cannot aid the restrictivist.

The Wolf/Dennett slide *is* a slide, and it is not well-motivated; the fact that doing A would be crazy does not (in itself and without further argumentation) imply that anyone who had the *ability* to do A would be crazy. Just as agents with the *power* to be gluttonous need not *be* gluttons, agents with the *power* to act crazily need not be considered crazy.

3 Is transfer necessary?

I have argued that van Inwagen has not succeeded in showing that Transfer (apart from any special assumptions about causal determinism or God's existence) is *sufficient* for significant lack of control. I now wish to argue that it is not *necessary* either. That is to say, I will argue that the incompatibilist's challenge to our view of ourselves as having genuinely open alternatives can be generated *without* the Transfer Principle.

The argument begins with two ingredients employed in the first version of the incompatibilist's challenge: the Principle of the Fixity of the Past (FP) and the Principle of the Fixity of the Laws (FL):

(FP)   For any action Y, agent S, and time t, if it is true that if S were to do Y at t, some fact about the past relative to t would not have been a fact, then S cannot at t do Y at t.

(FL)   For any action Y, and agent S, if it is true that if S were to do Y, some natural law which actually obtains would not obtain, then S cannot do Y.

Now consider some act X which agent S actually does at $t2$. Take determinism (as above) to be the thesis that a complete description of the state of the world at t in conjunction with a complete formulation of the laws entails every subsequent truth. Now if determinism is true, and $s1$ is the total state of the world at $t1$, one of the following conditionals must be true:

(1)   If S were to refrain from doing X at $t2$, $s1$ would not have been the total state of the world at $t1$.

(2)   If S were to refrain from doing X at $t2$, then some natural law which actually obtains would not obtain.

(3)   If S were to refrain from doing X at $t2$, then either $s1$ would not have been the total state of the world at $t1$, or some natural law which actually obtains would not obtain.

But if (1) is true, then (via FP) S cannot refrain from doing X at $t2$. Similarly, if (2) is true, then (via FL) S cannot refrain from doing X at $t2$. Finally, if (1)'s truth implies that S cannot refrain from doing X at $t2$ and (2)'s truth implies that S cannot refrain from doing X at $t2$, then it follows that if (3) is true, S cannot refrain from doing X at $t2$. The conclusion of this argument is that if determinism is true, then S cannot do anything other than what he actually does at $t2$. Generalizing this result, the incompatibilist claims that if determinism is true, none of us is free to do other than what he actually does.

I now wish to develop a similar version of the argument for the incompatibility of God's existence (construed as above) and human control (in the sense that requires freedom to do otherwise). Again, we suppose that God exists and that S does X at $t2$. Now it is plausible to say that one of the following three conditionals must be true:

(1) If S were to refrain from doing X at $t2$, then God would have held a false belief at $t1$.
(2) If S were to refrain from doing X at $t2$, then God would not have existed at $t1$.
(3) If S were to refrain from doing X at $t2$, then God would have held a different belief from the one He actually held at $t1$, i.e., God would have believed at $t1$ that S would refrain from doing X at $t2$.

But (1) must be false, in virtue of God's essential omniscience. Further, if (2) were true, then it would follow that S cannot refrain from doing X at $t2$. This would seem to follow from (FP); but even if it turned out that (FP) does not apply to (2), it would seem that one could argue from God's counterfactual independence of possible human action to the conclusion that if (2) were true, then S cannot refrain from doing X at $t2$.[42] Finally, if (3) were true, then it would seem to follow in virtue of (FP) that S cannot refrain from doing X at $t2$.

The structure of this version of the argument is as follows. There are three apparent possibilities: (1), (2), and (3). But (1) is not a genuine possibility – it cannot be true. And if (2) or (3) were true, it would follow that S cannot refrain from doing X at $t2$. Thus S cannot refrain from doing X at $t2$, and this result is easily generalizable to any human action. For obvious reasons, I shall call this version of the argument (in both the case of causal determinism and God's existence) the Conditional Version of the Argument for Incompatibilism.[43]

I believe that the Conditional Version shows that the Transfer Principle's role in arguments for incompatibilism is more peripheral than some have supposed. The Conditional Version implies that even if there were some strong objection to the Transfer Principle, this would *not* in itself decisively impugn incompatibilism. That is to say, even if there emerged some strong reason to reject Transfer – a general theoretical argument similar to the sort offered by Slote, or a counterexample – this would not in itself be a reason to reject incompatibilism; the incompatibilist's argument can be developed without Transfer, and there is no good reason to suppose that the problems with Transfer will necessarily infect the reformulated argument.

In response, someone might insist that all formulations of the argument for incompatibilism, even those which aren't *explicitly* formulated using Transfer, must *implicitly* depend upon *some* rule of inference similar to Transfer. Such a response is suggested by van Inwagen's own claim that all three of his formulations of the argument in *An Essay on Free Will* should "stand or fall together."[44] This claim is particularly germane to this discussion, because only van Inwagen's third argument explicitly depends upon Transfer. Nevertheless, he writes: "I am quite sure that any specific and detailed objection to one of the arguments can be fairly easily translated into specific and detailed objections to the others; and I think that any objection to one of the arguments will be a good objection to *that* argument if and only if the corresponding objections to the others are good objections to *them*."[45]

Van Inwagen is not alone in holding this view. Even some compatibilists, who in other respects want to take issue with van Inwagen's reasoning, agree with his intuition that any respectable form of the argument for incompatibilism must depend upon some type of inference akin to Transfer. One such theorist, Michael Slote (whose strategy we considered in the previous section), writes: "I want to argue, in particular, that the arguments of GLVW [Carl Ginet, James Lamb, Peter van Inwagen, and David Wiggins] all rest on the questionable form of inference, the very inference from the double modality of 'Np' and '$N(p \supset q)$' to 'Nq' which marks the superiority of the new kind of argument to earlier defenses of incompatibilism."[46]

Nevertheless, I want to suggest that the claim that all versions of the argument for incompatibilism depend on Transfer is false. (I do not know exactly how to *argue* for its falsity.) Admittedly, many formulations of the argument for incompatibilism do depend upon modal principles similar to Transfer. However, the argument for incompatibilism can be formulated in such a way that it does not explicitly make use of Transfer and does not appear implicitly to rely upon Transfer; one such formulation is the Conditional Version. Hence, I would claim that the onus rests on the theorist who claims that such arguments do, in fact, commit their proponents to accepting Transfer.[47]

There is another approach which claims that Transfer is not necessary in order to generate the incompatibilist's argument. Bernard Berofsky has recently argued that one can develop the argument without the use of Transfer.[48] Berofsky presents what he calls a "system of contingent necessity." This sort of system validates the following kind of principle, with certain restrictions:

$$p$$
$$N_{S,t} (p \supset q)$$
hence, $N_{S,t} (q)$

Whereas it is often alleged that this sort of move involves a modal fallacy, Berofsky attempts to justify this inference (suitably restricted), and he claims that it provides a way of formulating the incompatibilist's argument in a valid fashion. Of course, I share with Berofsky the claim that the incompatibilist's argument does not require Transfer. But if I am correct, then the incompatibilist's argument does not even require the validity of Berofsky's principle and his system of contingent necessity.[49] It is useful to see that the incompatibilist's argument does not require *any* modal principle similar to Transfer.[50]

4 Conclusion

In the first section I argued that, despite the intriguing argument presented by van Inwagen, Transfer is not sufficient to generate the conclusion that (across a wide range of cases) we lack the sort of control that involves alternative possibilities. Thus, if one seeks to generate this result, one will have to add such assumptions as that causal determinism obtains, that God exists, that the past is fixed, and that the natural laws are fixed.

If, as I have argued, Transfer is not in itself sufficient to generate the conclusion that we lack control (in a significant range of cases), then the focus of our attention should at least in part be upon these other ingredients in the challenges to our view of ourselves as free and responsible: the possible truth of causal determinism, the possible existence of

God, the Principle of the Fixity of the Past, and the Principle of the Fixity of the Laws. The latter two will receive considerable attention in the following chapters. That these matters should be *central* is supported by my argument that Transfer is not even *necessary* to generate the challenges to our view of ourselves as persons.[51]

4

The Laws and the Past:
The Conditional Version of
the Argument

1 Introduction

In the previous chapter I argued that the Transfer Principle is not
necessary in order to generate the anxieties about our personhood. I
showed how other elements – in particular, the Principle of the Fixity of
the Laws and the Principle of the Fixity of the Past – can be combined
in the manner of the Conditional Version of the Argument for Incompatibilism to generate the worries. In this chapter then I wish to
consider these principles and this mode of combination.

2 The fixity of the laws

It is undeniable that the laws of nature place certain constraints on our
abilities. But it will emerge that the precise form of these constraints is
a contentious matter. Recall the version of the Principle of the Fixity of
the Laws I employed in the Conditional Version of the Argument for
Incompatibilism:

(FL) For any action Y, and agent S, if it is true that if S were to do
Y, some natural law which actually obtains would not obtain,
then S cannot do Y.

I believe this goes some distance toward crystallizing the common-sense
understanding of the relationship between the natural laws and our
abilities. But the Principle of the Fixity of the Laws needs to be interpreted carefully. It will be revealing to consider various examples which
have been adduced to attempt to establish the principle.

First, consider some examples of van Inwagen. Van Inwagen claims that from the proposition that

(A) Jones, a physicist, can construct a particle accelerator that would cause protons to travel at twice the speed of light

it would be correct to deduce that

(B) It is not a law of nature that nothing ever travels faster than the speed of light.[1]

Also, van Inwagen says:

> Suppose a bureaucrat of the future orders an engineer to build a spaceship capable of travelling faster than light. The engineer tells the bureaucrat that it's a law of nature that nothing travels faster than light. The bureaucrat concedes this difficulty, but counsels perseverance: 'I'm sure,' he says, 'that if you work hard and are very clever, you'll find some way to go faster than light, even though it's a law of nature that nothing does.' Clearly his demand is simply incoherent.[2]

Similarly, van Inwagen asks us to suppose that, as a matter of fact, if any human being is deprived of vitamin C, he develops scurvy. Now he says:

> ... suppose also that there is a certain group of biologists and bureaucrats who want to institute a program of selective breeding that is intended to produce a population of human beings who are able to get along without vitamin C. Let us further suppose that wise counsel prevails, and these people are disuaded from this idiotic and immoral undertaking: but suppose that *if* they had been allowed to have their way, they (or their descendants) *would have* succeeded: eventually there *would have been* human beings who did not [need vitamin C in order to avoid scurvy]. In that case, it seems to me, we should hardly want to say that [it is a law of nature that if a human being is deprived of vitamin C, he gets scurvy].[3]

Van Inwagen's examples appear to render (FL) plausible. Consider also an example due to Carl Ginet.[4] Ginet points out that I clearly cannot cause my word-processor to be on Jupiter one minute from now. If I were to do so, I would be causing protons to travel faster than the speed of light. Thus, there is a straightforward explanation of why I cannot cause my word-processor to be on Jupiter one minute from now: my doing so would require a violation of a law of nature. Thus, (FL) is extremely attractive.

2.1 Local Miracle Compatibilism

But the matter is not so simple. (FL) appears to explain the examples in a natural way, and it also provides an element in the argument for incompatibilism. But I shall suggest that (arguably, at least) the examples can be just as adequately explained by a similar but *weaker* principle – one that cannot play the required role in the argument for incompatibilism. Let us explore this possibility.

The examples invite us to consider the relationship between our views about natural laws and human powers. (FL) is a crystallization of one idea of this relationship. But note that in all the examples the individuals would be performing acts which *themselves would be or cause a law-breaking event.* This raises the possibility that someone seeking to capture the intuitive conception of the relationship between the natural laws and human powers could agree that no human agent can perform an act that would be or cause a law-breaking event, but nevertheless deny (FL). Indeed, a certain sort of compatibilist, the "Local Miracle Compatibilist," will want to say that an agent might be able so to act that some natural law that actually obtained would not have obtained; but it appears he can say this *without* having to say that an agent can perform some act which would be or cause a law-breaking event.[5]

To flesh out this possibility, consider again the case in which S does some ordinary act X at $t2$. Say that S mows his lawn at $t2$. Suppose, also, that causal determinism obtains. According to the Local Miracle Compatibilist, it is possible that S be able to refrain from mowing the lawn at $t2$. And, more specifically, if S were to refrain from mowing the lawn at $t2$, then some natural law that actually obtained would not have obtained (perhaps *immediately prior to t2*). Let us imagine that if S were to refrain from mowing the lawn, he would have gone to the movies instead. The Local Miracle Theorist will argue that there is no reason stemming from considerations of the fixity of the natural laws to suppose that S cannot go to the movies at $t2$. The reason is that, whereas if S were to go to the movies at $t2$, some actually-obtaining natural law would have had to have been (at some point) violated, S's going to the movies would *not* itself be or cause a law-breaking event. Of course, S couldn't have gone to the movies faster than the speed of light. (Even on Southern California freeways, this is too fast!) If in going to the movies S would have moved faster than the speed of light, then his going to the movies would *itself* have been a law-breaking event. And of course S couldn't have built a car which could subsequently take him (or anyone) to the movies faster than the speed of light. If the car would go faster than the speed of light, then S would have *caused* some event which would be a law-breaking event. But what is envisaged is the normal sort of trip to the movies, and there is no reason to think that such a trip would be or cause a law-breaking event. Thus, argues the Local Miracle Compatibilist, there is no reason (stemming from the fixity of the laws) to suppose S cannot go to the movies at $t2$.

I have argued that it is important to distinguish (FL) from the weaker claim that no agent can perform an act which would be or cause a law-breaking event. Of course, by a "law-breaking event" I do *not* mean any event the occurrence of which, in the context of past states of the world, implies the falsity of some actual law of nature; *this* understanding of "law-breaking event" would clearly not be useful to a compatibilist. Rather, I mean by "law-breaking event" an event whose occurrence is incompatible with the laws of nature. The weaker claim, which I shall call the "Compatibilist's Principle of the Fixity of the Laws (CFL)," could be expressed as follows:

(CFL) For any action Y, event b, agent S and times $t1$, $t2$, and $t3$ ($t1 \leqslant t2 \leqslant t3$), if (1) Y's occurring at $t2$ is inconsistent with the laws of nature, or (2) Y's occurring at $t2$ would cause some event b's occurring at $t3$ and b's occurring at $t3$ is inconsistent with the laws of nature, then S cannot at $t1$ do Y at $t2$.

So I can't now do anything to cause my word-processor to be on Jupiter one minute from now, since my doing that now would cause protons to travel faster than light in the next minute, which is inconsistent with the laws of nature. And this interpretation is consistent with the denial of (FL) and thus with compatibilism: if determinism is true and S doesn't mow the lawn and instead goes to the movies, then his going to the movies need not be identical to or cause anything inconsistent with the laws of nature. Rather, it might be the case that if S were to go to the movies at $t2$, then some law would have had to have been violated prior to $t2$ (perhaps immediately prior to $t2$).

(CFL) embodies the idea that one cannot begin to do something at some time t which then involves a violation of an actually-obtaining natural law *at t or after*. Of course, this leaves it open that one can sometimes begin to do something at a time the occurrence of which would require a violation of an actually-obtaining natural law at some time *prior* to t. Thus, the compatibilist is here committed to a certain sort of temporal asymmetry: miracles (violations of actually-obtaining laws of nature) are permitted *before* the time of the beginning of the act in question, but *not after* this time.

But now it must be asked how a compatibilist could justify this alleged asymmetry. That is, how – apart from the need to explain the examples without eviscerating compatibilism – could one justify the claim that miracles are permitted immediately prior to the beginning of the relevant action but not after this time? Without such a justification, the Local Miracle Compatibilist's ploy will seem *ad hoc*. Why isn't Local Miracle Compatibilism just an ingenious ploy contrived to save a theory?

2.2 A defense of Local Miracle Compatibilism

I now wish to sketch a possible response to this worry on behalf of the Local Miracle Compatibilist. That is, I will be defending this view against the specific worry that it is *ad hoc*. The asymmetry in question is what David Lewis has called the "asymmetry of counterfactual dependence" – the past is counterfactually independent of the present while the future is counterfactually dependent on the present.[6] And Lewis has attempted to explain this asymmetry in terms of his approach to evaluating counterfactual conditionals. If Lewis is correct, then there is some hope that the compatibilist's move can be construed so that it is not egregiously *ad hoc*. On this approach, the asymmetry of counterfactual dependence is explained in terms of a general theory of counterfactuals (together with facts about our world and the relevant range of other possible worlds), and *not* in terms of intuitions about the relationship between abilities and natural laws. This is the crucial point of the defense of Local Miracle Compatibilism. Of course, on the approach which simply adverts to intuitions about the relationship between human abilities and natural laws, it would be absolutely mysterious why miracles should be allowed prior to the beginning of the act in question but not after!

It will be worthwhile to sketch certain aspects of Lewis' view of counterfactuals. Consider Lewis' formulation of the truth conditions for counterfactuals:

A counterfactual 'If it were that A, then it would be that C' is (non-vacuously) true if and only if some (accessible) world where both A and C are true is more similar to our actual world, overall, than is any world where A is true but C is false.[7]

Of course, there are various issues that might arise in an evaluation of this sort of approach. Most of these are beyond the scope of my discussion. Here I simply wish to assume that Lewis' approach is a very promising general strategy for analyzing and giving the truth conditions for counterfactual conditionals, and I wish to focus on a particular problem for it.

Various philosophers have presented the "future similarity objection" to this analysis. Here is Kit Fine's statement of the objection:

> The counterfactual, 'If Nixon had pressed the button there would have been a nuclear holocaust' is true or can be imagined to be so. Now suppose there never will be a nuclear holocaust. Then that counterfactual is, on Lewis' analysis, very likely false. For given any world in which antecedent and consequent are both true it will be easy to imagine a closer world in which the antecedent is true and the consequent false. For we need only imagine a change that prevents the holocaust but that does not require such a great divergence from reality.[8]

In "Counterfactual Dependence and Time's Arrow" Lewis responds to this very important criticism. I shall lay out Lewis' response rather carefully. (At points I follow Lewis' own presentation fairly closely.) Lewis takes the supposition that Nixon pressed the button as implicitly referring to a particular time t. Now Lewis considers world $w0$ which may or may not be ours.[9] Let determinism hold in $w0$. At $w0$, Nixon does not press the button at t and no nuclear holocaust occurs. Also in $w0$ the button is connected to a perfectly working system such that once it is set in motion, no one can stop the nuclear attack. Lewis agrees that at $w0$ Fine's counterfactual is true: if Nixon had pressed the button, there would have been a nuclear holocaust.

Now Lewis considers various possible worlds in which Nixon (or rather, a "counterpart" of Nixon) presses the button at t. One class of such worlds has $w1$ as a member. Until shortly before t, $w1$ matches $w0$; but shortly before t, $w1$ diverges from $w0$. As Lewis puts it, "The deterministic laws of $w0$ are violated in some, simple, localized, inconspicuous way. A tiny miracle takes place."[10] As a result of this miracle, Nixon presses the button. But no further miracle takes place after t; $w1$ now goes its separate way and the holocaust takes place.

In other worlds (typified by $w2$) there are *no* miracles. At $w2$ Nixon presses the button at t, and the same laws which hold at $w0$ hold at $w2$. Recall that causal determinism obtains at $w0$. So $w2$ differs from $w0$ indefinitely into the past. These worlds, Lewis argues, should be considered less similar to $w0$ than those typified by $w1$. For my purposes here, it will be appropriate to move to a discussion of the class of worlds typified by $w4$.

At $w4$ there is a perfect match with $w0$ until shortly before t; then there is a tiny divergence miracle and the button is pressed. But now there is a very widespread and complicated second miracle after t; this prevents the holocaust and wipes out all traces of Nixon's button-pressing (which otherwise would have been magnified eventually into significant divergence from $w0$). This second miracle is quite complex; the reconvergence miracle is a big miracle composed of many small miracles:

> The fingerprints vanish, and the sweat returns to Nixon's fingertips. Nixon's nerves are soothed, his memories are falsified, and so he feels no need of an extra martini. The click of the tape is replaced by innocent noises. The receding light waves cease to bear their incriminating images. The wire cools down, and not by heating its surroundings in the ordinary way. And so on, and on, and on.[11]

Lewis claims that worlds such as $w4$ should be considered less similar to $w0$ than are worlds such as $w1$. He crystallizes the following lesson: ". . . avoidance of big miracles counts for much more than avoidance of small miracles. Miracles are not all equal."[12] Thus, the similarity relation which, when combined with Lewis' analysis of counterfactuals, will give the correct account of the truth conditions for counterfactuals must embody the idea that it is of the first importance to avoid big, widespread, diverse violations of law. (This appears to make Lewis' approach a bit like that of the Republican Party!)

Lewis points out that the asymmetry of counterfactual dependence arises not solely from the analysis of counterfactuals nor from the standards of similarity; it also arises from the range of candidate worlds (and their relationship to ours). A small miracle prior to t permits divergence from $w0$; but convergence to $w0$ after t is purchased only at the expense of a massive miracle. Lewis' approach is "reductive" in the sense that he attempts to reduce the asymmetry of counterfactual dependence to other, more basic facts. Other theorists have explicitly built the asymmetry of counterfactual dependence into their analyses of the truth conditions of counterfactuals.[13]

The upshot of Lewis' approach to counterfactuals is that when we consider a counterfactual under the "standard resolution of vagueness" we generally allow minor miracles shortly before the relevant time t and then hold the laws fixed after t. This asymmetry of miracles follows from the analysis of the truth conditions of counterfactuals, the similarity metric, and the nature of the actual world and relevant other worlds.

And the asymmetry of miracles explains the asymmetry of counterfactual dependence.

Recall again van Inwagen's examples discussed above. It seems that Lewis' approach can suggest an alternative pattern of explanation of these cases (i.e., one that does not rely upon [FL]). Consider again van Inwagen's two propositions,

> (A) Nothing ever travels faster than light.
> (B) Jones, a physicist, can construct a particle accelerator that would cause protons to travel at twice the speed of light.

Van Inwagen's claim is that we can employ (FL) to get the result that (B)'s truth entails that (A) is not a law of nature. But our discussion suggests an alternative explanation. Break (B) into two components:

> (B1) Jones, a physicist, can construct a particle accelerator of type R.
> (B2) If Jones were to construct a particle accelerator of type R, it would cause protons to travel at twice the speed of light.

Making the implicit time reference in (B2) explicit, and assuming that Jones never does build the machine, we get:

> (B2) If Jones had constructed a particle accelerator of type R at t, then (after t) it would have caused protons to travel at twice the speed of light.

Now on the theory of counterfactuals developed above, in order to evaluate a conditional such as (B2), assuming that causal determinism obtains, we allow a small "miracle" – violation of the *actual* natural laws (or natural laws of the world in which (B2) is being evaluated) – to take place (before t) so that Jones constructs a particle accelerator of type R at t, and then we hold the laws fixed after t (that is, we require the propositions that are natural laws in the actual world to obtain after t in the relevant other world.)[14] But it follows straightforwardly from this approach that any world in which (B2) is true does not contain the law, "Nothing ever travels faster than the speed of light." That is, if the laws (of the world in which the counterfactual [B2] is being assessed) are held fixed after t (in the relevant other world) and (B2) is true, it follows that (A) is not a law of nature (at the world relative to which [B2] is being assessed). Thus, we have an explanation of (B)'s entailing that (A) is not a law of nature which does *not* refer to (FL) at all.

Recall, also, van Inwagen's example of the bureaucrat and the engineer. The bureaucrat tells the engineer

(B3) You can build a spaceship of type U, and
(B4) If you were to build a spaceship of type U, it would travel faster than the speed of light.

Now if the engineer tells the bureaucrat that it is a consequence of some law of nature that nothing travels faster than light, why is it inappropriate for the bureaucrat to say, "Build the spaceship anyway!"? It might be thought that one needs to appeal to (FL) here, but there is another explanation of the oddity of telling the engineer to build the spaceship. Given the information about the laws of nature and the normal way of assessing the truth of a conditional such as (B4), it would turn out that (B4) would be *false*. And this fact would be straightforwardly available to the bureaucrat. Hence the bureaucrat would know he would not be getting the sort of spaceship he had envisaged, if he persisted in his request. Thus, the bureaucrat would (or at least should) know that this request would be foolish (and self-defeating). Again, the Local Miracle Compatibilist can produce an explanation of the example which doesn't rely upon (FL).

And note that this explanation fits well with the compatibilist's overall position. Such a theorist asks us to envisage an ordinary case in which an agent does not go to the movies at t. We assume that determinism is true and that intuitively at least the agent is free to go to the movies at t – there are no special circumstances which would impair the agent. The Local Miracle Compatibilist claims that the person is able so to act that a natural law which does obtain would not have obtained. That is, the agent can go to the movies at t, and if the agent were to go to the movies at t, then a tiny miracle would have occurred just prior to t. But this is *not* to say that a human agent can so act at t that some law-breaking event would occur *at or after t*.

The strategy I have been presenting construes certain statements of the form, "S can bring about such-and-such," as implicitly involving *conjunctions*. The two conjuncts are a "can-claim" such as "S can do X," and a conditional, such as "If S were to do X, then Y would occur." Indeed, it has been *crucial* to my strategy for explaining Local Miracle Compatibilism (and defending it against the worry that it is *ad hoc*) that I have construed these statements as conjunctions involving conditionals of this sort, rather than atomic statements (or combinations of such statements) *prefixed by operators*. In contrast, if one construes them (say) as statements prefixed by some sort of unanalyzable "ability" or "power" operator, it becomes completely mysterious how one could defend Local Miracle Compatibilism against the charge. Consider, for example, the claim that you can build a spaceship that would travel faster than the speed of light. If you simply focus on intuitions about the relationship between human powers and natural laws (as many incompatibilists tend to do), then it will seem mysterious how to distinguish this sort of case from a case in which the envisaged violation of law occurs just prior to the relevant action.[15] And yet when the pertinent statements are construed as conjunctions one of whose conjuncts is a *conditional* (of the relevant sort), then the explanation (of the non-*ad hoc* nature of the application of the distinction between miracles prior to the action and after the action) in terms of the general theory of counterfactual conditionals becomes available.

My purpose in this section has been to lay out the Local Miracle response to (FL) (and thus to the incompatibilist's argument), and to argue that it is not obviously *ad hoc*. I do *not* however wish to suggest that Local Miracle Compatibilism is correct. There are at least the following worries about this approach. First, it is not uncontroversial that in the context of causal determinism the local miracle conditional would be true rather than the backtracking conditional. That is, it is not uncontroversial that if (for example) S were to refrain from mowing the lawn and go to the movies instead at $t2$, then a tiny miracle would have occurred just prior to $t2$; some would insist that if S were to go to the movies at $t2$, then the past would have been different from what it actually was "all the way back."[16] Also, even if Lewis is correct that the "local miracle" conditional would be true in such a context, it is not uncontroversial that Lewis has offered us the correct analysis of such conditionals; of course, a more complete evaluation of Lewis' approach (and related ones) is beyond the scope of this project. Finally, there may be cases in which the only explanation of an agent's inability to perform some act is precisely that his performing it would require a violation of a natural law *just prior to the beginning of the act*.

To assess this possibility, consider the following example due to Carl Ginet:

> Suppose that at some time before t, S ingested a drug that quickly causes a period of complete unconsciousness that lasts for several hours. Suppose that, because of the drug, there is true of S a certain proposition of the form
>
> At t, S's neural system was in state U

and it follows from this proposition and the laws of nature that S was unconscious for at least thirty seconds after t. If we let

bt = At t, S's neural system was in state U
at = Beginning at t plus five seconds, S voluntarily exerted force with her right arm for ten seconds,

then our supposition about the laws of nature here is that they entail that if bt, then not-at. If we know all this, then we are surely entitled to deduce that it was not open to S to voluntarily exert force with her arm in the five seconds after t.[17]

Ginet's point is that it appears as if the only available explanation of S's inability to exert force with her arm beginning five seconds after t is that if she were to do so, there would have to have been a violation of a natural law immediately prior to this time (given that we hold fixed the ingestion of the drug). That is, this seems to be a case in which intuitively an agent is unable to do something precisely because her doing it would require a violation of a natural law just *prior* to the time of the beginning of the action; if so, then Local Miracle Compatibilism is in jeopardy. It is in jeopardy because it is committed to the existence of cases in which it is entirely unproblematic both that an agent is able to do something and her doing it would require a violation of a natural law just prior to the time of the beginning of the action.

It is important to note however that the Local Miracle Compatibilist is *not* committed to the claim that *whenever* it is true that an agent's performing some action at a time would require a tiny miracle just prior to the time, it follows that the agent *can* do the act. Rather, the claim is that this requirement does not in itself rule out the ability in question. What the compatibilist must say is that there is some *other* reason why in Ginet's case S cannot voluntarily exert force with her arm beginning five seconds after t. Ginet's point is that our believing (CFL) fails to explain our judgment of inability in this case and it is unclear what explains it if it is not our believing (FL). Ginet (not unreasonably) expresses skepticism about the possibility of such an alternative explanation, although I am not certain that the prospects for such an explanation are so bleak.

To take stock. The incompatibilist's argument employs (as one ingredient) an assumption designed to capture our intuitive conception of the natural laws as out of our control: (FL). I have laid out a strategy of response according to which our intuitive conception can be captured by a weaker principle (CFL) which cannot play the required role in the incompatibilist's argument. I explained the structure of this response (Local Miracle Compatibilism), and I argued that it is not *ad hoc*. However, I conceded that it is also not obviously a successful response to the incompatibilist.

Notice the difficulty of *establishing* Local Miracle Compatibilism in a more decisive way. Above, I have laid out such a compatibilist's picture. On this picture, if causal determinism obtains and S refrains from mowing the lawn at *t2* and goes to the movies instead, then a tiny divergence miracle would have occurred just prior to *t2*. Of course, the incompatibilist will respond that under such circumstances, S *cannot* go to the movies at *t2* insofar as his so acting would require there to have been a violation of the natural laws. The Local Miracle theorist could simply *insist* that nevertheless S *can* go to the movies, since no special circumstance occludes his going to the movies; but this would clearly be question-begging. Given the difficulty of decisively establishing the Local Miracle view and also the strong view of some that the backtracking conditionals are true in the context of causal determinism, it is worthwhile now to turn to an evaluation of the Principle of the Fixity of the Past.

3 The fixity of the past

As I suggested in chapter one, the incompatibilist's challenge to our common-sense view of ourselves as having a certain kind of control over our behavior employs ingredients that purport to crystallize ordinary and plausible views. One such view is that the past is out of our control now. But as with the case of the natural laws, there are importantly different ways of capturing this intuitive view, and it will be revealing to consider these in some detail.

Consider again the version of the Principle of the Fixity of the Past employed in the Conditional Version of the Argument for Incompatibilism:

(FP) For any action Y, agent S, and time t, if it is true that if S were to do Y at t, some fact about the past relative to t would not have been a fact, then S cannot at t do Y at t.

It will be useful to distinguish a causal and non-causal interpretation of (FP):

(FPc)   For any action Y, event e, agent S, and time t, if it is true that if S were to do Y at t, S would thereby initiate a causal sequence issuing in the non-occurrence of some event e which actually occurred in the past relative to ˇt, then S cannot do Y.

(FPnc) For any action Y, event e, agent S, and time t, if it is true that if S were to do Y at t, some event e which actually occurred in the past relative to t would not have occurred, then S cannot at t do Y at t.[18]

Most philosophers (although perhaps not all) would readily assent to (FPc). But it is (FPnc), and not (FPc), which plays a role in the incompatibilist's argument (as it is presently being construed). And whereas (FPc) is relatively uncontroversial, (FPnc) is highly controversial; indeed it is precisely a denial of (FPnc) which characterizes the "Multiple-Pasts Compatibilist."

The proponent of (FPnc) argues as follows. If it really is the case that an agent's performing a particular act would require the past to be different from the way it actually was, then the agent cannot perform that act. As (FPnc) makes clear, the idea here is that there is alleged to be a certain sort of relationship between the relevant "backtracker" (backtracking conditional) and the relevant "can-claim." That is, it is claimed that the truth of the relevant backtracker *implies* the falsity of the paired can-claim.

Of course, we have already considered an approach which contends that in the context of causal determinism the backtrackers would typically be false; on this view, the local-miracle counterfactuals would instead typically be true. But for the sake of argument we can here concede that the backtrackers would typically be true. The point of controversy now is whether the truth of the backtracker *rules out* the truth of the associated can-claim.

(FPnc) does seem very attractive. One could perhaps reason as follows. If the past is fixed in the sense specified by (FPc), why not *also* suppose that it is fixed in the sense specified by (FPnc)? That is, *if* it is extremely plausible to think that we cannot initiate backward-flowing causal chains that issue in something different from what occurred in the actual past, why not *also* think that we cannot now do anything which is such that if we were to do it, the past would have been different from what it actually was? If the crucial issue is the fixity of the past, then what does causation add? And why should causation make the crucial difference? As with Local Miracle Compatibilism, doesn't the denial of (FPnc) seem simply to be an ingenious ploy to save compatibilism?

Various philosophers have however sketched a strategy that appears to show that certain can-claims and their associated backtrackers are *compatible* (and thus that [FPnc] is indeed false). This strategy involves the presentation of examples with a certain distinctive structure. John Turk Saunders offers a number of examples that putatively are counter-examples to (FPnc).[19] Here is one such example:

> Suppose that I know that my friend believes that I will do *X*, and that I am the sort of person who, in a situation like this, would not want to let down, and would not let down, a friend who believes that I am going to do *X*. Suppose that I am the sort of person who, in a situation like this, would want to refrain from *X*, and would refrain from *X*, only if my friend had not believed that I was going to do *X*. Then we may properly say that I would refrain from *X* only if the past had been different, i.e., only if my friend had not held a belief that in fact he did hold. I have the power to refrain from *X*, and this is a power that I would want to exercise, and would exercise, only if the past had been different in that a belief that was held had not been held. So my power to refrain from *X* is a power so to act that (to perform an act such that if it were performed) the past would have been different in that a belief that was held would not have been held. And what is contradictory in this?[20]

Consider, also, Saunders' similar example of the "careful historian":

> Suppose, for example, that Ben Franklin would have been President of the United States only if George Washington had not existed. Suppose that I am the sort of person who, in a situation like my current situation, would assert that Franklin was President only if Washington had not existed. I have the ability (know-how and resources) to make this as-sertion and the conditions for its exercise are quite normal. So it is in my power to make this assertion. I therefore have the power to perform an act that I would perform only if the past had been different in that a person who did exist had not existed. Thus it is proper to say that I have the power so to act that (to perform an act such that if I were to perform it) the past would have been different in that a person who did exist would not have existed.[21]

I should like also to offer my own example of this sort.[22] Consider the salty old seadog. Each morning at 9:00 a.m. (for the past forty years) he has called the weather service to ascertain the weather at noon. If the "weatherman" says at 9:00 that the weather will be fair at noon, the seadog always goes sailing at noon. And if the weatherman says that the weather won't be fair at noon, the seadog *never* goes sailing at noon.

The seadog has certain extremely regular patterns of behavior and stable psychological dispositions – he is careful to find out the weather forecast, is not forgetful, confused, or psychologically erratic, and whereas he loves to go sailing in sunshine, he detests sailing in bad weather.

Further, let us not make any assumptions about God's existence. Also, assume that causal determinism does *not* obtain. That is, let us imagine that various factors (values, desires, beliefs, etc.) explain or rationalize the seadog's choices and actions, but do not *causally determine* them. (We may even assume that there is universal causation without its being *deterministic* causation.)

It is now noon, and at 9:00 this morning the seadog called the weather service and was told that the weather at noon (and after) would be horrible, that there would be torrential rains. The seadog is healthy and alert, and his sailboat is ready to go. Bearing in mind the weather forecast, he decides at noon not to go sailing. But *can* he at noon go sailing this afternoon? Given that the seadog is not coerced, hypnotized, manipulated electronically, deceived, etc. (and causal determinism is false), it seems that the seadog certainly *can* go sailing at noon. He simply *doesn't* go sailing at noon: he makes a rational choice not to do something which he, nevertheless, has the *power* to do. He has the freedom, as it were, to be crazy (or at least to act crazily).

It might be suggested that

(C1) If the seadog were to go sailing at noon, then the weatherman would have told him at 9:00 that the weather would be fair at noon

is true in the example. If so, then it would appear that we would have a counterexample to (FPnc): we have a situation in which there is a true conjunction of a can-claim and its associated backtracking counterfactual.

But it is not so clear that (C1) is true in the example. After all, if the seadog were to go sailing at noon, it might have been the case that the seadog misunderstood the weatherman at 9:00, or that he forgot at 9:30 what the weatherman had said at 9:00 (and falsely believed that he had said that the weather would be fair at noon), and so forth. That is, if the seadog were to go sailing at noon, any of an indefinite number of things might have gone differently prior to noon. So, it seems that

(C2) If the seadog were to go sailing at noon, then *some* fact about some time prior to noon would not have been a fact.

And if (C2) is indeed true in the example, then it would still seem that we have a non-question-begging counterexample to (FPnc) – an example in which it would have to be conceded (even by the incompatibilist) that both the pertinent can-claim and the backtracking conditional are true.

In all three examples it is alleged that it is uncontroversially the case that the relevant can-claims and the associated backtrackers are true. If this is correct, then (FPnc) is false, since (FPnc) claims that if the backtracker is true, then the can-claim must be false. This sort of example has convinced various philosophers that (FPnc) can be shown to be false in a non-question-begging manner.[23]

But not so fast. In all three cases, it is not absolutely evident that the backtracking conditional is true. This is because in all three cases one might be attracted to the view that if the agent had acted otherwise, then he would have had to be acting out of character in some way (but the past would have been just the same as the actual past). So, in Saunders' case of the careful historian, one might be inclined to the view that if I had said that Ben Franklin was the first President, I simply would have been wrong! (Perhaps I would have been uncharacteristically careless or simply misinformed.) Of course, I am not here claiming that *this* view (about which conditional is true) is obviously correct; I am simply pointing out that in light of this view it certainly is not evident that we have here an *uncontroversial* case of the joint truth of a can-claim and its paired backtracker.

The case of Saunders' solicitous friend is similar. It is a case in which Saunders alleges that if I were to refrain from doing X, the past would have been different from what it actually was (in that my friend would not have had the belief that I would do X). But why not suppose that if I were to refrain from doing X, I would be acting out of character? That is, why not think that if I were so to act, I would be exhibiting some temporary character flaw or inexplicable failure to live up to my ordinary high standards of concern for my friends? So also with the seadog. Why not say that if he were to go sailing at noon, he would be acting out of character? Why not say that if he were to go sailing at noon, he would be flouting his usual conservatism and casting his fate to the wind (and rain!)? Again, I certainly do not believe that it is *obvious* that these are the true conditionals (rather than the competing backtrackers). But what does seem obvious is that in light of the view that these are the true conditionals it would be inappropriate to think that the backtrackers are *uncontroversially* true (and thus that the examples provide relatively clear examples of the compatibility of can-claims and their associated backtrackers). Again, we seem to have come to a "dead-end." It is difficult to see how the proponent of either the backtrackers or the non-backtracking conditionals could decisively establish his case.[24]

3.1 Dialectical stalemates

It will not have escaped one's notice that we have at various points above reached situations in which there is a certain sort of standoff. I wish to say a few words about these situations. Frequently in philosophy we are engaged in considering a certain argument (or family of arguments) for some claim C. The argument employs a principle P. Allegedly, P supports C. Now the proponent of the argument may be called upon to support the principle, and he may do so by invoking a set of examples (or other considerations). Based on these examples (or other considerations), he argues that the principle and thus also the philosophical claim are to be accepted.

But the opponent of the argument may respond as follows. The examples are not sufficient to establish the principle P. One could embrace all the examples and not adduce P to explain them: rather, it is alleged that a weaker principle, $P^\star$, is all that is decisively established by the examples (or other considerations). Further, $P^\star$, in contrast to P, does not support C. Finally, it is very hard to see how one could decisively establish P. One reason it is so difficult is that it at least appears that one cannot invoke a particular example which would *decisively* establish P without begging the question in a straightforward fashion against either the opponent of P or the opponent of C. Further, it *also* seems that one cannot invoke a particular example which would *decisively* refute P without begging the question against the proponent of P or the proponent of C. These conditions mark out a distinctive – and particularly precarious – spot in dialectical space.

I shall call contexts with roughly the above form, "Dialectical Stalemates." We have seen various examples of Dialectical Stalemates in our discussions of aspects of the free will problem and also the problem of epistemic skepticism. Recall again the situation in regard to the fixity of the natural laws. Van Inwagen and Ginet adduce a number of examples which seem to establish (FL), which supports incompatibilism. But the opponent of incompatibilism points out that a weaker principle (CFL) will adequately explain the examples (but cannot be employed to argue for incompatibilism). And it is hard to see how one could either decisively establish or refute (FL). I suggest that the same sort of situation characterizes the fixity of the past.

Also, consider again the structurally similar modal principles: Closure of Knowledge Under Known Implication and the Principle of the Transfer of Powerlessness. Recall that I pointed out that Closure can be employed by the skeptic to show that we don't know that we are not (say) brains in a vat. I also said (in effect) that someone could turn this argument on its head and point out that insofar as we obviously know we are *not* brains in a vat, it follows that the Closure principle is invalid. But I further claimed that this strategy seems straightforwardly to beg the question against the skeptic, since the issue of whether we can know we are not brains in a vat is precisely what is at issue. The skeptic invokes Closure to establish his skepticism; it is then inappropriate to argue against Closure in a way which simply presupposes the falsity of skepticism.[25] The context of epistemic skepticism is replete with Dialectical Stalemates.

Similarly, consider Transfer. Various considerations seem to render Transfer plausible. And Transfer can be invoked to support incompatibilism. But not everyone wishes to adopt Transfer. As I argued above, it is difficult decisively to establish or refute this principle. Suppose someone attempted to refute it by pointing to an ordinary context (say) in which S mows the lawn at $t2$ and determinism obtains. Here, it is alleged, it is *obvious* that S can at $t2$ refrain from mowing the lawn (and, say, go to the movies instead). But if this is so, then this case may constitute a decisive counterexample to Transfer. For, since determinism obtains, arguably S has no choice about the relevant state of the world in the past and no choice about its leading to his mowing the lawn at $t2$. And yet he (allegedly) has a choice about his mowing the lawn at $t2$. But of course this strategy defeats Transfer only at the price of begging the question against incompatibilism; one cannot (without begging the question at issue) simply assume that although determinism obtains S is nevertheless free at $t2$ to refrain from mowing the lawn.

My suggestion is that one of the most salient characteristics of a perennial philosophical problem is that it involves a Dialectical Stalemate.[26] Further, it seems that the free will problem is a true philosophical classic in part because it is an environment rich in Dialectical Stalemates. I do not however think that Dialectical Stalemates should issue in philosophical despair. An opponent of the principle under consideration may demand that its proponent provide examples which absolutely *require* one to accept the principle. But I would claim that this is *unreasonable*. It may even be true that it is *necessarily* the case that if a philosopher argues for a certain general principle by giving examples, a weaker principle can be found that is the strongest principle the examples support (strictly speaking). The crucial issue becomes whether it is plausible to accept the stronger principle, if one accepts the weaker principle. Considerable philosophical ingenuity can be displayed in generating examples which invite one to accept the *stronger* principle as well as the weaker principle, or in explaining in a non-*ad hoc* fashion exactly why one should *only* accept the weaker principle. Alternatively, philosophical creativity can issue in a restructuring of the problem; that is, one might find some other principle P^* which can be employed to establish C, or perhaps one can show in some way that C wasn't that interesting after all.[27]

Although free will is a focal point for Dialectical Stalemates, this need not cause us to despair. Wisdom in philosophy consists partly in recognizing that one should not expect decisive arguments in most contexts. Rather, strong plausibility arguments are all that it is reasonable to hope for. Contrasting his style of philosophy with "coercive philosophy" (which seeks only knockdown arguments), Robert Nozick says:

> At no point is the person forced to accept anything. He moves along gently, exploring his own and the author's thoughts. He explores together with the author, moving only where he is ready to; then he stops. Perhaps, at a later time mulling it over or in a second reading, he will move further.[28]

In the next chapter I shall develop precisely a *restructuring* of the free will problem. We saw above that there are Stalemates pertaining to questions about the relationships between "can-claims" and various conditionals – "local-miracle conditionals" and "backtrackers." The restructuring that I shall develop has the potential of allowing us to *avoid* these Stalemates. I do not claim that this will issue in an immediate and uncontroversial resolution of the underlying problems; there will be new disagreements, given the new contours of the debate. I do claim however that substantial progress will have been made by taking the perspective suggested by the restructuring.

4 Conclusion

In chapter three I argued that the basic intuitive views that drive the Transfer Version of the Argument for Incompatibilism can be crystallized in the Conditional Version of the Argument. This version employs distinctive formulations of the Fixity of the Past Principle and the Fixity of the Laws Principle; these formulations rule out the coherence of certain conjunctions. In the case of the Principle of the Fixity of the Past, the conjunctions in question are of can-claims and (counterfactual) backtracking conditionals. In the case of the Principle of the Fixity of the Laws, the conjunctions in question are of can-claims and conditionals specifying in the consequent that some actual natural law would not have obtained. Employing the Conditional Version of the Argument allows us to avoid the Transfer Principle.

Unfortunately, the Conditional Version can lead to certain Dialectical Stalemates. Specifically, the local-miracle compatibilist will say that there are cases in which both a can-claim and a local-miracle conditional are true, whereas the incompatibilist will insist that if the local-miracle conditional is indeed true, then the can-claim must be false. Similarly, the multiple-pasts compatibilist will say that there are cases in which both a can-claim and a backtracking counterfactual conditional are true, whereas the incompatibilist will insist that if the conditional is indeed true, then the can-claim must be false. It can seem as if we have reached a dialectical dead-end, where nothing fruitful can be said to dislodge the parties to the dispute. It has seemed to many that we have here reached an irresolvable, basic disagreement.

This appearance, however, is misleading. It may indeed be impossible *directly* to resolve the standoff. But it is nevertheless worthwhile to consider a *restructuring* of the problem which promises to move the debate forward quite significantly. Of course, it is unreasonable to demand that any useful restructuring of a problem lead immediately to a decisive resolution. But, short of a decisive resolution, a restructuring may render one or another position clearer, more natural, or perhaps significantly more plausible. One way in which it may do this is by exhibiting the structure of the problem in such a way that the competing positions are naturally associated with competing "intuitive pictures." It is this sort of restructuring I aspire to give.

5

The Basic Version and Newcomb's Problem

1 Introduction

In the previous chapter I described a set of Dialectical Stalemates in which the compatibilist and incompatibilist may find themselves. The ingredients of the Conditional Version of the Argument for Incompatibilism – the Conditional Version of the Fixity of the Past and the Conditional Version of the Fixity of the Laws – express certain relationships between conditionals and associated can-claims. The parties to the dispute disagree deeply about the nature of these relationships and thus the plausibility of the ingredients in the argument.

In this chapter I shall develop a version of the incompatibilist's challenges which can allow us to *avoid* the problems that issued in the Stalemates described above. As I believe this is the most powerful version of the incompatibilist's argument, I will call it the Basic Version of the Argument for Incompatibilism. It employs the intuitive views which also underlie the Transfer Version and the Conditional Version, but it gives expression to these ideas in a slightly different way. I shall begin by laying out the new version of the argument in a fairly informal fashion and explaining informally how it can help us to avoid one of the Dialectical Stalemates. I shall then give a slightly more formal analysis.

In developing the Basic Version of the Argument for Incompatibilism, I shall show precisely how even an incompatibilist can *agree* that there are cases in which (for example) both a backtracker and its associated can-claim are *true* and nevertheless argue plausibly for incompatibilism. Thus, I shall show how the Dialectical Stalemates can be avoided. Further, I shall highlight a very plausible interpretation of the fixity of the past. Given this interpretation, I shall develop a distinctive approach to the notoriously intractable Newcomb's Problem. Accepting this version of the fixity of the past allows us both to give a powerful version of the argument for incompatibilism – a version that allows us to avoid the Stalemates described in the previous chapter – and to illuminate a host of puzzles about practical reasoning (of which Newcomb's Problem is an example).

2 Informal presentation

The Basic Version of the Argument for Incompatibilism employs the following very simple idea: an agent can do X only if his doing X can be an extension of the actual past, holding the laws fixed.[1] Put metaphorically, if an agent can do X, then one could in principle "trace a path" (along which the actual natural laws obtain) between the actual past and his doing X. Imagine various pathways into the future. The point is that the only such paths that indicate what an agent has it in his power to do are the ones which are extensions of the actual past and along which the actual natural laws obtain: these are paths whose initial segments correspond to the actual world up to the relevant time of the action.[2]

I can now develop the Basic Version of the Argument for Incompatibilism. I start with the assumption of causal determinism. Suppose, as above, that S mows his lawn at $t2$. It follows from causal determinism that the state of the world at $t1$ together with the natural laws entail that S mows the lawn at $t2$. But we have supposed that an agent can perform an act only if his performing that act could be an extension of the actual past, holding the natural laws fixed. And since S's refraining from mowing the lawn at $t2$ cannot be an extension of the actual past, holding the laws of nature fixed, it follows that S cannot refrain from mowing the lawn at $t2$. Given the truth of causal determinism, one could not even in principle trace out a path along which the natural laws obtain from the actual past to S's (say) going to the movies at $t2$. Thus, S cannot (say) go to the movies at $t2$.

The argument can also be developed in the context of the assumption of God's existence. So, begin with the assumption that God (as envisaged above) exists. And, again, imagine that S mows the lawn at $t2$. It follows that God believed at $t1$ that S would mow the lawn at $t2$. Given the assumption of God's essential omniscience, God's belief at $t1$ entails that S mows the lawn at $t2$. Thus, S's refraining from mowing the lawn at $t2$ cannot be an extension of the actual past. It follows that S cannot refrain from mowing the lawn at $t2$. One could not even in principle trace out a path from the actual past (which of course includes God's belief)[3] to S's (say) going to the movies at $t2$. Hence, S cannot (say) go to the movies at $t2$.

I believe these (admittedly compressed and rather informal) formulations capture the leading ideas of the incompatibilist. I am of course not claiming that I have *established* these ideas or this particular way of giving them expression. But I do claim the ideas have considerable natural appeal. I now wish to show how this approach can help us to avoid some of the Stalemates discussed above. In particular, I wish to argue that the Basic Version of the Argument can avoid the Stalemate concerning the coherence of conjunctions of can-claims and backtrackers.

Recall the set of examples (presented in the previous chapter) which purport to establish the coherence of certain can-claims and their associated backtracking conditionals: the Solicitous Friend, the Careful Historian, and the Salty Old Seadog. As we have seen, some wish to argue that in these examples both the can-claims and the backtrackers are true, whereas others deny this possibility. We have seen that it is difficult decisively to establish either position. It is then felicitous that the Basic Version of the Argument for Incompatibilism gives us a way of side-stepping this issue.

Remember that in the example of the Careful Historian it is alleged that I would assert that Franklin was President only if Washington had never existed. (And it is further alleged that I have it in my power to assert that Franklin was President.) Thus, this is alleged to be a case in which I can perform some act which is such that if I were to perform it, the past would have been different from the way it actually was. Assuming here the *falsity* of causal determinism, the incompatibilist can *grant* the claims in question. That is, he can grant that there are cases (perhaps this is one) in which both the can-claim and its associated backtracker are true.

To explain. The incompatibilist would here point out that (given the falsity of causal determinism and given that it is not assumed that God exists) there is no reason to deny that one could trace out a path (along which the actual natural laws obtain) from the actual past to my asserting that Ben Franklin was President. And this is compatible with the truth of the conditional, "If I were to assert that Ben Franklin was President, then George Washington would not have existed." Of course, the actual past includes the existence of George Washington; thus, when one traces the path from the actual past to the assertion one holds fixed the existence of George Washington. But when one evaluates the backtracker, one need not hold fixed the existence of George Washington.

This kind of "shift" is precisely what renders plausible the position that in such a case both the can-claim and the backtracker are true. Finally, note that nothing here implies any sort of threat to the Basic Version of the Argument for Incompatibilism; indeed, its resources were employed to structure and analyze the example perspicuously.

Indeed, the above discussion suggests the following kind of informal analysis of the examples. First, one thinks about the "can-claim," and here one holds fixed the actual past. So, for example, in the case of the Solicitous Friend, when one thinks that it is really true that I have the power to refrain from doing X, one is implicitly holding fixed the actual past and supposing that I have the power to: refrain from doing X even though my friend believed I would do X. Indeed, this fits with the incompatibilist's view that in assessing can-claims one always holds fixed the actual past and natural laws. Then, one thinks about the backtracking conditional, and here one need not hold fixed the actual past. This shift in the conditions of assessment of the two claims renders them compatible.

2.1 A (slightly) more formal presentation

In developing the analysis a bit more formally, I shall focus primarily on the example of the seadog. (I believe the discussion applies equally to all the examples.) In the example, it is alleged that the seadog can at noon go sailing at noon, and if he were to go sailing at noon, then some fact about the past relative to noon would not have been a fact.

Now one way of analyzing the "can" of freedom is in terms of the relationship between the actual world and other possible worlds. That is, very roughly, it is not unreasonable to say that an agent can do X just in case there exists a possible world suitably related to the actual world in which the agent does X.[4] Of course, there is considerable disagreement about how to specify the "suitable relationship" referred to here, but the general idea is that can-claims, being modal claims of a certain sort, correspond to claims about possible worlds.

Also, a subjunctive conditional, being another kind of modal claim, is very naturally given a possible-worlds semantics.[5] On this sort of approach, a conditional, "If P were the case, then Q would be the case," corresponds to the following kind of claim: in the possible world(s) in which P is true which bears a kind of *proximity* relation to the actual world, Q is also true. The proximity relation may be "most similar to," or "minimally different from," etc. I shall assume, then, that the semantics of the conditional, "If P were the case, then Q would be the case," are: in all the possible worlds in which P is true which are most similar to the actual world, Q is also true.[6]

Now, using the apparatus sketched above, let us see how to describe the example of the seadog. The incompatibilist claims that the possible-worlds analysis of freedom must be filled in (partially) as follows: An agent S can at t do X at t only if there exists a possible world with the same past relative to t and the same natural laws as in the actual world and otherwise "suitably related" to the actual world in which S does X at t. This corresponds to the intuitive idea developed above that an agent can do X only if his doing X can be an extension of the actual past, holding the laws fixed.

It is important to see exactly how this sort of analysis of freedom can underwrite the truth of the can-claim in the example of the seadog (as well as the other examples) compatibly with the truth of the backtracker. Let us see how this works. The can-claim states that the seadog can at noon go sailing at noon. On the suggested analysis, it follows that there is some possible world w with the same past (relative to noon) and laws as the actual world and otherwise suitably related to the actual world in which the seadog does go sailing at noon. And the backtracker states that if the seadog were to go sailing at noon, then the past would have been different from what it actually was. On the possible-worlds analysis, it follows that in all possible worlds in which the seadog goes sailing at noon which are most similar to the actual world, the past (relative to noon) is different from that of the actual world.

It is important to see that the two possible-worlds statements (which purport to analyze the can-claim and the backtracker) are *consistent*. Of course, in order for them to be consistent, it must be the case that the possible world w posited by the analysis of the can-claim is *not* in the set of possible worlds in which the seadog goes sailing at noon which are *most similar* to the actual world. That is, it requires more of a departure from the actual world to get to a possible world with the same past as the actual world (relative to noon) in which the seadog goes sailing at noon than it does to get to a world with a different past (relative to noon) than in the actual world in which the seadog goes sailing at noon. The "can" of freedom and the subjunctive conditional are both modalities, but *different* ones, and they point us to different possible worlds; the possible world in virtue of which the can-claim is true need not be in the set of possible worlds relevant to the assessment of the conditional.[7] This shift in the relevant possible worlds corresponds to the shift (identified above) between the assumption of the fixity of the past inherent in the assessment of the can-claim and the lack of this assumption in the assessment of the backtracker.

Note that the examples discussed above provide absolutely no reason to think that my way of filling in the analysis of can-claims is false. That is, in the example of the seadog, it seems uncontroversial and clearly acceptable (even to the incompatibilist) that the seadog can go sailing at noon, even though he was actually told at 9:00 that the weather would be bad at noon. We think that the seadog *can* at noon act irrationally and out of character, knowingly doing what he normally wouldn't do. (Of course, we also know that he *won't* do so.) What is uncontroversially and clearly true, then, is that the seadog can actualize a possible world whose past relative to noon is *just like* that of the actual world but in which he goes sailing at noon. If the world he can actualize had a different past from the actual one, then it wouldn't be true that the seadog can act out of character – that he has the power to act crazily. But *this* is the sort of can-claim that is uncontroversially true in the example; and *this* is what is envisaged when we suppose intuitively that, despite being told at 9:00 that the weather would be bad, the seadog can nevertheless go sailing at noon. In fact, *none* of the examples provides any reason to deny that the past must be held fixed in ascertaining can-claims. All they indicate is that certain can-claims may be compatible with their paired backtrackers. "History," Steven Daedelus said, "is a nightmare from which I am trying to awake."[8] It is clearly a nightmare from which the compatibilist cannot so easily awake.

Let me finish this section with a few brief words about my conception of the possible-worlds apparatus I have employed above. The important point is that I view the possible-worlds framework as a *heuristic device*. That is, employing this framework may help to clarify and perspicuously analyze a given range of phenomena; it can help to bring out more clearly the "structure" of a set of claims – the relationships among the claims, and the implications of those claims. For example, confronted with a set of complicated claims about necessity and contingency, one might not know intuitively how they fit together (if at all); in this context, the possible-worlds framework can give a clear and useful model by reference to which the claims can be evaluated. Also, confronted with a counterfactual conditional or set of them, one might be at a loss to evaluate them – one might have conflicting intuitions about the truth value of the conditional (or conditionals); in this kind of context, the possible-worlds framework may provide a more effective way of coming to the task of evaluating the conditionals. For example, it might shift our attention from confused and conflicting intuitions about the conditionals themselves to more specific questions about similarities among various possible worlds. And whereas this shift may not decisively decide the question, it may help to clarify it and ultimately to make it more tractable.[9]

I wish to emphasize that I employ the possible-worlds framework *solely* as a heuristic device. Thus, I do not think I can prove (nor do I have any interest in proving) that talk of freedom *commits* one to the existence of other possible worlds, or to any particular account of their nature. Rather, I simply employ the framework as a particularly useful way of giving a picture which structures and clarifies a puzzling philosophical context. *In principle, one should be able to make the relevant points within alternative frameworks.* So, for example, I do not believe one *need* accept the possible-worlds analysis of can-claims or conditionals in order to adopt the position I have adopted about the relevant can-claims and conditionals; it is simply that the possible-worlds framework gives a useful way of setting out this position, exhibiting its structure, and perhaps even part of its motivation.

2.2 Restructuring the debate

Above I have sketched what I have called the Basic Version of the Argument for Incompatibilism. I have shown how this version of the argument allows us to sidestep the Dialectical Stalemate pertaining to the question of whether it is coherent to assert both a can-claim and a paired backtracker; the Basic Version allows an incompatibilist to *concede* that there are cases in which such claims can both be true *without* in any way vitiating the thrust of incompatibilism.

Further, the Basic Version requires that the natural laws be held fixed *at all times* in the scenarios pertinent to the assessment of can-claims. Thus, even if the Local Miracle Strategy were successful (in showing how the asymmetry of counterfactual dependence is not *ad hoc*), this would not in any way vitiate the thrust of incompatibilism. Note how the analysis I have developed applies to the context of the laws of nature. The Local Miracle Compatibilist claims that there are cases in which both a local-miracle conditional and its associated can-claim are true. Given the analysis, an incompatibilist can concede this point. But, again, the worlds pertinent to the assessment of the conditional will not include the world in virtue of which the can-claim is true. The *most similar* possible worlds to the actual world in which the agent performs the action in question (which of course he does not actually perform) have a "local miracle" just prior to the time of the action; that is, in these worlds just prior to the time of the action some actual natural law does not obtain. But in the world which renders true the claim that the agent has the power to perform the action all the actual natural laws obtain.

The Basic Version of the Argument for Incompatibilism thus *restructures* the debate in a useful manner; progress can be made in avoiding Dialectical Stalemates. And the Basic Version gives a crisp, perspicuous, and natural formulation of the underlying intuitive ideas that drive the incompatibilist. (As I shall go on to show, the naturalness of the formulation helps us to get a clearer picture of the issues, and helps us to make useful connections with other debates.) The following is one way of understanding the overall flow of the dialectic thus far. The uncertain status of the Transfer Principle, together with the fact that the Argument for Incompatibilism can be formulated in the Conditional Version, motivates a scrutiny of the Conditional Version. But the Dialectical Stalemates inherent in the Conditional Version help to motivate the development and evaluation of the Basic Version. The Transfer Version and the Conditional Version can be construed as approximations to the Basic Version of the Argument for Incompatibilism.

3 Reasons, the past, and the future

The analysis I have developed in previous sections can help to shed light on a notorious and fascinating puzzle: Newcomb's Problem. In some of the examples discussed above, the consequents of the backtracking counterfactual conditionals express the fact that some relatively innocuous or at least "neutral" feature of the past would not have obtained. For example, it is not of great moment whether or not (say) my friend was told to expect me at a certain place and time. But the example of the seadog is a bit different. Here the consequent of the backtracking counterfactual conditional expresses the idea that some *unfortunate and undesirable* feature of the past would not have been the case. This raises interesting questions about our practical reasoning and how to take into account such information. I shall begin by presenting two more examples which share this key aspect with the example of the Salty Old Seadog. I shall then employ and extend the form of analysis developed above to understand these examples. Finally, I shall proceed to Newcomb's Problem.

3.1 Two examples

Consider the example of the Icy Patch. Sam saw a boy slip and fall on an icy patch on Sam's sidewalk on Monday. The boy was seriously injured, and this disturbed Sam deeply. On Tuesday, Sam must decide whether to go ice-skating. Suppose that Sam's character is such that if he were to decide to go ice-skating at noon on Tuesday, then the boy would not have slipped and hurt himself on Monday.

The situation is puzzling. It seems that Sam is able to decide to go and to go ice-skating on Tuesday. And it also appears plausible that if he were to decide to go skating on Tuesday, the terrible accident would not have occurred on Monday. So it appears that Sam *ought* to decide to go ice-skating on Tuesday. And yet, given that Sam knows that the accident did in fact take place on Monday, it also seems *irrational* for Sam to decide to go ice-skating on Tuesday on the basis of a reason flowing from the truth of the backtracker. Nothing *prevents* Sam from deciding to go and from going ice-skating on Tuesday; and if he were to decide to go ice-skating, the accident would not have occurred. And yet it seems inappropriate for Sam to decide to go ice-skating. To do so would seem to exemplify something akin to "wishful thinking."

Perhaps the puzzle can be resolved by denying that the backtracker would be true in these circumstances. So perhaps it would be true that if Sam were to decide to go ice-skating, then he would have forgotten about the accident, or would be acting out of character in a certain way, etc. I believe that the example can be filled in to make it more plausible that the backtracking conditional is in fact true, but I certainly do not believe that it is *evident* that the backtracker can be established as uncontroversially true in such circumstances. It is essentially contentious whether the backtracker or one of the competing conditionals is true in these sorts of cases. Thus, it is open to someone to avoid the puzzle by insisting on the falsity of the backtracker.

But, given that it is controversial which conditional is true, it is useful to have another method of resolving the puzzle. And the approach sketched above suggests a promising way of doing this. Above I argued for a certain way of capturing the intuitive conception of the fixity of the past. On this approach, an individual can do X only if his doing X can be an extension of the actual past. Alternatively, one might say that an agent can actualize only those possible worlds which share the past of the actual world. Thus, it seems reasonable for an agent to restrict his attention in deliberating to the reasons present in such worlds (i.e., those possible worlds which share the past with the actual world). This seems to be a reasonable restriction on the relevant reasons (given the intuitive picture of the fixity of the past), quite apart from one's particular view about how one ought to combine and weigh these reasons. If one accepts some sort of maximization of expected utility as rational, then one ought to choose that action associated with the possible world whose past is just like ours with the greatest expected utility.

In the example of the Icy Patch, then, one could concede the truth of the can-claim and the associated backtracker: Sam can decide to go ice-skating, and if Sam were to decide to go ice-skating, the terrible accident would not have occurred. Further, there is no obstacle to saying that Sam can know that both the can-claim and the associated backtracking counterfactual conditional are true. Nevertheless, one need not conclude that Sam ought to decide to go ice-skating. This is because Sam should be concerned *not* simply with what would be the case if he were to perform an action which he can perform. Rather, he needs to be concerned with extensions of the actual past. In terms of the heuristic device of possible worlds, it may be that the "closest" worlds to the actual world in which Sam decides to go ice-skating on Tuesday are worlds in which the accident did not occur on Monday. But it does not follow from this and the fact that Sam can go ice-skating on Tuesday that these worlds are "accessible" to Sam, and that Sam can *actualize* these worlds. Given that the accident did in fact occur on Monday, it seems appropriate for Sam to focus his attention in his deliberations only on those worlds in which the accident occurred on Monday. After all, these are the only possible worlds Sam can actualize; these are the only possible worlds that are extensions of the actual past.

My suggestion, then, is that it is reasonable to restrict one's attention to those possible worlds one can actualize: the only reasons that are relevant to practical reasoning are reasons that obtain in the possible worlds one can actualize (or which are accessible to one). This idea, combined with the claim that one can only actualize those possible worlds which are extensions of our world (in the sense that they share the past of the actual world) allows us to resolve the puzzle. And it is resolved without insisting on an essentially controversial view about which conditional is true in the example.

I should like to motivate my point about the restriction of relevant reasons to those in accessible worlds by considering a simple example. Imagine that you and I are climbing a path upward toward a mountain peak (which is our goal). It is noon, and we started at seven in the morning. I begin to tell you about another path. That is, I begin to describe the lovely scenery along that path – the beautiful views of the valley below, the exquisite stream that runs alongside it, and so forth. But when you inquire further about it, I point out that we cannot get to that trail from where we are, because of a deep gorge which separates us from the other path. To get there we would have had to have started out on that different path at seven in the morning. Given this, it is obvious that the reasons for taking that other trail for the rest of the day are simply irrelevant to our current deliberations. They may be of great interest to us and help us pass the time as we walk, but you would be correct to tell me that these reasons – compelling as they may be – should not play any (straightforward) role in our deliberations about the rest of our day.

Consider, now, another example which is similar in structure to the Icy Patch example. It is the morning of 25 April 1980, and President Jimmy Carter has received reliable word that the United States rescue mission in Iran failed miserably on 24 April, and the American hostages remain in Tehran. Let us suppose that the plan was for Carter to dispatch a plane on 25 April to Cairo in order to pick up the hostages, who would have been transported to Cairo on the 24th, had the rescue mission been a success.

Now surely Carter has it in his power on 25 April to dispatch the plane to Cairo. And suppose Carter's character is such that if he were to dispatch the plane on the 25th, then the rescue mission would have succeeded on the 24th. (Carter is not a fool, and does not wish to waste resources; thus, if he were to order the plane to Cairo on the 25th, then it must have been the case that the rescue mission was a success on the 24th.) Given these facts, it seems that Carter *should* decide to dispatch the plane to Cairo. And yet this is evidently irrational.

We now have the machinery to resolve this puzzle (again without insisting on the falsity of the backtracker). It can be conceded that both the can-claim and the backtracker are true in the example (given a suitable specification of detail). That is, Carter can on 25 April dispatch the plane to Cairo, and if he were to do so, the hostages would successfully have been rescued on 24 April. And yet Carter need not decide to send the plane, since in his deliberations the only reasons that are relevant obtain in worlds *which are extensions of the actual world*. That is, on 25 April he can actualize only worlds in which the rescue mission failed on 24 April, and these worlds should be the sole focus of his attention (in his deliberations).

Precisely the same sort of analysis applies to the case of the Salty Old Seadog. In the example of the Seadog, his choosing to go sailing at noon would quite probably have very bad consequences. In contrast, in the two new cases the parallel choices – Sam's deciding to go ice-skating on Tuesday and Carter's choosing to dispatch the planes on 25 April – may not have such bad consequences. (We may assume that Sam's going ice-skating would in fact not produce great anxiety and pain, and that Carter could keep the purpose of the mission relatively quiet.) This fact gives even *more* impetus to the temptation to make the relevant choices! But even so, we have a strong intuition that the choices would be *inappropriate* and *irrational*; and my analysis explains exactly why this is so.

3.2 Newcomb's Problem

The problem It is interesting to note that the structure of the above examples is similar to that of Newcomb's Problem. I shall argue that the analysis developed above can be helpful in coming to grips with Newcomb's Problem. Here is Newcomb's Problem, as first described by Robert Nozick:

> Suppose a being in whose power to predict your choices you have enormous confidence. (One might tell a science-fiction story about a being from another planet, with an advanced technology and science, who you know to be friendly, etc.) You know that this being has often correctly predicted your choices in the past (and has never, so far as you know, made an incorrect prediction about your choices), and furthermore you know that this being has often correctly predicted the choices of other people, many of whom are similar to you, in the particular situation to be described below. One might tell a longer story, but all this leads you to believe that almost certainly this being's prediction about your choice in the situation to be discussed will be correct.
>
> There are two boxes, (B1) and (B2). (B1) contains $1000. (B2) contains either $1,000,000 ($M) or nothing. What the content of (B2) depends upon will be discussed in a moment.
>
> ... You have a choice between two actions:
>
> (1) taking what is in both boxes
>
> (2) taking only what is in the second box.
>
> Furthermore, and you know this, the being knows that you know this, and so on:
>
> (I) If the being predicts that you will take what is in both boxes, he does not put the $M in the second box.
>
> (II) If the being predicts you will take only what is in the second box, he does put the $M in the second box.
>
> The situation is as follows. First the being makes its prediction. Then

it puts the $M in the second box, or does not, depending upon what it has predicted. Then you make your choice. What do you do?[10]

There are two conflicting views about what should be done. The first view claims that if I choose both boxes, then the predictor will have predicted this, and so I will get only $1,000. But if I choose the second box, the predictor will have predicted this, and so I will get $M. Hence I should take what is in the second box. This is the "one-box" strategy.

The second strategy starts with the idea that the predictor has *already* either put the $M in the second box or not. Now a "dominance argument" favors taking what is in both boxes. If the $M is in the second box, then I get the $M + $1,000 if I take what's in both boxes, whereas I get only $M if I take only what is in the second box. If the $M is not in the second box, and I take what is in both boxes, I get $1,000, whereas if I take only what is in the second box, I get nothing. Hence I should take what is in both boxes. This is the "two-box" strategy.

Newcomb's Problem is vexing: both the "one-box" and the "two-box" strategies appear to be compelling, and yet they are incompatible. It is difficult to see how decisively to argue for one strategy rather than the other. Also, it appears as if the dominance strategy embraced by the two-boxer is in conflict with the strategy of expected-utility maximization embraced by the one-boxer; and yet both sorts of strategy seem to be valid, powerful forms of reasoning.

Lewis and Horgan   In order to frame the issues on which I wish to focus, I shall lay out the competing views of David Lewis and Terence Horgan. As I pointed out above, David Lewis has argued that the standard way of resolving the vagueness of conditionals implies that the backtracking conditionals are false; in contrast, the standard resolution of vagueness implies that the local-miracle conditionals are true. On Lewis' view, standardly we believe in an asymmetry of counterfactual dependence: the past is counterfactually independent of the present, whereas the future is counterfactually dependent on the present. Above I sketched the views about similarity of possible worlds which Lewis invokes to support the standard resolution (where it is appropriate). Lewis believes that in certain (atypical) contexts a *special* resolution of vagueness is appropriate. This resolution allows for the truth of the backtrackers. But Lewis does not believe that a Newcomb situation is such a context.[11] And Lewis (like various other philosophers) holds that the dominance strategy (and thus the two-box conclusion) is clearly appropriate, given the falsity of the relevant backtrackers.

So, for example, consider backtrackers such as, "If I were to choose both boxes, then the predictor would have predicted this," and "If I were to choose the second box, the predictor would have predicted this." If these backtrackers are false, or at least if I am not entitled to have confidence that they are true, then the one-box strategy is vitiated. Thus, Lewis' general theory of conditionals lends support to the two-box strategy.

In an interesting paper, Terence Horgan argues against Lewis' view and in favor of a one-box strategy.[12] Horgan's argument is that the Newcomb situation is precisely the sort of situation in which a special resolution of vagueness (allowing for the truth of backtrackers) is appropriate. Put abstractly, Horgan's argument is as follows. Horgan points out that some are attracted to the standard resolution of vagueness of the relevant conditionals and thus deny the truth of the backtrackers, and others are attracted to a special resolution and thus embrace the backtrackers. For Horgan, this is the crucial issue involved in Newcomb's Problem; he believes that if the backtrackers are true, then the one-box strategy would have been vindicated. Further, Horgan believes that there is a way of breaking the deadlock between these two competing views about the conditionals. That is, he believes that there is a compelling "meta-level" argument open to the one-boxer to support his favored resolution of the vagueness of conditionals, whereas there is no such "meta-level" argument open to the two-boxer. (Horgan argues that the initially attractive meta-level arguments available to the two-boxer are question-begging.) The details of Horgan's argument are not important for my purposes here; it suffices to map out his position abstractly.

In a later piece, Horgan retreats a bit, admitting that the debate between the one-boxers and the two-boxers is a "hopeless stalemate."[13] He here points out that the two-boxer can reasonably resist the claim that he *needs* a meta-level justification of a certain sort for his view that the standard resolution of the vagueness of conditionals is appropriate. It is interesting to note that the debate between Horgan and Lewis about Newcomb's Problem is structurally similar to the debates about free will discussed above: the crucial issue appears to be whether we here have a conjunction of a true can-claim and its associated backtracker. And because of this similarity, it seems to me that the analysis I developed above can help to resolve the "hopeless stalemate" about Newcomb's Problem.

Analysis   As above, I believe that the two-boxer can *concede* that both the backtrackers and the can-claim are true in Newcomb situations without undermining his position. Thus, as above, we can bypass the vexatious and intractable issue of precisely which conditional is true. I have suggested that a fair interpretation of the intuitive view of the fixed past implies that one can do X only if one's doing X can be an extension of the actual past. Alternatively, one might say that an individual can actualize only those possible worlds which share the past of the actual world. And the worlds pertinent to the backtracker (the *closest* possible worlds in which the antecedent is true) may not include the world in virtue of which the can-claim is true. These worlds may not be accessible to the agent – he may not be able to actualize them. Further, it seems appropriate for an agent to focus his attention (in his practical reasoning) on the worlds he can "get to from here," i.e., the worlds he can actualize. More specifically, I have suggested – and the explication of the intuitive picture of the fixity of the past makes this plausible – that the reasons relevant to an individual's deliberations are those which obtain in the worlds that are extensions of the actual past.

Given this sort of analysis, the stalemate with regard to Newcomb's Problem can be resolved. Although the conjunction of the can-claim and the backtracker can (although of course it need not) be granted, this does *not* in itself imply the one-box strategy. And given that the only reasons that are relevant are the ones that obtain in worlds with the same past as the actual world, a convincing argument (employing the dominance strategy) can be developed for the two-box strategy.

I am to reason as follows. I don't know whether the predictor put the $M in box (B2) or not. First, I assume that he did in fact put the money in box (B2). Then the only possible worlds I can now actualize have in their past that this is so. Thus, clearly I should choose both boxes, as I get more than I would if I simply choose box (B2). Second, I assume that the predictor did not put the money in box (B2). Then the only possible worlds I can now actualize have in their past that this is so. Thus, clearly again I should choose both boxes, as I would at least get something rather than nothing. The fixed-past worlds (given the current assumption, the worlds in which the predictor did not put the money in the box) in which I choose both boxes are to be preferred to the fixed-past worlds in which I choose the one box. Of course, the fixed-past world in which I choose both boxes will not be the *closest* possible world to the actual world in which I choose both boxes, for in *that* world, the predictor would have put the money in the box. But lamentably I do not have access to that world – I cannot get there from here. (Note that I am here assuming that there can be possible worlds in which the predictor is *wrong* and thus it is not part of the predictor's *essence* that he is always right. That is, the assumption here is that the predictor is *inerrant* but not *infallible*. I turn to the possibility that the predictor is infallible below.)

Again, think of the future as a garden of forking paths, or a branching tree-like structure in which various possible futures fork off a single past. All the possible future paths are *extensions* of the actual past, and thus the only paths I can take share the actual past. Hence, in my deliberations the reasons that are relevant are the ones that obtain along these paths: I should restrict my attention to these reasons in my deliberations, and the fact that there is some reason that obtains along a path which is not an extension of the actual past cannot be relevant to my practical reasoning. Thus, even if I know that I can pick box (B2), and that if I were to pick box (B2), then arguably at least the predictor would have placed the $M in it, it does *not* follow that I should pick box (B2). This is because I do not know that I have access to (can actualize) the scenario in which the money is in box (B2), since I do not know that this scenario is an extension of the actual past.

This type of analysis also suggests a reconciliation of the apparently conflicting forms of reasoning issuing from the expected utility maximization approach and the dominance approach. Expected utility maximization should enjoin such maximization with regard to all *relevant* worlds, i.e., all those worlds to which the agent has access. And the intuitive picture of the fixity of the past suggests that an agent has access only to those possible worlds that are extensions of the actual world. This suggests that the expected utility approach should restrict the relevant options to those that follow paths that are extensions of the actual world. Given this natural and intuitive restriction, there is no conflict between employment of the principle of maximization of expected utility and the dominance strategy pertinent to Newcomb's Problem.

Reasons   I believe the approach I have sketched is more natural than the approach which restricts the reasons that are relevant to deliberation to those one brings about or causes. This widely-accepted approach, "causal decision theory," would issue in the same benefits as the approach I have suggested, but it seems to me somewhat *ad hoc*.[14] Whereas it does resolve the puzzle, it does not explain why I shouldn't be interested in reasons that obtain in the scenarios apparently relevant to my deliberations, even if I do not (or would not) cause them to obtain. Why am I not interested in *all* the reasons there will be along future paths, not just the ones which I can cause? Suppose, somewhat fancifully, I know I can perform some simple action, and I know that if I were to do it, something wonderful would obtain (but not as a result of my action – the wonderful thing is caused by someone else or simply mysteriously would appear). Why should I not *do* the thing in question? Why should I desist if someone points out that, after all, I would not be *causing* the wonderful thing to obtain? In contrast, the approach I have developed explains the restriction on reasons in a natural, appealing way – by reference to the intuitive picture of the future as necessarily being an extension of the past.

I believe this approach analyzes a related kind of example in a perspicuous way. Here is the example, as presented by Gibbard:

> It is discovered that the reason for the correlation between smoking and lung cancer is not that smoking tends to cause lung cancer. Rather, the cause of lung cancer is a certain genetic factor, and a person gets lung cancer if and only if he has that factor. The reason for the correlation of lung cancer with smoking is that the same genetic factor predisposes people to smoke.
>
> A smoker who knows these facts is trying to decide whether to give up smoking. . . . He likes to smoke, but wants much more to avoid cancer than to continue to smoke.[15]

Now I am not a smoker, and I do not in any way wish to encourage this habit! But the example is supposed to be one in which it is intuitively clear that the smoker should not decide to stop simply because this will be a sign or indication that he does not have the genetic predisposition to cancer; this does not seem to be a good reason to stop, even if there are other good reasons.

Given the analysis I have been developing, it should be evident how the smoker should reason (given the hypothesized facts). Whether or not he has the genetic factor is determined by some past event. Assume first that this event did impart to him the genetic factor. Then the only possible worlds accessible to the smoker are ones in which he does have the factor, and thus he should go ahead and smoke (and enjoy what remaining time he has). Assuming that the event did not occur and he thus does not have the genetic factor, then all of the accessible future paths contain the smoker *sans* genetic factor. Thus, again, he should smoke (assuming of course that this is part of maximally enjoying his future). We can thus say the intuitive and natural thing about this example without making *ad hoc* or esoteric assumptions about what can count as reasons or about the causal structure of the world. For example, we can say the correct thing without introducing the assumption that one cannot take as a reason for action that some condition would be a mere sign or indication of some other condition that is itself desired.

A related point. Suppose I believe that my choice itself is an extremely reliable sign or indication that something *else* is true. Further, imagine that I consider this "something else" highly desirable. May I take the fact that my choice is such an indicator as a *reason* to make the choice? May I take this fact as a reason, even if I concede that my choice is *only* a sign, and does not *cause* the "something else"? Of course, the causal decision theorists have insisted that it is inappropriate to treat this sort of fact as a reason for making the choice. But surely it is contentious whether we should accept this constraint on reasons. Gregory Kavka says,

> It is not obvious . . . that the proposed stricture on practical rationality – while initially very plausible – is correct. Determining whether it is would ultimately require an ascent to the uncharted and dizzying heights of the metatheory of practical rationality, wherein the criteria for adequate theories of practical rationality are set forth.[16]

The analysis I have proposed allows us to *sidestep* this issue about reasons and thus avoid at least *these* dizzying heights. Indeed, we can, for the sake of the argument, accept that non-causal connections between choices and desirable states of affairs *may* count as reasons for the choices and still defend a plausible solution to Newcomb's Problem and Newcomb-type problems. Indeed, the analysis shows that even if one is quite permissive in one's views about what can count as reasons, the two-box approach can still be defended very naturally. (The defense proceeds as above. The crucial point is that the reasons relevant to an agent's deliberations must obtain in worlds that are extensions of the actual past.)

I wish briefly to consider an objection to the form of analysis I have been developing. I have claimed that the Basic Version of the Principle of the Fixity of the Past is at least a plausible and natural way of construing the intuitive idea that the past is fixed. I have then employed this principle to generate a certain way of resolving Newcomb's Problem (as well as some of the Dialectical Stalemates pertaining to free will). I claimed that my analysis will break the deadlock between Horgan and Lewis; but in fact Horgan (and various compatibilists) would not accept the fixed-past requirement, and thus he would not accept my purported resolution of Newcomb's Problem.[17]

Since I do not have a decisive argument for the Basic Version, I can only put forward my form of analysis as plausible and natural, but I do not claim that it is ineluctable. One could look at the situation as follows. If one rejects the Basic Version, one gives up the natural and intuitive idea that accessible futures must be extensions of the actual past. (I bring this point out more forcefully in chapter nine.) Further, I look at it as a considerable advantage of adopting the fixed-past requirement (apart from its manifest intuitive plausibility) that it helps to resolve an otherwise recalcitrant stalemate about Newcomb's Problem. Given its natural plausibility and its fruitful application to various puzzles, it is hard to know what more in the way of support it would be reasonable to require.

Inerrancy and infallibility Finally, I wish to consider Newcomb's Problem with an *infallible* (rather than a merely inerrant) predictor. (An infallible predictor has as part of his *essence* that he is never wrong; it is thus in a broad sense metaphysically impossible that he be wrong. Some have identified this predictor with God.) I believe that the form of analysis developed above will be instructive here. The simple point I wish to make is that the move from inerrancy to infallibility is *significant*; it is not innocuous, as many have supposed. Further, once it is assumed that God is the predictor (or that the predictor is essentially omniscient), then it is contentious whether the puzzle conditions are coherent; specifically, it is essentially contentious whether I have more than one genuinely open alternative, given that God (or an essentially omniscient predictor) knows in advance what I will do. Indeed, given the context of a discussion of the problem of the relationship between God's existence and human freedom, it would seem question-begging simply to assume that one does have such options, given that God is the predictor.[18]

Further, the analysis developed in the discussion of such cases as the Salty Old Seadog above can explain exactly *why* the move from inerrancy to infallibility is so problematic. Recall the seadog; although he was told at nine that the weather would be bad, we said above that he nevertheless is able to decide to go sailing at noon. Of course, this is to say that he is able to act crazily and out of character; that is, he is able to actualize a world in which he was told at nine that the weather would be bad and nevertheless he decides to go sailing at noon. More specifically, when we affirm the can-claim here, it is relative to a fixed past: when we say that the seadog can go sailing at noon, we are implicitly saying that his going sailing at noon can be an extension of the past which includes the bad forecast at nine. Similarly, when one affirms the pertinent can-claims in the Newcomb situation with a merely inerrant predictor, one implicitly assumes that either choosing one box or two boxes could be extensions of the actual past. So suppose the predictor predicted that I would choose one box. Nevertheless it is imagined that I can choose two boxes; corresponding to this thought is a possible world in which the predictor is wrong. It is supposed that there *are* such worlds, if the predictor is merely inerrant. But there are *no* such possible worlds, if the predictor is infallible. Thus, it seems that, if the predictor is genuinely infallible, the puzzle conditions are not coherent: it cannot be blithely assumed that I can either take one box or two. After all, *one* of the two predictions is part of the actual past, and given the infallibility of the predictor, there can only be *one* relevant extension of this past. The form of analysis developed above can illuminate precisely *why* the move from inerrancy to infallibility is so problematic.

But we can surely imagine a revised Newcomb's Problem in which it is *not* supposed that I can choose either one box or two boxes. Rather, the assumption would simply be that, although I can in fact only choose one of these options, I do not know in advance of making my decision which option I can in fact take. So let us think of this as the appropriate formulation of Newcomb's Problem, given an infallible predictor.

Under such circumstances, it seems rational to choose the one box. And, indeed, the reasoning sketched above on behalf of the two-box solution is clearly unavailable here, since the predictor is here taken to be infallible. That is, given that one of the two predictions has actually been made and that the predictor is genuinely infallible, there is no meta-physically possible extension of the actual past in which the predictor is wrong. Thus, there is just one relevant extension of the actual past, whatever it in fact was. I do not know precisely which past was the actual past, but I know it is better for me if the predictor predicted that I would choose just the contents of the one box.

The one-box strategy is the correct solution for the case of an infallible predictor, and the two-box strategy is correct for the case of a merely inerrant predictor. (This position was embraced, but not defended, by Nozick.) In contrast, both Lewis and Horgan believe the appropriate strategy is invariant with respect to the distinction between inerrancy and infallibility: Lewis is an invariant two-boxer, and Horgan an invariant one-boxer (at least in his earlier work). The form of analysis developed above shows precisely why there is a crucial asymmetry between the case of inerrancy and infallibility.[19]

Finally, I wish to apply my analysis to a puzzle concerning the Calvinist view that it is rational to live virtuously as a kind of "sign" that one has already been saved. This can seem very puzzling; after all, if one has already been saved (or not), one might as well enjoy life to the fullest and not bother with moral rules! But, given the analysis developed above, a defense of this aspect of Calvinism can be mounted. The opponent of the Calvinist view emphasizes that the decision about one's salvation has *already* been made; but whereas this is true, the further claim that it is now rational to disobey the moral rules (when convenient) tacitly assumes that God is less than infallible. But, as I argued above, there is a crucial asymmetry between an inerrant predictor and a genuinely infallible predictor; if the predictor is genuinely infallible, the one-box solution is rational. And if God is infallible (as the Calvinist would surely suppose), then obedience to the moral rules is similarly rational.[20] Thus, the form of analysis I have offered can illuminate and structure the puzzling debate about Calvinism: the opponent is tacitly assuming mere inerrancy (or less), whereas the Calvinist must be relying upon God's infallibility.

Newcomb, Wolf, and free will   What exactly is the relationship between Newcomb's Problem and compatibilism about God's foreknowledge and human control (in the sense that requires freedom to do otherwise)? William Lane Craig has argued that Newcomb's Problem is the "final vindication of the [compatibilist]."[21] Craig believes (as do I) that it is rational to choose the one box, if the predictor is infallible. So let us suppose that I opt for choosing the one box. It follows that the predictor (let us say, God) knew this in advance. Thus, I did something such that if I were to do it, God would have put the $M in the one box. This is then an example in which a certain backtracking conditional is true, but note that the example goes no distance toward establishing compatibilism. For, as I argued above, in this case it is plausible that I cannot do otherwise than I actually do. Since God is infallible, there is only one possible extension of the actual past (in which God believed that I would do what I actually do, namely, choose the one box). Thus, Newcomb's Problem cannot legitimately be invoked to *establish* any sort of compatibilism. The key insight is that nothing in Newcomb's Problem can be used to argue that an agent can be free in any sense to make it the case that the past is *different* from what it actually was. Newcomb's Problem is not, then, the "final vindication of compatibilism"; it is more like Saddam Hussein's "Mother of All Victories."

In my view, precisely the same problem afflicts Susan Wolf's suggestion for a response to a version of the skeptical challenge from causal determinism to our freedom to do otherwise. In *Freedom Within Reason*, Wolf offers what she calls the "Leibnizian Story," which is intended to illustrate two morals: first, that the ability to do otherwise which is relevant to responsibility is a psychological ability, not a physical one; second, that such a psychological ability to do otherwise is compatible with causal determinism.

The story, briefly summarized, runs as follows. Imagine there is a Leibnizian-type God who chooses to create the best of all possible worlds. In this world, God wants there to be persons who have the ability to exercise practical and theoretical reason, and who are able to deliberate and act on the basis of their deliberations. It is also extremely important to God that these persons not be psychologically determined to choose and act as they do. After considering all possible worlds, God actualizes the best one, and, for reasons not specified, this world happens to be one in which the psychologically undetermined persons are "composed of stuff that is subject to completely deterministic physical laws."[22] In this best of all possible worlds, Wolf tells us, there is a professor named Rose who chooses one evening to watch a movie on TV rather than grade her students' exams. And the question Wolf asks is whether Rose could have done otherwise – whether she could have graded papers instead of watching the movie. Wolf readily concedes that given the details of her story, it is both physically and, so to speak, divinely impossible for Rose to grade the papers. Nevertheless, Wolf insists that in a sense relevant to an assessment of Rose's freedom and responsibility, she could have done otherwise.

In support of this claim Wolf emphasizes that Rose was created such that it is compatible with "her psychological history up to the moment in question, in conjunction with all the psychological and psychophysical laws that apply to her, that she choose TV, and it is also compatible with these that she choose to grade papers."[23] Since at the level of psychological explanation Rose is able to do otherwise, Wolf argues that she is responsible, and further that it is not relevant that Rose is physically unable to do otherwise. After all, Wolf asks, "Do the physical facts make Rose choose (or explain why she chooses) to watch TV, or does Rose's choice to watch TV make (or explain why) the physical facts come out as they do"?[24] And to this question Wolf answers, "Given God's basis for choosing which world to create, the latter seems more reasonable than the former. For God's choice of the physical facts does not condition but rather is conditioned *by* His choice of the psychological or personal facts."[25]

Wolf writes, "this line of argument [i.e., that the story shows the physical level of explanation is not more basic than the psychological level] might be used as part of a response to the Ginet–van Inwagen argument for incompatibilism."[26] To support this claim, Wolf notes that this argument depends upon the premise that it is not in anyone's power to affect the laws of nature or the past, and

> curiously, there is a sense in which the persons in the story might be said to have the power (by way of God's foreknowledge and interests) to affect the laws of nature or states of the world prior to their birth. Thus, one might argue that the Ginet/van Inwagen argument does not apply to the persons in the story. If this were admitted, however, along with the conclusion that these persons were free though determined, it would throw doubt on the strength of the argument even in our own case. If the psychological abilities possessed by the people in the story are sufficient for their freedom and responsibility, why wouldn't those same abilities be sufficient for us?[27]

Admittedly, Rose's psychologically undetermined choices are one of the factors which lead God to actualize this best of all possible worlds, and in this "curious" sense it might be said that Rose's choice to watch TV affects (via God's foreknowledge) the states of the world before her birth. But there are two important points to keep in mind. First, surely Rose's freedom not to watch TV but to grade her papers instead *requires* the physical freedom to do otherwise, and the Leibnizian Story presents no reason to think that Rose can affect the past or laws in any way that would give her an ability physically to do anything other than watch TV. Second, even if the pertinent ability is merely the ability to *choose* to grade the papers rather than watching TV, the Story gives no reason to suppose Rose can have this sort of ability. This is because God knows (and thus believes) in the past that Rose will choose to watch TV. I can grant, for the sake of argument, that Rose's choice in some "curious" sense affects the past (i.e., affects God's belief states and thus also the physical states of the world in the past). But this point goes *no* distance toward showing that Rose *could have chosen otherwise* and thus *so acted that the past would have been different from what it actually was*. Indeed, if all the possible futures must be extensions of the actual past, the supposition of Rose's psychological freedom is clearly ruled out (given God's foreknowledge). Further, Wolf's Story provides absolutely no reason to call into question the natural and plausible assumption that all possible futures must branch off the actual past. As far as I can see, Wolf's appeal to "psychological indetermination" is entirely ineffective in addressing the skeptic's challenge.

4 Conclusion

In this chapter I have argued that we can *again* recast the argument for incompatibilism. Further, I have argued that the Basic Version of the Argument can avoid some of the Dialectical Stalemates associated with the Conditional Version, and the reasoning it employs can illuminate a host of other puzzling examples, including Newcomb's Problem.[28]

Undeniably, the assumptions of the Basic Argument for Incompatibilism resonate with common sense. It is clearly a basic tenet of common sense that all of the possible futures branch off one actual past and that these possible futures are *not* associated with more than one possible past (in the sense of "possible" relevant to control). On this view, if I can take a certain possible pathway into the future, this would be an extension of the actual past – it would not have a different past of its own. The future may be a garden of forking paths, but the past is not.

6

The Facts

At the March 1984 Pacific Regional meeting of the Society of Christian Philosophers, Pike presented a discussion of Fischer's paper, which was responded to by Marilyn Adams and Fischer, so that the conferees were treated to hearing Adams on Pike on Fischer on Adams on Pike, and Fischer on Pike on Fischer on Adams on Pike. 'Enough!' you may well cry. And yet the beat goes on.

William P. Alston[1]

1 Introduction

In previous chapters, I have presented and refined an argument that contends that causal determinism (and God's foreknowledge) are incompatible with the sort of control which requires alternative possibilities. I have attempted to crystallize and give clear expression to the engines that drive the argument. One such engine is the intuitive idea of the fixity of the past. I have suggested that we can construe this idea as requiring that any scenario which is a possible future for an agent (in the sense relevant to control) be *an extension of the actual past.* Thus far, I have not paused to discuss the delicate matter of what precisely the actual past consists in. To this set of issues I now turn.

2 Hard and soft facts

Imagine, as above, that some ordinary agent S does something ordinary X at $t2$. The argument presented above suggests that, despite the common-sense view to the contrary, S cannot refrain from doing X at $t2$, if causal determinism obtains or God exists (and is construed as above). Part of the argument involves the claim that the past is fixed. But, as noted above, this sort of claim (on some interpretations) can appear to lead to *fatalism* – the doctrine that quite apart from any assumption about causal determinism or God we lack the freedom to do otherwise.

To see this, imagine (again) that S does X at $t2$. Arguably, it follows that it is true at $t1$ that S does X at $t2$. But then S's doing otherwise at $t2$ would require that some fact about the past – that it is true at $t1$ that S does X at $t2$ – would not have been a fact. Thus, the argument goes, S cannot refrain from doing X at $t2$. But there is a glaring problem with the argument: the intuitive idea of the fixity of the past does not apply to such facts as the fact that it is true at $t1$ that S does X at $t2$. Typically, then, a response to the fatalist's argument involves making a distinction between temporally relational or "soft" facts and temporally nonrelational or "hard" facts. Intuitively, a hard fact, as opposed to a soft fact, is "fully accomplished and over-and-done-with" at the relevant time.[2] The temporal relationality of soft facts is analogous to the spatial relationality of facts such as the fact that I am sitting a mile away from an orange grove. Given this distinction between hard and soft facts, it is attractive to suppose that the idea of the fixity of the past applies *only* to *hard* facts; this assumption was implicit in previous chapters, and I now make it explicit.

Let us begin to think about how to characterize the intuitive distinction between hard and soft facts. My alarm clock rang at seven this morning (Tuesday); I quickly turned it off! The fact that the alarm clock rang is a hard fact about seven. In contrast, the fact that the alarm clock rang two hours prior to my typing is a soft fact about seven. It is not "fully accomplished and over-and-done-with" at seven – indeed, it seems to involve or at least imply the occurrence of certain sorts of facts about times *after* seven o'clock. Both "It is true at $t1$ that S does X at $t2$" and "The alarm clock rings at seven, two hours prior to Fischer's typing" entail that certain sorts of facts obtain at times *after* the relevant time (the time the fact is allegedly "about"). This suggests some sort of entailment criterion of soft facthood: a soft fact (as opposed to a hard fact) entails that a certain kind of fact obtains in the future (or after the time the fact is allegedly about).

But it is a delicate matter to specify precisely the relevant sort of fact (entailment of which renders the entailing fact soft). Arguably, any fact entails that *some* facts obtain in the future. So, for example, the fact that the alarm clock rings at seven on Tuesday entails that the alarm clock does not ring for the first time at eight on Tuesday.[3] And yet this does not show that the fact that the alarm clock rings at seven is not a hard fact about seven. Various philosophers have attempted to specify the relevant sort in a precise way.[4] Rather than pursuing this approach, I shall adopt the position suggested by Alvin Plantinga.[5] On Plantinga's view, we say that it is a *mark* of a soft fact that it entails that a certain sort of fact, which we can intuitively identify but may not be able to reductively define – obtains in the future. Plantinga says:

> . . . I say that none of ["Eighty years ago, the proposition *Paul will mow his lawn in 1999* was true," "Eighty years ago, the sentence 'Paul will mow his lawn in 1999' expressed the proposition *Paul will mow his lawn in 1999* and expressed a truth," and "God knew eighty years ago that Paul will mow in 1999"] is a hard fact about the past, because each entails ["Paul will mow his lawn in 1999"]. In so saying, however, I am not endorsing a *criterion* for hard facthood; in particular I am not adopting an 'entailment' criterion, according to which a fact about the past is a hard fact about the past if and only if it entails no proposition about the future. No doubt *every* proposition about the past entails *some* proposition about the future . . . What I *am* saying is this: No proposition that entails [*Paul will mow his lawn in 1999*] is a hard fact about the past . . .[6]

This view about the entailed facts is similar to United States Supreme Court Justice Potter Stewart's view about obscenity. Admitting his inability to formulate a coherent test for obscenity, Stewart said, "I know it when I see it" (*Jacobellis v. Ohio*, 1964). For the purposes of this discussion, I shall adopt Plantinga's view about soft facts. I shall call this the "Entailment View" or "Entailment Criterion," but I shall adopt the explicit understanding that it is *not* the unrefined entailment approach suggested by Adams, but rather the entailment view suggested by Plantinga.

The Entailment View nicely captures the intuitive feeling that such facts as "It is true at $t1$ that S does X at $t2$" and "The alarm clock rings at seven two hours prior to Fischer's typing at nine" are soft facts about the relevant times. But it raises a pressing problem: it now seems as if facts about God's prior beliefs are soft facts about the past! More specifically, the fact that God believes at $t1$ that S will do X at $t2$ now appears to be a soft fact about the past and thus not within the purview of the fixity of the past. It seems now that the argument for the incompatibility of God's existence and human freedom to do otherwise is relevantly similar to the fatalistic argument and crucially different from the argument from causal determinism.

William of Ockham made a distinction rather like the distinction between hard and soft facts. Further, he claimed that only the hard facts are fixed in virtue of being in the past. The following quotation provides at least some support for attributing to Ockham the view I shall below call "Ockhamism":

> Some propositions are about the present as regards both their wording and their subject matter (*secundum vocem et secundum rem*). Where such propositions are concerned, it is universally true that every true proposition about the present has (corresponding to it) a necessary one about the past: *e.g.*, 'Socrates is seated', 'Socrates is walking', 'Socrates is just', and the like.
>
> Other propositions are about the present as regards their wording only and are equivalently about the future, since their truth depends on the truth of propositions about the future. Where such (propositions) are concerned, the rule that every true proposition about the present has corresponding to it a necessary proposition about the past is not true.[7]

Ockham's "propositions about the present as regards both their wording and their subject matter" correspond to hard facts, and his claim is that they are fixed at later times. Ockham's "propositions about the present as regards their wording only" correspond to soft facts, and his claim is that they need not be fixed at later times.

The Ockhamist's position, then, is that (a) facts which only appear to be strictly about the past but are really also about the future do not carry the necessity of the past, (b) God's beliefs are precisely this sort of fact. The Ockhamist then agrees with the incompatibilist (as opposed to the Multiple Pasts Compatibilist) that facts which *are* strictly about the past (hard facts) are indeed now *fixed* and out of our control. But he claims that God's prior beliefs are *not* in the class of such facts, and that there is no other reason stemming from the fixity of the past to deny that we can be free to do otherwise. Thus, the Ockhamist is a certain sort of compatibilist.

I shall concede that there is a superficial difference between the argument from God's existence and the argument from causal determinism, but I shall argue in this chapter that at a deep level they are similar. That is, I shall concede that the pertinent fact about the past in the argument from God's existence ("God believes at $t1$ that S does X at $t2$") is a *soft* fact, whereas the parallel fact in the argument from causal determinism is a *hard* fact. Nevertheless, I shall argue that the fixity of the past implies that God's existence is on a par with causal determinism in threatening our freedom to do otherwise. Thus, I propose to call

Ockhamism into question. I shall attempt to capture the feeling that the fact about God's belief is similar in certain ways to the paradigmatic soft facts, and yet importantly different from them: although the fact about God's belief shares with the paradigmatic soft facts the property specified by the Entailment View of soft facts, it just "feels" different. I shall show precisely why it is indeed different.

3 Hard-core soft facts

To begin to see the problems with Ockhamism, note that it does *not* follow from a fact's being a soft fact about the past that one can so act that it would not be a fact. Suppose, for instance, that I am chained to my chair and thus intuitively it is quite clear that I cannot leave my office. It is a fact about yesterday that it was true then that I went to the store a day prior to being chained to a chair. Thus, if I were to leave my office, I would be falsifying this soft fact. Nevertheless, I cannot leave the office. Indeed, whenever it is envisaged that I do other than I actually do, one thereby envisages something that implies that I falsify *some* soft fact about the past; thus, it is quite clear that the falsification of a soft fact cannot be deemed *sufficient* for the relevant can-claim.

It is evident then from the above discussion that there are soft facts which are nevertheless fixed. They may be fixed for reasons other than the fixity of the past. Consider, for example, the fact that Judy sits at $t1$ prior to the sun's rising at $t2$. This is a soft fact about $t1$ which is nevertheless fixed at $t2$: there is nothing any human agent can do about this fact at $t2$. Thus, it is very important to distinguish two sets of issues: first, temporal nonrelationality and relationality (i.e., hardness and softness), and second, fixity and non-fixity (i.e., being out of one's control and being in one's control). I shall argue that God's prior beliefs are in the class of soft facts which are nevertheless fixed. Thus, they are similar in an important way to the fact that at $t1$ Judy sits prior to the sun's rising at $t2$. But it will turn out that they (unlike this fact about Judy) are fixed precisely in virtue of the fixity of the past.

Ultimately, it will emerge that there is a relatively simple and general reason why God's prior beliefs are plausibly taken to be fixed, no matter *how* we construe the nature of God (within a certain range of possibilities). But I will start in this section with a particular construal. Specifically, I will here depart from my previous practice of taking "God" to be a name of an individual. Let us here begin by assuming that "God" is a role-term that specifies a position characterized by the divine attributes (such as essential omniscience, essential omnipotence, and so forth). Further, let us suppose that the individual who is God in this world (if anyone is) is named "Yahweh." I assume further that it is logically and in a broad sense metaphysically possible that Yahweh have existed and not filled the role of God; thus, it is not essential to the personal identity of Yahweh that he be God (or, let us add, that he have any of the divine attributes). Further, I here assume that it is logically and in a broad sense metaphysically possible that some other individual have been God.

I have been speaking rather loosely about "falsifying facts." Let us pin this down a bit more specifically. Let us say that an agent can at some time t falsify a fact F insofar as he can at t actualize some scenario (or possible world) in which F is not a fact. That is, although F is actually a true proposition, there is an extension of the actual past that is accessible to the agent in which F is not true.

Now suppose (as above) that S does X at $t2$. It follows from God's essential omniscience that God believes at $t1$ that S will do X at $t2$. And, of course, given the Entailment View, this fact about God's belief is a soft fact about $t1$. We may further assume that, although it is metaphysically possible that Yahweh not have been God, it is not within S's power to make it the case that Yahweh is not God. Thus, the only way in which S can falsify the fact that God holds the belief at $t1$ is by falsifying the fact that Yahweh holds that belief at $t1$. But the fact that Yahweh holds the belief at $t1$ is a hard fact about $t1$; this fact does *not* entail the relevant sort of fact about the future. In this case it appears that S's falsifying the soft fact would *require* falsifying the hard fact.[8]

To see what is going on in this argument, note that a particular fact F might be thought to have various elements or parts. Perhaps the elements are "smaller" or "constituent" *facts F1, F2, F3*, and so forth. Now it may turn out that, relative to an agent and a time, the only way in which some fact F can be falsified is by falsifying a certain element. If this is the case, I shall call the element in question a "kernel element" (relative to the agent and time). Thus, the set of kernel elements of a fact (relative to an agent and time) are the elements which *must* be falsified (or, as I shall explain later, affected) if the agent is to falsify the fact (at the time in question). This set of kernel elements is the *baggage* of the fact (relative to the agent and time).

Now if the fact that Yahweh believes at $t1$ that S will do X at $t2$ is taken as part of the fact that God holds this belief at $t1$, then the fact that God holds this belief at $t1$ is a "hard-core soft fact" about $t1$. Such a fact is a soft fact some of whose component facts are kernel elements (relative to the agent and time) which are *hard facts*. The problem with such facts is that the only way in which the relevant agent can falsify them (at the relevant time) would be to falsify some *hard* fact about the past. And if it is plausible to say that hard facts about the past are now fixed, then it is equally plausible to say that hard-core soft facts about the past are now fixed. Thus, even though the fact about God's prior belief is soft, it is plausibly taken to be fixed. The problem for the Ockhamist (on the current construal of "God") is the problem of excess baggage.

4 Hard-type soft facts

4.1 God's beliefs as hard-type soft facts

When "God" is construed as a title term and "Yahweh" names an individual who is actually God but does not possess the divine attributes essentially, then the problem of excess baggage developed above is pressing. But there is of course another picture according to which either "God" is a name or "Yahweh" names the individual who is actually God and *essentially* possesses the divine attributes. In this section I shall assume that "God" is a name for an individual who essentially possesses the divine attributes. On this view, one cannot divide the fact about God's beliefs at $t1$ into components, one of which is a kernel element (relative to S at $t2$) which is a hard fact about $t1$.[9] (This is because now the fact that Yahweh holds a certain belief about the future at $t1$ will not be deemed a hard fact about $t1$, given the Entailment View.) Nevertheless, I shall argue that even on this view of the nature of God, Ockhamism is untenable. It will turn out that even here Ockhamism is saddled with the problem of excess baggage.

It is important now to distinguish two ways of dividing up facts: first, into smaller component facts, and second, into individuals and properties (and perhaps times). On the first approach to division (sketched above), the components of a fact are themselves facts; the combination of the components comprises the "larger" fact. On the second approach to division, the components of a fact are an individual (or perhaps set of individuals) and a property (or set of properties); the individual's having the property (perhaps at a time) comprises the fact.

Above, I said that an agent can at some time t falsify a fact F insofar as he can actualize some scenario which is an extension of the actual past in which F is not true. Similarly, I shall now say that an agent can at some time t affect a property insofar as he can at t actualize a scenario which is an extension of the actual past in which some individual who actually has the property does not have the property (or in which some individual who actually does not have the property has it).

As stated above, a particular fact F might be thought to have various elements or parts. Perhaps the elements are facts $F1$, $F2$, and $F3$, and so forth. Or perhaps they include an individual I and a property P. In any case, it may be that, relative to an agent and a time, the *only* way in which the fact can be falsified is by affecting a certain element. Above, I explained that a fact may be a kernel element. Now it should be evident that a property may also be a kernel element of a fact (relative to an agent and a time).

Above, I pointed out that there is a distinction between temporally nonrelational and relational facts (hard and soft facts). I argued that this gives rise to the possibility of hard-core soft facts: soft facts with hard kernel facts. Now I shall point out that there is a parallel distinction between temporally nonrelational and relational *properties* (hard and soft properties). I shall argue that this in turn gives rise to the possibility of "hard-type soft facts": soft facts with hard kernel properties. Specifically, I shall develop an argument that God's prior beliefs (where "God" is a name) are just such facts: hard-type soft facts (relative to the relevant agents and times).

First, I simply point out that there appears to be a distinction between temporally nonrelational and relational *properties* which is parallel to the distinction between temporally nonrelational and relational *facts*. So, whereas "Judy sits at $t1$" is a hard fact about $t1$, "Judy sits at $t1$ prior to having lunch at $t2$" is a soft fact about $t1$. And, similarly, whereas the property, "sitting," is a temporally nonrelational or "hard" property relative to $t1$, the property, "sitting prior to having lunch at $t2$," is a temporally relational or "soft" property relative to $t1$. Temporally relational or soft properties are the temporal analogues of spatially relational properties, such as "standing a mile west of a burning barn," and so forth. Regrettably, it is not an easy task to provide an account of the distinction between temporally nonrelational and temporally relational properties.[10] But, in the absence of a general account, it will suffice here to rely upon intuitive considerations and relatively clear cases on each side of the distinction.

Given that there is a distinction between hard and soft properties, I shall now offer some considerations that should incline one to think that believing a certain proposition at a time is a *hard* property relative to that time. I begin with some properties that are paradigmatic hard and soft properties. Recall that at seven o'clock my alarm clock rang and at nine o'clock I was typing. So, at seven my alarm clock had the hard property of ringing, and the soft property of ringing prior to Fischer's typing at nine. Intuitively, a soft property is *dependent* (in a certain way) upon future states of the world. To bring out this sort of dependence, note that the particular physical state of the alarm clock at seven counted as part of ringing prior to typing at nine, given that I typed at nine; but this physical state of the alarm clock would *not* have counted as part of ringing prior to typing at nine, if I had not typed at nine. In contrast, this particular state of the alarm clock at seven would have counted as ringing, no matter what I (or anyone else) would have done after seven. The asymmetry to which these rough intuitive considerations point may help to explain the difference between hard and soft properties.

Consider now the fact that some human being H knows at $t1$ that S will do X at $t2$. Note that the state of H's mind at $t1$ that actually counts as part of knowing that S will do X at $t2$ would *not* so count, if S were to refrain from doing X at $t2$. That is, it is *not* the case that one and the same state of H's mind at $t1$ would count as part of knowing that S will do X at $t2$, whether or not S does X at $t2$. Thus, the fact that this state of H's mind counts as knowledge of a future proposition exhibits a kind of *counterfactual dependence on the future* which appears to rule out the possibility that knowing this proposition is a hard property relative to $t1$.

But, in respect of this counterfactual dependence on the future, belief appears to be crucially different from knowledge. Suppose now that H merely believes at $t1$ that S will do X at $t2$. The state of H's mind that counts as his belief would *not* count as a different belief (or no belief at all), if S were to refrain from doing X at $t2$. Note that the situation here is importantly different from the situation with regard to knowledge: here, one and the same state of H's mind at $t1$ would count as believing that S will do X at $t2$, no matter what S (or anyone else) does at $t2$. The fact that the particular state of H's mind at $t1$ counts as believing that S will do X at $t2$ is *resilient* to future states of the world. Thus, it appears that softness is associated with a certain kind of counterfactual dependence on the future, whereas hardness is associated with a certain sort of resilience to the future.

I can see no good reason to deny that the property of believing exhibits this sort of resilience when possessed by God. That is, I maintain that the property of believing is in this respect the same when applied to humans and God. When God believes at $t1$ that S will do X at $t2$, His mind is in a certain state at $t1$. Further, my contention is that being in this state would still count as believing that S will do X at $t2$, even if S were to refrain from doing X at $t2$. Believing a proposition just is not counterfactually dependent on the future: it is *not* the case that one and the same state of mind would count as one belief given one future, and another belief (or no belief at all) given another future. Of course, if God believes at $t1$ that S will do X at $t2$, then it is (according to the assumptions adopted here) metaphysically impossible for *God's* mind to be in the same state and S not do X at $t2$. But this does *not* show that "believing that S will do X at $t2$" is not a hard property relative to $t1$; at most it helps to show that "God believes at $t1$ that S will do X at $t2$" is not a hard *fact* about $t1$.

4.2 God's beliefs and human beliefs

So far I have relied largely on intuitive formulations in presenting my argument that believing a certain proposition should be considered a hard property, even in the case of God. Let me attempt to make the idea behind it a bit more precise. The main idea is that God's beliefs (His states of believing) are here being construed as *similar* to human beliefs in an important respect. Jerry Fodor has argued that human beliefs must be constrained by what he has called the "formality condition."[11] Roughly, this constraint implies that two human thoughts "can be distinct in content only if they can be identified with relations to formally distinct representations. . . . mental states can be (type) distinct only if the representations which constitute their objects are formally distinct."[12] That is, Fodor's constraint is quite similar to the main idea behind my argument; he is suggesting that one and the same mental representation (formally specified) cannot count as one belief, if one proposition about the future obtains, and another belief (or not a belief at all) if a different proposition about the future obtains.

Of course, Fodor assumes that human mental representations have some *physical realization* in the human brain. Thus, the problematic notion of "formality" can be cashed out, in some way or another, in physical terms. In contrast, of course, God's mental states are *not* physical; God is not related to physical representations when He is in the state of believing some proposition. My suggestion is, however, that there is *some* notion of formality that applies to God's mental states. That is, my contention is that God's belief states somehow involve mental representations, and that in a very broad sense these representations have formal properties. Indeed, it is hard to see how to dispense with something like the contention that God's belief states involve mental representations; for example, Zemach and Widerker say

> *Our* beliefs consist in our using some symbols (words, pictures, etc.) to stand for certain states of affairs which we take to exist. If God's beliefs are fashioned in a *radically* different way, we cannot say that He has *beliefs*. To have beliefs *about* something, He must use some symbols to represent that something.[13]

I am not sure I understand a notion of belief that does not involve the representation of the world to the agent as being of such and such a sort. Further, if the world is represented to two agents in exactly the same way, it is difficult to see how they could be in two different belief states. But here it is appropriate to consider a problem raised by the sorts of arguments presented by Putnam and others that meanings and the contents of beliefs "ain't in the head."[14] According to Putnam, the state of my mind that actually constitutes my believing that water is wet would have constituted a different belief – for example, the belief that "XYZ" is wet – if lakes and oceans on earth had been filled with XYZ rather than water. On this picture, the same internal state (formally specified) would indeed count as different beliefs, given different "environmental niches." Thus, someone who adopted this picture of the determination of the content of belief could *deny* my claim that one and the same state of God's mind would not count as different beliefs, given different events concerning S in the future.

Zemach and Widerker wish to do precisely this. They say:

> Fischer pays surprisingly little attention to the functionalist account of the mental . . . Functionalists, however . . . say that what we know as the mental content of an item *is* its function in a certain kind of system. Therefore, for the functionalist, the same state or item can *be* different mental states if lodged in different sociological or biological systems. Thus a certain state m which in fact is a belief that p, may have realized, in different surroundings, a different propositional content . . . If this is so, then, for all we know, the fact that p may be such an environmental necessary condition for the internal state of God, m, to count as a belief that p.[15]

I am inclined to make (at least) two points about this sort of objection. First, the different possibilities for future events concerning S seem to me to be very different from the different environmental niches envisaged by such philosophers as Putnam (and, following him, Zemach and

Widerker). Whereas causal contact in the past with different kinds in nature might well help to give different content to our beliefs, it is not at all plausible to suppose that whether or not (say) S does X at $t2$ will have this sort of effect on the content of anyone's beliefs. That is, even if rather more global issues such as causal contact in the past with certain natural kinds does in fact help to determine the content of our beliefs, holding these global factors fixed, it does not seem that whether or not someone does something in the future will have a comparable effect on the content of our beliefs. One way of putting the point is that I am not actually envisaging a variation in the "environmental niche"; rather, I am holding this fixed, and varying certain events which take place within the context of this niche.

Second, there is an important distinction, even if it is rather difficult to specify crisply, between what has been called "narrow content" and "wide content" of belief.[16] Very roughly speaking, narrow content is "what's in the head." Thus, if two agents have the world represented to them in the same way "from the inside," then their beliefs have the same narrow content. Again, roughly, two agents with the same phenomenological character to the belief states will have the same narrow content.

In contrast, two agents who have the same internal states may be in belief states with different "wide content." So, for example, I and my *doppelgänger* on Twin Earth (in which the wet stuff is XYZ) may be molecule-for-molecule identical – and thus be in exactly the same brain state – but be in belief states with different wide content: I believe that water is wet, and he believes that XYZ is wet. It might seem, then, that the debate about the nature of God's belief states is really a debate about whether the pertinent notion of content is wide or narrow. The analogue of the formality constraint is appropriate to God's beliefs, in the sense of narrow content; but it is inappropriate, if God's beliefs are construed in the sense of wide content. Clearly, Zemach and Widerker are thinking of God's beliefs in terms of wide content.

I have no interest in denying that God's beliefs have wide content. In general, ascribing wide content to belief states is appropriate in certain contexts and for certain purposes. It is just that the *relevant* notion of content here is narrow content. This is because narrow content is relevant to the explanation of behavior in a way in which wide content is not. That is, narrow content appears to be what is explanatorily relevant; if two agents are in belief states with exactly the same narrow content, any difference in their behavior must be attributed to differences in their preferences, desires, or intentions; invocation of wide content here appears explanatorily worthless. Indeed, if one imagines two agents with the same complex of "pro-attitudes" and the same beliefs in the sense of narrow content, it would seem hard to understand or explain any differences in behavior; specifically, invocation of belief in the sense of wide content would appear to be unpromising. Intuitively, it should be clear that what explains behavior must be "in the head."[17]

Further, God should be in a position to act differently based (say) on different prospective actions by S. Imagine, for example, that God is in the same belief state at $t1$ in the sense of narrow content in the following two scenarios. In Scenario One, S will do X at $t2$, and in Scenario Two, S will not do X at $t2$. Surely, this is an etiolated and implausible picture of God's belief states at $t1$. Further, it seems to make it impossible for God to consider intervention in a reasonable way. If there is no difference between the two scenarios that is accessible to God in terms of what is internal to His belief states, how can He reasonably consider appropriate actions of His own?

To see the problem more clearly, suppose that in Scenario One (in which S does X at $t2$), God warns S of some possible danger, and that in Scenario Two (in which S refrains from doing X at $t2$), God does not issue the warning, since it would be unnecessary. If the narrow content of God's beliefs is the same in both cases, how can we explain the difference in God's behavior? Is it simply luck or accident? And surely it is not helpful to point out that God had different beliefs in the wide sense in the two scenarios, for by hypothesis these differences are *inaccessible* to God: they are not reflected in any "internal" differences. Adopting the view that only the wide notion of content is relevant to God's beliefs seems to make such possible differences in God's behavior essentially mysterious.

Of course, greater mysteries have been associated with God, and I do not think that I have presented a knockdown argument for the relevance of the narrow sense of belief content. But we do wish to avoid ascribing mysterious and baffling properties and powers to God. Perhaps my point could be put as follows. Human beliefs, insofar as they are relevant to the explanation of behavior, appear to be governed by something like Fodor's formality condition. Similarly, if God's beliefs are relevant to the explanation of His behavior, they should also be governed by an analogue of the formality condition.[18]

A particularly salient departure from this idea is found in Edward Wierenga's book, *The Nature of God: An Inquiry Into Divine Attributes*. He supposes that, when Jones (sorry to S!) mows his lawn at $t2$, God's mind is in the state $m^\star$ at $t1$. Now Wierenga says:

... Fischer assumes that if $m^\star$ is an instance of *God's believing at t1 that Jones will mow his lawn at t2*, it is essentially so. Why, if Jones does not mow his lawn at *t2*, would it be false that $m^\star$ occurs but is not an instance of *God's believing at t1 that Jones will mow his lawn at t2?* ... Why could not $m^\star$ be the state of God's believing every truth? In that case, if Jones mows his lawn at *t2*, then $m^\star$ is an instance of *God's believing at t1 that Jones will mow his lawn at t2*, but if Jones were not to mow his lawn at *t2*, then $m^\star$ would be an instance of *God's believing at t1 that Jones will not mow his lawn at t2*.[19]

On Wierenga's view, God's belief states are *maximally* etiolated: no matter what happens, God is in the *same* belief state (narrowly construed). But this makes His cognitive capacities, and His related capacities to plan, deliberate, and intervene in the world, maximally obscure.

As I said above, my view *commits* me to the idea that God's beliefs involve a mental representation with formal properties of some sort or another. I take formal properties to be (at least) properties which are not *semantic*, i.e., which do not pertain directly to the relationship of mental states to the external world. If the representation is physical, then perhaps the notion of formality can be explained physically (in terms of differences in "shape" or "structure" or other physical properties). Difficult as this project is, it is even more difficult to explain the notion of formality as applied to God's representations. But then again I do not need to give a full characterization of the notion. I need, at least, to claim that there is some *analogy* between the formal features of a physical representation and those of a nonphysical representation. (Zemach and Widerker construe God as being related to [presumably nonphysical] "symbols.") Further, presumably the formal features of God's mental representations are those which He has access to and which make it "appear" or "seem" to Him that the world is one way rather than another. Of course, God's mental representations do not have a certain "shape"; but they have some features in virtue of which they make it appear to God that the world is a certain way rather than another.[20] When these features are the same in two cases, and thus the world appears to God to be the same, then it is hard to see how we could attribute to God two different belief states (in the narrow sense).

At one point Fodor suggests that not even God will violate the formality constraint (in a certain way).[21] And he is right: not even God will violate the formality constraint. That is to say, the notion of God's belief contents that is relevant to the argument for incompatibilism is *narrow* content. Any other notion will not be connected in a suitable way with God's possible behavior. And thus any other notion of belief content will not render God's beliefs relevantly similar to human beliefs.

If the relevant notion of belief involves narrow content, and God does indeed have some sorts of mental representations or symbols (or analogues to these), then it becomes quite clear why an interesting argument of Jonathan Kvanvig misses the mark.[22] Kvanvig points out that there is a state of God's mind at $t1$ that exhibits the sort of counterfactual dependence upon the future which is characteristic of soft properties: the state of believing the truth. God's believing the truth would count as believing that S will do X at $t2$ if S will indeed do X at $t2$, and the same state would count as believing that S will not do X at $t2$, if S will not do X at $t2$. But Kvanvig admits that there is *another* state (in addition to the state of believing the truth), which he calls the state of believing (a particular proposition). He however points out that there is no plausible way of arguing that the state of believing is more "ontologically basic" than the state of believing the truth, and thus he suggests that no good argument can be made that the important state of God's mind is a hard property.[23]

But I do not think the issue of ontological basicality is relevant here. No doubt, the state of believing the truth is not a hard property, particularly when it is realized by some state of belief about the future. And I do not deny that God's mind is in the state of believing the truth. But my contention is that He is *also* in a particular state of believing (say) that S will do X at $t2$. My response to Kvanvig involves two elements. First, given that this particular state involves some mental representation, then it emerges that God *is* in *some* state that is a hard property relative to $t1$. Second, this property is a *kernel* element: the property would have to be affected, if S were to do otherwise at $t2$. The point is *not* that this particular state is more "ontologically basic" than the more general state of believing the truth. Rather, the point is that God *must* be in the more particular state, if His beliefs are relevantly similar to human beliefs, and if God's beliefs are to play the required role in His mental economy. And this property would *have* to be affected, if S were to do otherwise at $t2$.

4.3 A slightly more formal presentation

The considerations developed above suggest a slightly more general way of presenting the constraints on hard facts and hard properties (which I have been sketching in an informal fashion). First, return to the context of facts. I said that "Judy sits at $t1$" is a clear case of a hard fact about $t1$, whereas "Judy sits at $t1$ prior to having lunch at $t2$" is a soft fact about $t1$. Note that there is a physical fact which obtains at $t1$ which is such that it would count as Judy sitting, no matter what happens in the future. This suggests that a fact $F1$ is a hard fact about $t1$ only if some fact $F2$ which intuitively obtains at $t1$ counts as (part of) $F1$ and would count as (part of) $F1$, no matter what happens after $t1$. Hard facts are in this way resilient to the future. In contrast, consider the fact that Judy sits at $t1$ prior to having lunch at $t2$. There is a physical fact which intuitively obtains at $t1$ and which in fact counts as part of Judy sitting prior to having lunch at $t2$. But this physical fact would *not* count as part of this fact, no matter what happens in the future. Thus, "Judy sits at $t1$ prior to having lunch at $t2$" is not a hard fact about $t1$.

Now consider the context of properties. "Sitting" is a hard property relative to $t1$, whereas "sitting prior to having lunch at $t2$" is a soft property relative to $t1$. Note that there is a state of Judy's body which in fact counts as sitting, and which would so count, no matter what happens in the future. This suggests that a property p is a hard property relative to $t1$ only if some state of the world at $t1$ in fact counts as (part of) p, and would so count no matter what happens in the future. Hard properties are in this sense resilient to the future. In contrast, consider the property of sitting prior to having lunch at $t2$. There is a state of Judy's body which in fact counts as part of sitting prior to having lunch at $t2$. But this state would *not* so count, no matter what happens in the future. Thus, "sitting prior to having lunch at $t2$" is not a hard property relative to $t1$.

Finally, I apply this more general formulation to God's beliefs. As I have pointed out, "God" can be construed either as a role-term or a name. If "God" is a role-term and "Yahweh" picks out the individual who in fact is God (but is not necessarily God), then God's prior belief will turn out to be a hard-core soft fact (as I argued above). This is because the fact that Yahweh believes at $t1$ that S does X at $t2$ is deemed a hard fact about $t1$: there is a fact (which involves Yahweh's mind) which intuitively obtains at $t1$ and which actually counts as the fact that Yahweh believes that S does X at $t2$ and which would so count, no matter what happens in the future.

And if "God" is taken to be a name, then God's prior belief will turn out to be a hard-type soft fact. This is because the property of believing that S does X at $t2$ is deemed a hard property relative to $t1$: there is a state which intuitively obtains at $t1$ (a state of God's mind) which in fact counts as believing that S does X at $t2$, and which would so count, no matter what happens in the future. Of course, if S were to refrain from doing X at $t2$, then *God* could not be in the state He actually is in; but this does not render it false that *that type* of state would count as that belief, no matter what happens in the future.

At the beginning of this chapter, I claimed that I would argue that Ockhamism is untenable because the facts about God's prior beliefs are relevantly different from the standard sorts of soft facts. I said facts about God's prior beliefs "just feel different" from the paradigm soft facts. Now the explanation for this inchoate difference emerges more clearly: God's prior beliefs are either hard-core or hard-type soft facts. In either case they come with excess baggage: they cannot be falsified without affecting some genuine feature of the past.

This *distinguishes* facts about God's beliefs from standard soft facts. Consider (again) two such standard soft facts: "It is true at $t1$ that S does X at $t2$" and "Judy sits at $t1$ prior to having lunch at $t2$." Neither of these facts is burdened with excess baggage, and thus they are crucially different from the facts about God's prior beliefs.

Although these two soft facts are similar in lacking excess baggage, it is interesting to see that they are in one respect different. The latter fact – that Judy sits at $t1$ prior to having lunch at $t2$ – is a "soft-type soft fact": it is a soft fact with a constitutive property which is soft ("sitting at $t1$ prior to having lunch at $t2$"). But note also that a soft-type soft fact need not be "thoroughly soft" (lacking any hard aspects or elements on *any* of the methods of division). To see this, divide the fact about Judy according to the method of division which decomposes larger facts into *smaller facts*. On this approach, we get the fact that Judy sits at $t1$ and the fact that Judy eats lunch at $t2$. Thus, the larger fact *does* have a component fact which is hard relative to $t1$: the fact that Judy sits at $t1$. Thus, the larger fact is in this respect *different* from the thoroughly soft fact that it is true at $t1$ that S does X at $t2$. But note also that the hard component fact is not a *kernel element* of the larger fact (relative to the relevant agent and time). Thus, although the two soft facts are different in one respect, they are similar in lacking excess baggage.

Compare, now, four facts: (1) It is true at $t1$ that S does X at $t2$, (2) Judy sits at $t1$ prior to S doing X at $t2$; (3) Judy sits at $t1$ prior to the sun's rising at $t2$ (the next morning); and (4) God believes at $t1$ that S does X at $t2$. They are all soft facts about $t1$. (1) is a thoroughly soft fact: it has no hard element (on any of the methods of division). (2) has a hard element, on one method of division (which decomposes larger facts into smaller facts); but there is no reason to think it is a kernel element relative to S and $t2$. On this method of division, then, it is a "soft-core soft fact." And on the other method of division, the fact consists in an individual and a *soft property* relative to *t1*: it is a soft-type soft fact. Either way, it does *not* have a hard kernel element (relative to the relevant agent and time). (3) however does come with excess baggage; it is impossible for any human agent to falsify this fact after *t1* without doing something no human being intuitively can do (cause the sun not to rise in the morning). (4) is in this respect similar to (3): it comes with excess baggage. I have argued that it is a specific kind of baggage – either a hard fact or a hard property; thus, the fact is either a hard-core or hard-type soft fact. It is impossible for any human agent to falsify (4) without doing something one cannot do *in virtue of the fixity of the past*.

God's beliefs are linked to human actions in virtue of God's essential omniscience. This linkage implies that (4) has excess baggage. In contrast, there is no such linkage in the case of (2). Because of this lack of linkage, *S* may have it in his power simply to separate his doing *X* (or not) from the prior event of Judy's sitting at *t2*. This lack of linkage explains the difference between (2) and (4). Because of this lack of linkage in (2), its second element (*S*'s doing *X* at *t2*) "floats free" of any temporally nonrelational encumbrances. In contrast, in virtue of the linkage between the elements of (4), there are precisely these sorts of encumbrances.

5 The facts: Taxonomy and conclusion

These are the facts. To begin: there are hard facts and soft facts. Hard facts exhibit a certain sort of resiliency with respect to the future, whereas soft facts are counterfactually dependent on the future. Hard facts, of course, are taken by the incompatibilist to be fixed at subsequent times; in contrast, it is generally agreed that not all soft facts are subsequently fixed.

Among the soft facts, some are totally and relentlessly soft – they have no aspects or components that are hard, on any method of division. Some such "thoroughly soft" facts are not fixed at the relevant times. So, for example, it is not plausible that the fact that it is true at *t1* that *S* does *X* at *t2* is fixed at (or just prior to) *t2*, despite the claims of certain fatalists.[24] Note that some thoroughly soft facts are indeed fixed (at the relevant times) in virtue of a component which is out of our control for reasons independent of temporal nonrelationality and the fixity of the past. So, for example, the fact that it is true at *t1* that the sun rises at *t2* (the next morning) is fixed at (or just prior to) $t2$, albeit thoroughly soft (relative to $t1$).[25] Thus, there are some soft facts which are fixed for reasons quite apart from the fixity of the past.

Other soft facts are *not* thoroughly soft: they have some "hardness" to them, on some method of division. Many soft facts have some components that are hard on at least some method of division, but which are not hard *kernel elements*. The fact that Judy sits at $t1$ prior to S doing X at $t2$ is just such a fact. This fact may well be within S's power to affect at (or just prior to) $t2$, since it lacks a *hard kernel element* relative to S at (or just prior to) $t2$. Since the hard elements of such facts are not kernel elements, there is a sense in which these facts have "handles."

Among the soft facts which are not thoroughly soft, however, are facts which *are* plausibly thought to be fixed at subsequent times. Some such soft facts have *components or aspects* which are hard kernel elements (either facts or properties). When the hard kernel element is a fact, the soft fact is a hard-core soft fact; and when the hard kernel element is a property, the soft fact is a hard-type soft fact. Hard-core and hard-type soft facts have excess baggage. And soft facts with excess baggage are plausibly taken to be fixed precisely in virtue of the fixity of the past.

It emerges from this sort of taxonomy that there is a crucial difference between God's beliefs and other soft facts. If my analysis of God's beliefs is correct, then facts about God's beliefs are either hard-core or hard-type soft facts. Thus, facts about God's beliefs are crucially different from other soft facts to which the Ockhamist typically assimilates them.

My basic contention has been that there are important differences among the various sorts of soft facts. Seeing this, we can give more concrete expression to the inchoate feeling with which I started: facts about God's beliefs really are crucially different from the "standard" or "paradigmatic" soft facts to which they are frequently compared by compatibilists. Now let me apply this insight to two arguments which employ resources provided by Alvin Plantinga.[26] As I pointed out above, Plantinga develops and endorses the Entailment View of Soft Facthood, according to which a fact is a soft fact insofar as its obtaining at a time entails the obtaining of a certain sort of fact at a subsequent time. Further, Plantinga points out that facts about God's beliefs are similar to other soft facts in this respect, i.e., in satisfying the Entailment Criterion. But clearly it would be a mistake to conclude from this similarity that God's beliefs are *relevantly similar* to other soft facts (which are intuitively not taken to be fixed at the relevant times). The fixity characteristics of a fact are partly a function of a fact's internal structure, and thus it would be too crude to group all soft facts together as regards their fixity. The entailment idea may be a useful tool for demarcating softness, but it is obviously too coarse-grained to give us an adequate indication of fixity.

Second, consider the "equivalence argument" suggested by Plantinga. Plantinga points out that, on the assumption that God exists necessarily, the facts, "God believes at $t1$ that S does X at $t2$" and "S does X at $t2$" are necessarily equivalent. Since "S does X at $t2$" is clearly not a hard fact about $t1$, and this fact is necessarily equivalent to "God believes at $t1$ that S does X at $t2$," one might conclude that the fact about God's belief is not a hard fact about $t1$.

I grant the conclusion of the equivalence argument. Any fact necessarily equivalent to a soft fact may well be a soft fact. But again I must point out that this does *not* entail that the facts are *relevantly similar*. It remains open that the fact about God's belief (as opposed to the fact about S) is a soft fact with excess baggage. Thus, the equivalence argument is not sufficient to vindicate Ockhamism.

The distinction between hard and soft facts is useful, but it is too coarse. Whereas it reveals something, it also conceals something. More precisely, an excessive preoccupation with the distinction – with its explicit articulation and with classifying facts as hard or soft – can conceal the complexity of the internal structure of soft facts. While certain philosophers have developed intricately ramified accounts of the distinction and have triumphantly noted, at the end of the day, that these accounts imply that God's beliefs are soft facts, they have failed to see that more work needs to be done, in order to defend Ockhamism. Indeed, they have failed to see that the Ockhamist's own view that temporally nonrelational features of the past are fixed threatens to vitiate the entire enterprise.

In this chapter I have begun to provide a subtler, more fine-grained understanding of the facts that are relevant to freedom. When the true complexity of these facts is revealed, it emerges that the incompatibilist arguments from causal determinism and God's existence are importantly *similar* at a deep level. Granted, the pertinent past fact in the argument from causal determinism is a hard fact, whereas in the argument from God's existence it is a soft fact. But in both cases it is plausible to say that an agent's doing otherwise would require *some* hard (temporally nonrelational) feature of the past to be other than it actually was. In both cases an agent's doing otherwise cannot be *an extension of the actual past*. Thus, at a deep level, the arguments are on a par.

7

Responsibility and Alternative Possibilities

1 Introduction

In previous chapters, I have elaborated (at some length) a set of challenges to the intuitive and natural picture of ourselves as having a certain sort of control. This sort of control implies that we have various genuinely open pathways branching into the future. The basic problem with this picture is that it may require us to have an implausible power over the past or the natural laws. Thus, it is not clear that we do in fact have the sort of control that implies alternative possibilities. And if moral responsibility and personhood require this sort of control, it is not clear that we can legitimately hold each other morally responsible for our behavior and indeed conceive of each other as persons. Because of the power and persistence of the skeptical challenges to our having the sort of control that involves alternative possibilities, perhaps it is advisable to ask whether we really *do* require this sort of control, after all.

2 Frankfurt-type examples

Imagine, if you will, that Black is a quite nifty (and even generally nice) neurosurgeon. But in performing an operation on Jones to remove a brain tumor, Black inserts a mechanism into Jones' brain which enables Black to monitor and control Jones' activities. Jones, meanwhile, knows nothing of this. Black exercises this control through a sophisticated computer which he has programmed so that, among other things, it monitors Jones' voting behavior. If Jones were to show any inclination to vote for Bush, then the computer, through the mechanism in Jones' brain, intervenes to assure that he actually decides to vote for Clinton and does so vote. But if Jones decides on his own to vote for Clinton, the computer does nothing but continue to monitor – without affecting – the goings-on in Jones' head.

Suppose that Jones decides to vote for Clinton on his own, just as he would have if Black had not inserted the mechanism into his head. It seems, upon first thinking about this case, that Jones can be held morally responsible for his choice and act of voting for Clinton, although he could not have chosen otherwise and he could not have done otherwise.[1] That is to say, Jones is rationally accessible to – an appropriate candidate for – the reactive attitudes on the basis of his choice and his action. Of course, it need not follow that we ought to praise him (or blame him); rather, he is an *appropriate candidate* for such attitudes – these attitudes are not ruled out (as they would be in the context of direct manipulation of the brain or certain sorts of coercion, and so forth).

Clearly, the Frankfurt-type example just presented is an unusual case. We are fairly certain that "counterfactual interveners" such as Black generally do not exist. And yet an unusual case can point us to something very mundane – but also very important. It can cause us to focus with increased clarity on what makes us morally responsible in quite ordinary cases.

It seems to me that the conclusion tentatively adopted above is correct: moral responsibility does not require the sort of control which involves the existence of genuinely open alternative possibilities. But this is not to say that moral responsibility does not require control of any sort. Indeed, it is important to distinguish two sorts of control, and it will emerge that moral responsibility for actions is associated with one (but not the other) kind of control.[2]

Let us suppose that I am driving my car. It is functioning well, and I wish to make a right turn. As a result of my intention to turn right, I signal, turn the steering wheel, and carefully guide the car to the right. Further, I here assume that I was able to form the intention *not* to turn the car to the right but to turn the car to the left instead. Also, I assume that had I formed such an intention, I would have turned the steering wheel to the left and the car would have gone to the left. In this ordinary case, I guide the car to the right, but I could have guided it to the left. I control the car, and also I have a certain sort of control *over* the car's movements. Insofar as I actually guide the car in a certain way, I shall say that I have "guidance control." Further, insofar as I have the power to guide the car in a different way, I shall say that I have "regulative control." (Of course, here I am not making any special assumptions, such as that causal determinism obtains or God exists.)

To develop these notions of control (and their relationship), imagine a second case. In this analogue of the Frankfurt-type case presented above, I again guide my car in the normal way to the right. The car's steering apparatus *works properly* when I steer the car to the right. But unbeknownst to me, the car's steering apparatus is broken in such a way that, if I were to try to turn it in some other direction, the car would veer off to the right in precisely the way it actually goes to the right.[3] Since I actually do not try to do anything but turn to the right, the apparatus functions normally and the car's movements are precisely as they would have been, if there had been no problem with the steering apparatus. Indeed, my guidance of the car to the right is precisely the same in this case and the first car case.

Here, as in the first car case, it appears that I control the movement of the car in the sense of guiding it (in a certain way) to the right. Thus, I have guidance control of the car. But I cannot cause it to go anywhere other than where it actually goes. Thus, I lack regulative control of the car. I control the car, but I do not have control *over* the car (or the car's movements). Generally, we assume that guidance control and regulative control go together. But this Frankfurt-type case shows how they can at least in principle pull apart: one can have guidance control without regulative control. That is, one can have a certain sort of control without having the sort of control that involves alternative possibilities.

The Frankfurt-type cases, unusual as they are, may well point us to something as significant as it is mundane. When we are morally responsible for our actions, we *do* possess a kind of control. So the traditional assumption of the association of moral responsibility (and personhood) with control is quite correct. But it need not be the sort of control that involves alternative possibilities. The suggestion, derived from the Frankfurt-type cases, is that the sort of control necessarily associated with moral responsibility for action is *guidance control*. Whereas we may intuitively suppose that regulative control always comes with guidance control, it is not, at a deep level, regulative control that grounds moral responsibility.

I have not sought to give a precise (or even very informative) account of the two sorts of control. Rather, I have relied on the intuitive idea that there is a sense of control in which I control the car when I guide it (in the normal way) to the right. Further, I have employed the Frankfurt-type example to argue that this sense of control need not involve any alternative possibilities. Then, I have simply contrasted this sort of control with a kind of control which does indeed require alternative possibilities. Below, I shall attempt to say more about the first sort of control – guidance control – but for now it will suffice to simply have in mind a fairly intuitive distinction between the two sorts of control.

Above I pointed out that, because of the power and persistence of the skeptical challenges to the idea that we have the sort of control that involves alternative possibilities, it would be desirable if moral responsibility did not require this sort of control. It is the beauty of the Frankfurt-type examples that they suggest precisely that moral responsibility for our actions does *not* require the sort of control that involves alternative possibilities – regulative control. If this is indeed so, then a line of argument opens that has at least some chance of answering the skeptic's challenges to our moral responsibility and personhood.

3 The flicker of freedom strategy

3.1 The strategy and its significance

A lot, then, is at stake in evaluating the Frankfurt-type examples. They suggest that (perhaps in conjunction with the satisfaction of certain epistemic conditions) the presence of guidance control is sufficient for moral responsibility. They thus suggest a way of meeting the skeptic's challenge, because this challenge is based precisely on the assumption that alternative possibilities are required for moral responsibility and personhood.

But exactly because of the beauty and power of the idea that guidance control is the "freedom-relevant" condition sufficient for moral responsibility for action, we should not be too hasty in the analysis of Frankfurt-type cases.[4] The Frankfurt-type cases seem at first to involve no alternative possibilities. But upon closer inspection it can be seen that, although they do not involve alternative possibilities of the normal kind, they nevertheless may involve *some* alternative possibilities. That is to say, although the counterfactual interveners eliminate most alternative possibilities, arguably they do not eliminate *all* such possibilities: even in the Frankfurt-type cases, there seems to be a "flicker of freedom." Thus, there is an opening to argue that these alternative possibilities (the flickers of freedom) *must* be present, even in the Frankfurt-type cases, in order for there to be moral responsibility.

To motivate the flicker of freedom strategy for responding to the Frankfurt-type cases, let us go back to the second car case presented above. I pointed out that, in virtue of the malfunctioning steering apparatus, it is plausible to say that I had guidance control but not regulative control; although I controlled the car, I didn't have control over its movements. But certainly I possessed *some* alternative possibilities: for example, apart from any special assumptions, there is no reason to deny that I could have formed the intention to guide the car in some *other* direction than right, and I could have attempted to steer the car in this other direction, and so forth. Thus, I had *some* alternative possibilities, even if I could not change the path of the car.

Now this sort of worry is part of the motivation for the elaborate set-up of the case of Jones and Black. In this case, should Jones show any indication that he is about to choose to vote for Bush, Black will intervene to assure that he does not even *choose* to vote for Bush. Thus, in contrast to the car case, in the case of Jones and Black regulative control over *choice* and the formation of intention is also absent.

But, still, one might somehow be unsatisfied with the claim that there are *no* alternative possibilities in the case of Jones and Black. After all, consider again part of the description of the case: "If Jones were to show any inclination to vote for Bush, then the computer, through the mechanism in Jones' brain, intervenes to assure that he actually decides to vote for Clinton and does so vote." This suggests that, at the very least, Jones must be taken to have the power to "show an inclination" to vote for Bush (or perhaps to choose to vote for Bush). But then here is the flicker of freedom! Exiguous as it may be, here is the space – the elbow room – that must exist, if we are legitimately to be held morally responsible for what we do.

Before developing the flicker strategy in greater detail, I pause to ask why it is so important to isolate the flicker of freedom. Recall that the skeptic about our moral responsibility urges that, for all we know, we do not have *any* alternative possibilities. More specifically, it is evident that, if the incompatibilistic arguments are sound, then they show that (if causal determinism obtains or God exists) we have *no* alternative possibilities of *any* sort. Now suppose that there are flickers of freedom, even in Frankfurt-type cases. Then, even if these cases show that we can be morally responsible for what we do even in contexts in which we do not have alternative possibilities as they are traditionally conceived, they could *not* be employed straightforwardly to establish that we can be morally responsible for our actions in a causally deterministic world (or a world in which God exists). For in such a world there cannot be even a flicker of freedom (if the skeptical arguments are correct). Of course, causal determinism would extinguish not just a prairie fire of freedom, but also the tiniest flicker.

3.2 Four versions of the strategy

Having laid out the basic idea behind the flicker of freedom strategy and indicated what is at issue, I turn to the specific development of various versions of this strategy. In the above section I began to develop the first version of the strategy. Basically, on this approach we keep tracing "backward" in the relevant alternative sequences until we find a flicker of freedom.

To explain. Return to the case of Jones and Black. In this case Jones actually deliberates in the normal fashion, chooses to vote for Clinton, and does so on his own. Further, he cannot choose to do otherwise; nor can he do otherwise. But let us think about a possible alternative sequence in which he *begins* to choose to vote for Bush. If this should occur, Black would immediately intervene, but at least Jones *begins* to choose to vote for Bush and thus Jones can be said to have at least this power – the power to initiate (albeit not complete) the choice to do otherwise. Perhaps, then, this is the flicker of freedom.

But now it seems we can imagine another case in which Jones has a propensity to show some *sign* which reliably indicates his voting behavior prior even to his beginning to make a choice or form an intention. Suppose, that is, that Jones would blush red (or show some other sign that is readable by Black – perhaps a furrowed brow or raised eyebrow or even a complex and arcane neurophysiological pattern) prior to initiating any process of decision-making if and only if he were about to choose to vote for Bush. If Jones is like this, then Black could (by reading the sign) prevent him from even *beginning* to make the relevant choice or decision.[5]

But again a flicker emerges, for even here Jones has the power to show the relevant sign – to blush red or display the complex neurophysiological pattern, and so forth. And it is hard to see how a Frankfurt-type example could be constructed which would have absolutely *no* such flicker. For a Frankfurt-type case must have an alternative sequence in which intervention is triggered in some fashion or other, and it is hard to see how to avoid the idea that the triggering event can serve as the flicker of freedom. Thus, it appears that, no matter how sophisticated the Frankfurt-type example, if one traces "backward" (from the event caused by the agent and toward the agent, as it were) far enough, one will find a flicker of freedom.[6]

Another flicker strategy involves tracing in precisely the opposite way along the alternative sequence. On this approach, one proceeds "forward" (from the agent and toward the event caused by the agent) until one gets to the terminal point, and this constitutes the flicker of freedom. Here let us adopt the assumption that when an agent performs an action, he causes some concrete event to occur. I further suppose that when an agent is morally responsible for performing a particular act, he is morally responsible for causing the relevant concrete event to occur.

Crucial to this version of the flicker of freedom strategy is the adoption of some sort of essentialist principle of event individuation.[7] On the strongest version of this principle, all the actual causal antecedents of a particular event are essential to it; thus, if a given event *e* occurs in the actual world, then any possible event with any different causal antecedent would not be identical to *e*. For simplicity's sake, I start with this strong version of the essentialist principle.

Now consider again the original example of Jones and Black. Recall that Jones actually chooses to vote for Clinton and does vote for Clinton as a result of the ordinary sort of sequence. Imagine, however, contrary to fact, that Jones begins to show an inclination not to choose to vote for Clinton and this triggers the intervention by Black (and the subsequent choice to vote for Clinton and the vote for Clinton). Under these hypothetical circumstances, Jones would indeed have voted for Clinton. But, given the essentialist principle of event-individuation, Jones would have caused a *different* particular event of voting for Clinton from the actual voting event. That is, as things actually went, the neurologist Black played no role in the causal background of the voting event, whereas Black does play such a role in the alternative scenario; thus, on the essentialist principle, the actual particular event cannot be identical to the hypothetical event (in the alternative sequence). So it is *not* the case that Jones could not have caused another particular event to occur. This, then, is the flicker of freedom. Although Jones cannot bring it about that he doesn't vote for Clinton, he does possess the power to bring about a different event particular. And insofar as responsibility for action involves responsibility for bringing about a particular concrete event, responsibility for action involves alternative possibilities, even in the Frankfurt-type cases.

Note that strictly speaking the strong version of the essentialist principle of event-individuation is not required by the argument. A weaker version of the principle that specifies that certain *salient* or *significant* causal antecedents are essential to event-particulars would presumably also yield the same results, since whether or not an agent such as Black intercedes in the way envisaged is, on any plausible view, a salient or significant feature of the causal background of a particular event.

On this version of the flicker strategy, it is crucial to distinguish the notions of bringing about a particular concrete event and bringing about an event of a certain general type. Although Jones cannot avoid bringing about an event of the general type, "voting for Clinton," he can avoid bringing about the particular event he actually causes to occur. This suggests that the claim that the Frankfurt-type examples show that an agent can be held morally responsible for bringing about an event even though he cannot avoid bringing it about gains some illicit support from a failure carefully to distinguish between bringing about a concrete particular event and bringing about an event of a certain general sort.[8]

There is another set of considerations that issues in a distinctive version of the flicker of freedom strategy. These considerations are associated with the "libertarian" picture of agency. Of course, there are various different libertarian accounts of agency, and I cannot go into the details here. But I shall sketch enough of the basic intuitions of the libertarian to motivate this version of the flicker approach.

Here is one (although certainly not the only) libertarian picture of agency. On this model, what distinguishes an action from a mere event is that an action is preceded by a *volition*. But of course this claim in itself need not lead to the libertarian view. What is added is that the volition must be "agent-caused," where agent causation is a special sort of causation *not* reducible to event-causation. It is assumed that when an agent causes a volition via this special sort of causation – agent-causation – nothing causes the agent to cause the volition. That is, the agent's agent-causing the volition is incompatible with the agent's being caused by some external factor to cause the volition.

Suppose, for the sake of argument, that one adopts this picture of agency. Now the Frankfurt-type case of Jones and Black can be analyzed as follows. Insofar as Jones deliberates, chooses, and acts in the normal way, we can suppose that Jones agent-causes his volition to vote for Clinton. Now think about the alternative sequence. It is hypothesized that should Jones begin to show any inclination to choose to vote for Bush, Black would intercede and neurologically ensure that he choose to vote for Clinton. Under such a circumstance we can (again, for the sake of argument) grant that Jones would have some sort of mental state consisting in a choice or decision to vote for Clinton, but he clearly would *not* have agent-caused a volition to vote for Clinton (insofar as his volition is caused by some external entity).

Thus, according to this libertarian analysis, Jones possesses the power to refrain from agent-causing his volition to vote for Clinton. Although he does not have the power to agent-cause a volition to vote for Bush, he *does* have a flicker of freedom: although he actually agent-causes a volition to vote for Clinton, he has it in his power *not* to agent-cause this sort of volition. On this approach, it is not envisaged that Jones must have the power to act otherwise, or even form a different sort of volition, if he is to be deemed morally responsible for what he does. Rather, it is supposed that Jones must at least have the power not to form the sort of volition he actually forms. And it is alleged that Jones has precisely this power, even in the Frankfurt-type case.[9]

I do not believe that one needs to posit volitions or even agent-causation to get the sort of results just sketched. It may be simply that one believes that mental events cannot, as a conceptual matter, be caused in the way envisaged in the alternative scenario of the case of Jones and Black. If one holds this belief, one would simply deny that in the alternative scenario Jones genuinely chooses (or wills) to vote for Clinton. Thus, again, one can say that, although Jones does not have the power to choose otherwise, he does in fact have the power to refrain from choosing (or willing) to vote for Clinton. Here, again, is the flicker of freedom.

All of the above three flicker of freedom strategies start by taking a somewhat careful view of the alternative sequence and thereby generate an alternative possibility that might previously have gone unnoticed. The final strategy starts with a more careful look at the actual sequence. More specifically, it invites us to be more careful in our specification of *what* the agent is (putatively) morally responsible for. Seeing exactly what we hold the agent responsible for, it is alleged, will help us to see that there are indeed alternative possibilities, even in the Frankfurt-type cases.

Return to the original case of Jones and Black. Someone might claim that what we "really" hold Jones morally responsible for is *not* "voting for Clinton," or even "choosing or willing to vote for Clinton." Rather, what we hold Jones morally responsible for is something like "voting for Clinton on his own," or "choosing to vote for Clinton on his own," where we mean by "on his own" at least in part "not as a result of some weird intervention such as that of Black."[10] But clearly if this is indeed what we hold Jones morally responsible for, then there are alternative possibilities. For, obviously, in the alternative sequence Jones would not be choosing or voting "on his own."

These strategies, although different in interesting respects, have something important in common. They all suggest that the Frankfurt-type examples cannot be employed (at least straightforwardly) to argue that moral responsibility need not require alternative possibilities. Indeed, they suggest that, whereas the initial impression got from considering a Frankfurt-type case is that there are no alternative possibilities, in fact one can see that there *are* such possibilities, if one scratches below the surface just a bit. And although they may not be quite the alternatives traditionally envisaged, they are alternative possibilities nevertheless – and just the sort that would be ruled out (if the skeptical arguments are sound) by causal determinism or God's foreknowledge.

3.3 Response

Despite the undeniable appeal of the flicker of freedom strategy, I believe that ultimately it is not convincing. I do not have a decisive argument against it, but of course such arguments are few and far between in these realms. I wish now to develop a set of considerations which lead me to reject the flicker of freedom approach. The kind of argument I shall sketch will apply, *mutatis mutandis*, to all the versions of the flicker strategy presented above, but it will be most convenient to begin with the second version (and then apply the analysis to the other versions).

Recall the second version of the flicker of freedom strategy. On this approach, it is argued that (in the original Jones and Black case) Jones does indeed have an alternative possibility insofar as he has the power to bring about a *different particular event* (from the actual event he brings about). I am willing to grant to the flicker theorist the claim that there exists an alternative possibility here; but my basic worry is that this alternative possibility is not sufficiently *robust* to ground the relevant attributions of moral responsibility. Put in other words, even if the possible event at the terminus of the alternative sequence (in the case of Jones and Black) is indeed an alternative possibility, it is highly implausible to suppose that it is *in virtue* of the existence of such an alternative possibility that Jones is morally responsible for what he does. I suggest that it is not enough for the flicker theorist to analyze the relevant range of cases in such a way as to identify an alternative possibility. Although this is surely a first step, it is not enough to establish the flicker of freedom view, because what needs also to be shown is that these alternative possibilities *play a certain role* in the appropriate understanding of the cases. That is, it needs to be shown that these alternative possibilities *ground* our attributions of moral responsibility. And this is what I find puzzling and implausible.

Briefly think about the basic picture of control that underlies the alternative-possibilities view (and thus the flicker of freedom strategy).

Here the future is a garden of forking paths. At various points in life, it is envisaged that there are various paths that branch into the future, and one can determine which of these genuinely open pathways becomes the actual path of the future. The existence of *various* genuinely open pathways is alleged to be *crucial* to the idea that one has *control* of the relevant kind. But if this is so, I suggest that it would be very puzzling and unnatural to suppose that it is the existence of various alternative pathways along which one does *not* act freely that shows that one has control of the kind in question. How exactly *could* the existence of various alternative pathways along which the agent does *not* act freely render it true that the agent has the relevant kind of control (regulative control)? And notice that this is precisely the situation in the Frankfurt-type cases. In particular, note that even if it is granted that the terminus of the alternative sequence in the case of Jones and Black is a *different* event from the actual event of Jones' voting for Clinton, it also is evident that Jones would not be *freely* voting for Clinton in the alternative sequence.

The point might be put as follows. The proponent of the idea that regulative control is required for moral responsibility insists that there can be no moral responsibility, if there is but one path leading into the future: to get the crucial kind of control, we must add various alternative possibilities. Now it seems that the flicker theorist must claim that the addition of the sort of alternative possibility he has identified would transform a case of lack of responsibility into one of responsibility. But this seems mysterious in the extreme: how can adding an alternative scenario (or perhaps even a set of them) in which Jones does not *freely* vote for Clinton make it true that he actually possesses the sort of control required for him to be morally responsible for his voting for Clinton? This might appear to involve a kind of *alchemy*, and it is just as incredible.

Consider, also, another analogy with epistemology. As I shall explain a bit more carefully in the following chapter, certain accounts of knowledge imply that an agent knows that p only if he can distinguish a class of situations in which p obtains from a contrasting class in which p does not obtain. (Actually, our discussion of the Principle of Closure of Knowledge Under Known Implication in chapter two pointed us toward some such theories.) On this approach, knowledge requires a certain kind of *discriminatory capacity*; this model is clearly analogous with the view that moral responsibility requires regulative control. More specifically, on this approach to knowledge, an agent knows that p only if there exists a set of alternatives to the actual world in which the agent's beliefs line up with states of the world in the right way. What would be highly implausible would be to suppose that what transforms some case of lack of knowledge into a case of knowledge would be the existence of a range of alternative scenarios in which the agent *gets it wrong*!

Suppose, for example, that we are assessing the claim that a certain individual, Schmidtz, knows that there is a barn in front of him. Of course, some epistemologists urge that it is necessary that Schmidtz be able to distinguish the actual situation (in which there is a barn in front of him) from a class of relevant alternative scenarios (in which there is no barn in front of him), in order for Schmidtz to know that there is a barn in front of him. But it would surely be bizarre and unattractive to point to a set of relevant alternative scenarios in which Schmidtz comes to a *false* belief about states of the world and then to claim that it is in virtue of *this* set of alternatives that Schmidtz actually possesses knowledge! And arguably it is not much more plausible to suggest that it is in virtue of a set of alternative possibilities in which Jones does *not* act freely that he actually can be held morally responsible for his behavior. How could adding a set of alternatives in which Jones does *not* act freely make it the case that he *actually* acts freely?

The point can be put somewhat differently. On the traditional alternative-possibilities picture, it is envisaged that an agent has a choice between two (or more) scenarios *of a certain sort*. In one scenario, he deliberates and forms an intention to perform an act of a certain kind and then carries out this intention in an appropriate way. In at least one other possible scenario, he deliberates and forms an intention to perform a different kind of act (or no act at all) and carries out this intention in an appropriate way. This is what is involved in having robust alternative possibilities, and certainly this is the natural way to think about the sort of alternatives that allegedly ground moral responsibility.

But it is evident that in Frankfurt-type examples these conditions do *not* obtain: the alternative scenarios are not of the requisite kind. In the case of Jones and Black, in the alternative scenario Jones does *not* deliberate and then form an intention to vote for Bush (and then act on this intention in an appropriate way). Thus, even if there is a flicker of freedom in these cases, it does not seem to be *robust* enough to ground moral responsibility ascriptions. The traditional alternative-possibilities model links moral responsibility with *control* of a certain kind (regulative control); but for this kind of control to exist, surely the alternative possibilities which are invoked to ground the attributions of responsibility must be more robust.[11]

I have begun my critical discussion of the flicker of freedom strategy by focusing on the second version of the strategy. But I believe parallel considerations apply to the other versions. Consider now the third version (the "libertarian version"). On this approach, it is required that an agent have the power not to cause the volition he actually causes, in order for him to be morally responsible. And, as pointed out above, it is indeed true that in the case of Jones and Black, Jones has the power not to cause his volition to vote for Clinton (given the libertarian assumptions about agency). But note further that even so, in the alternative sequence Jones does *not* form an intention to refrain from causing the volition in question (the volition to vote for Clinton) and then proceed to carry out this intention in an appropriate way. Again, it may be granted that Jones has the power not to cause a volition to vote for Clinton. But in not causing such a volition he would of course *not* be acting freely; because of the nature of Black's intervention, it would *not* be true that Jones freely refrains from causing the volition to vote for Clinton. Thus, even if there is some sort of flicker of freedom here, it does not seem capable of playing the requisite role in grounding ascriptions of moral responsibility – it does not seem sufficiently robust.

Consider, also, the flicker strategy that insists that what Jones is "really" morally responsible for is "voting for Clinton on his own" (or perhaps "choosing on his own to vote for Clinton"). If this is the appropriate specification of the content of Jones' moral responsibility, then evidently there is an alternative possibility. But note again that this alternative possibility lacks robustness. After all, in the alternative sequence Jones does *not* freely refrain from "voting for Clinton on his own." Indeed, he does *not* freely behave in any fashion, and he certainly does *not* deliberate about and choose the possibility of not voting for Clinton on his own (but rather as a result of Black's intervention). Thus, again, it seems to me that the alternative possibilities so nicely generated by the strategy of redescription of the content of moral responsibility lack robustness.

I now turn to a response on behalf of the flicker theorist. Thinking about this response will lead us back to the issues raised by the first version of the flicker of freedom strategy. Let us think carefully about the alternative sequence in the original Jones and Black case. In discussing the second version of the flicker strategy, I pointed out that in the alternative sequence Jones does *not* freely *vote for Clinton*. Thus, I suggested that the alternative possibility here envisaged is not sufficiently robust. But the flicker theorist may respond that nevertheless there is at least the following thing in the alternative sequence which is freely done: Jones begins to initiate the process of making a choice to vote for Bush.

(Of course, this process is then cut off before it can be completed.) So we seem to have isolated at least *something* in the alternative sequence which can plausibly be thought to be freely done and which thus may be able to ground the ascriptions of responsibility. This move can be made to help bolster the second, third, and fourth versions of the flicker strategy, or it can be taken to indicate that the most "basic" version of the flicker strategy is the first: it does not really matter for my purposes.

The problem with this move – which finds something, let us call it an "initiating action" – which can be said to be freely done and which thus grounds the ascription of responsibility – is that it seems that we can systematically reconstruct the Frankfurt-type examples (as discussed above) so that there is some sign or indication which would *precede* the initiating action and which could be read by the "counterfactual intervener" (the analogue of Black). Further, and this is the important point here, the evincing of such a sign is not even an action, and is certainly not plausibly thought to be robust enough to ground responsibility ascriptions. Again, the problem seems to be the lack of robustness of the relevant alternative possibilities.

To explain. Suppose we again consider the version of the Jones and Black case in which Black can be alerted to Jones' future inclination to vote for Bush by the presence of some involuntary sign, such as a blush or twitch or even a complex neurophysiological pattern. So if Jones were (say) to blush red, then Black could intervene prior to Jones' doing *anything* freely and ensure that Jones indeed votes for Clinton. Here the "triggering event" (i.e., what would trigger the intervention of Black) is *not* any sort of initiating action, and thus cannot be said to be freely done. Again, precisely as above, this sort of triggering event appears to be not sufficiently robust to ground responsibility ascriptions.

A bit more specifically, here is the problem. On the current version of the flicker theory, the claim, first, is that if there is *no* alternative possibility, there cannot be the sort of control which grounds moral responsibility. Thus, some sort of alternative possibility must be added to what happens in the actual sequence to get the crucial kind of control. And, further, the claim is that precisely this sort of possibility is present in the Frankfurt-type case of Jones and Black: a certain sort of triggering event (a blush, a twitch, and so forth). But now in response it is reasonable to ask how the addition of an alternative possibility of *this sort* – a triggering event which is not even an *initiating action* – could possibly transform a case of no control (of the relevant kind) into a case of control. How exactly does the addition of an alternative possibility which is (say) an involuntary blush or twitch transform a case of lack of control into a case of control? The thought that the presence of this sort of etiolated alternative can make *this sort of difference* is puzzling.

If, then, the first version of the flicker strategy is the basic version, then the basic response is as follows. In principle, there is no decisive objection to specifying all Frankfurt-type examples so that they are like the second version of the case of Jones and Black (in which there is a sign that would "give away" the future choices). That is, they are all to involve some involuntary sign that would precede any voluntary initiating action in the alternative sequence. But the alternative possibilities in such examples are mere triggering events that are *not* voluntary initiating actions and thus not sufficiently robust to ground the ascription of moral responsibility.

But even now the flicker of freedom theorist has available one final move. The flicker theorist may not dispute the claim that the alternative possibilities in the Frankfurt-type examples are insufficiently robust to *ground* our ascriptions of moral responsibility. That is to say, he may not wish to argue that the existence of such alternatives in themselves supports our intuitive judgments that individuals are morally responsible for what they do. But he nevertheless may insist that alternative possibilities *must be present*, whenever an agent is legitimately held morally responsible for what he does.

To pursue this line of thought, note that a flicker theorist can point out that even the fanciest, most sophisticated Frankfurt-type example contains *some* alternative possibility, no matter how exiguous. And, indeed, it is hard to imagine how to construct any kind of non-question-begging example in which it is clear both that there are absolutely no such possibilities and the agent is morally responsible for his action. Thus, we have as yet no decisive reason to abandon the claim that moral responsibility requires the *presence* of alternative possibilities, even if the presence of these alternatives is not in itself what drives our judgments about moral responsibility. Further, it is important to note that, if the skeptical arguments developed above are correct, causal determinism or God's existence rule out the presence of *any* sort of alternative possibility (even one that does not in itself ground the pertinent responsibility ascriptions).

The flicker theorist's move could be formulated as follows. Even if the alternative possibilities are not what explain our intuitions about moral responsibility, nevertheless there may be some *other factor* which *both* grounds our responsibility ascriptions and *also* entails that there be some alternative possibility (thin and weak as it may be). And if this were so, then moral responsibility would require alternative possibilities, even thin and weak ones.

I do not see any decisive way to rebut the current move by the flicker theorist, but, again, I do not find it attractive. Specifically, I do not see why one would think that there is a factor of the sort described. What could it be? I grant that there is "conceptual space" for the claim that there is a factor of the sort in question, i.e., one whose presence in itself grounds our ascriptions of moral responsibility and also entails the existence of alternative possibilities, but it is implausible to me that there really is such a factor. Further, rumination about cases (actual and hypothetical) does not issue in any inclination for me to posit such a factor; that is, simply thinking about cases and seeking to understand the relationship between responsibility and alternative possibilities, I find I have no inclination whatsoever to posit such a factor.

Now of course one might say that there indeed must be such a factor: the falsity of causal determinism or the non-existence of God. And, again, there is certainly conceptual space for this position. But I do not see *why* one would say this, based simply on consideration of the relationship between moral responsibility and alternative possibilities in a wide range of actual and hypothetical cases. Of course, one could wish to invoke the falsity of causal determinism or the non-existence of God as the crucial factor because one is *independently* (and prior to a neutral consideration of a range of cases pertaining to the relationship between responsibility and alternative possibilities) committed to the notions that causal determinism (or God's existence) rules out moral responsibility. But, apart from this sort of *prior commitment*, I do not see why one would wish to posit the necessity of the sort of factor under consideration here for moral responsibility.

Perhaps it will now be evident that we have reached the sort of Dialectical Stalemate described in previous chapters. A number of examples have been invoked to support the general claim that moral responsibility does not require alternative possibilities. It has then been pointed out that they do not *decisively* establish the claim; the examples fall just short (in various ways) of absolutely establishing the claim. And any example which would decisively support the principle would seem (at any rate) to beg the underlying question of whether (say) causal determinism is compatible with moral responsibility. That is to say, if we simply imagined that *all* the alternative possibilities disappear by positing the truth of causal determinism (together with incompatibilism about causal determinism and alternative possibilities), we appear to beg the issue to which the claim about the lack of a requirement of alternative possibilities for moral responsibility was designed to apply. Thus, the sort of metaphysical gridlock characteristic of Dialectical Stalemates again rears its ugly head.

But, as in the above discussions of Dialectical Stalemates, I do not believe there is cause for alarm or despair. One should not expect decisive, knockdown arguments in most areas of philosophy. Indeed, the prevalence of Dialectical Stalemates helps to explain why the cluster of problems pertaining to free will has traditionally been so difficult and intractable. Also, it is the reason this cluster of issues has been such a "target-rich environment" for those who would "dissolve" the problems (or at least seek to "restructure" them).

But the fact that one cannot decisively resolve the dispute about the putative necessity of alternative possibilities for moral responsibility does *not* imply that one ought to suspend judgment about the issue. And I maintain that the arguments developed above against the flicker of freedom strategy are extremely plausible, albeit not ineluctable. I believe that the arguments come extremely close to establishing that alternative possibilities are not required for moral responsibility. I am convinced, even in the absence of a knockdown argument, that the alternative possibilities posited by the flicker theorist are simply not sufficiently robust to ground our ascriptions of moral responsibility. Thus, I conclude that moral responsibility does not require regulative control.

4 Causal determinism, God's existence, and moral responsibility

It does not however follow straightforwardly that guidance control is the freedom-relevant condition sufficient for moral responsibility. Note, to begin, that guidance control seems entirely compatible with causal determinism: when I guide my properly functioning automobile to the right in the standard case, my exercise of control does not appear to depend on the falsity of causal determinism. But now it emerges that it is one thing to say that regulative control is not necessary for moral responsibility, and quite another to say that guidance control is sufficient for moral responsibility. Indeed, someone could grant that the sort of control that involves alternative possibilities is not required for moral responsibility but still insist that the lack of causal determinism (or perhaps the non-existence of God) is *also* required.

For certain incompatibilists about causal determinism and moral responsibility, the reason why determinism threatens moral responsibility is that it rules out alternative possibilities. For such an incompatibilist the concession that moral responsibility need not require regulative control is fatal. But another sort of incompatibilist might grant that an agent can be morally responsible for an action although he has no alternative possibility. For this sort of incompatibilist, the reason why determinism threatens responsibility *need not* be that it undermines alternative possibilities.

To see that there is at least dialectical space for this kind of position, consider again the example of Jones and the "counterfactual intervener," Black. Suppose that the world actually proceeds via a sequence that is *not* causally deterministic; that is, although there are some causal laws, not all events are causally determined. Suppose further that the world proceeds in just the sort of way in which a libertarian says it must, if agents are to be morally responsible for what they do. Although an agent's desires and purposes explain his choices and acts, they do not causally necessitate them; the agent freely "identifies" with some of his desires, where this identification is not causally necessitated. Perhaps the identification is explained in terms of agent-causation, although this notion need not be invoked. In this sort of world, one in which human choices and actions are not causally necessitated, the libertarian can certainly say that Jones is morally responsible for voting for Clinton, even if Black *would have* brought it about that Jones vote for Clinton, if Jones had shown signs of deciding to vote for Bush. That is, nothing about Frankfurt's example *requires* the actual sequence issuing in the decision and action to proceed in a deterministic way; if it proceeds in a non-deterministic way that satisfies the libertarian, then Jones can be held responsible, even though he could not have done otherwise.

According to this sort of incompatibilist, the kernel of truth in Frankfurt-type examples is that moral responsibility attributions are based on what happens in the actual sequence. An incompatibilist about responsibility and determinism can agree with this and thus admit that, if determinism is false, an agent who couldn't have done otherwise might be responsible for his action. But of course this does not show that *causal determinism* is compatible with moral responsibility. After all, causal determinism is a doctrine about what happens in the actual sequence.

The point could be put as follows. There are two ways in which it might be true that one could not have done otherwise. In the first way, the actual sequence involves some factor that operates and makes it the case that the agent could not have initiated an alternative sequence. In the second way, there is no such factor in the actual sequence, but the alternative sequence contains some factor which would prevent the agent from doing other than he actually does. Frankfurt's examples involve such alternative-sequence factors. But since causal determinism implies the presence of an actual-sequence factor of the kind in question, the Frankfurt-type examples do not decisively establish that moral responsibility is compatible with causal determinism.

But I do not find this view attractive. I believe that even (as above) in the absence of a knockdown argument that moral responsibility is compatible with causal determinism, the Frankfurt-type examples (conjoined with other considerations) provide very strong reason to accept this conclusion. This is because it is hard for me to see why causal determinism would threaten moral responsibility for some reason apart from its relationship to alternative possibilities. That is, why exactly would causal determinism be thought to pose a threat to moral responsibility, if it is *not* in virtue of undermining the notion that we have alternative possibilities?

I do not know of a compelling answer to this question. I can think of various possible answers, but none is very appealing. For example, it might be thought that moral responsibility requires that an agent be "active" or in some sense "creative." But even if this is so, I do not see any reason to deny that an agent whose action is part of a causally deterministic sequence cannot be active and creative in any sense plausibly taken to be required for moral responsibility. Also, someone might insist that moral responsibility for an action requires that the action be the *agent's own*. Again, even if this is so, I do not see any reason to deny that an action that is part of a causally deterministic sequence can be the agent's own action, in any sense plausibly taken to be required for moral responsibility. Of course, there will be compatibilistic and incompatibilistic accounts of the relevant notions of being active (as opposed to passive), creativity, and ownership; but I do not see any reason, apart from a *prior commitment* to incompatibilism about determinism and moral responsibility, to opt for the incompatibilistic analyses.

Take, for example, the notion of creativity. First, consider creativity in the arts. Would we say that (for example) Goya or Picasso were *not* creative, if we discovered that causal determinism were true? Clearly, not; our ascription of creativity in the arts (and, I believe, quite generally) does *not* depend on the absence of causal determination. (Who could imagine saying that Kant was not original, if it turned out that the consortium of scientists is correct and causal determinism obtains?) Thus, there must be a sense in which an individual can be artistically (or intellectually) creative (or original) that is compatibilistic; why suppose that an indeterministic sense must be preferable or more natural?

Someone might say that in order for an agent to be morally responsible for an action, the agent must be creative in the sense of being a "self-initiator" or "self-originator" of the action. And the claim would be that these ideas require the absence of causal determination. Now I can see why someone might insist that responsibility requires this sort of incompatibilistic creativity, *if* one is committed to the idea that moral responsibility requires alternative possibilities, but I do not see any reason to insist on precisely *this* sort of creativity, *apart* from such a prior commitment.

Let us suppose a lightning bolt strikes a barn, thus (apparently) starting a fire. Would we say that in fact the lightning bolt did *not* start the fire, if it turned out that causal determinism were in fact true? For some purposes and in some contexts, perhaps we would withdraw our claim about the lightning bolt, if causal determinism were true; but surely there is a perfectly good sense in which it is true that the lightning bolt started the fire, even given the truth of causal determinism. Thus, there is a perfectly reasonable notion of "initiation" that is compatible with determinism; why suppose that the indeterministic sense is more appealing in the context of ascription of moral responsibility (*apart from considerations relevant to alternative possibilities*)?

Various philosophers have thought that some sort of indeterministic "initiating capacity" is required for moral responsibility (or at least for one's actions having the greatest amount of value). Robert Nozick argues for the importance of what he calls, "originative value." He says:

> A being with originative value, one whose acts have originative value, can make a difference. Due to his actions, different value consequences occur in the world than otherwise would; these were not in the cards already (with the person's action being one of the cards).[12]

About this notion of originative value, Nozick says, somewhat alarmingly, "Puppets and marionettes lack originative value (except in fairy stories), and the way we resemble them, if causal determinism is true, is that we lack originative value too."[13]

But it seems to me that the Frankfurt-type cases are precisely situations in which it is *not* the case that "due to the agent's action different value consequences occur in the world than otherwise would." Of course, in these cases the relevant agent does not *act* in the alternative scenario, although the same value consequences ensue. And one can imagine similar cases in which there is a different sort of fail-safe mechanism that does not proceed through the agent – perhaps *someone else* would bring about the same result, if the agent who actually brings it about were to refrain from acting. It seems that in these sorts of contexts the agent's actions lack "originative value" in the sense suggested by Nozick; the agent does not "make a difference" in the way specified. But nevertheless the agents are surely morally responsible for what they do.[14] Thus, "making a difference" (as defined by Nozick) cannot be invoked to help explain why we would want an indeterministic kind of creative capacity.

I see no promising strategy for arguing that causal determinism threatens moral responsibility apart from its allegedly ruling out alternative possibilities. Further, let me explain my general methodological commitment; this will lend further weight to the conclusion that there is no strong reason to suppose that causal determinism is incompatible with moral responsibility. I am seeking to find an account of moral responsibility that *systematizes* our clear intuitive judgments about cases in which an agent is morally responsible. That is, we have some fairly clear considered judgments about actual and hypothetical cases in which we are inclined to hold agents morally responsible for their actions (and in which we are *not* so inclined). I seek to elaborate a general account that (at least) captures these reflective intuitive judgments about relatively clear cases. Obviously, this methodology is similar to the Rawlsian methodology of seeking a "reflective equilibrium" in matters of distributive justice.[15]

I would hope that my general account of moral responsibility would imply that agents who act as a result of certain sorts of coercion, hypnosis, direct manipulation of the brain, neurological disorders, severe mental diseases, and so forth are *not* to be held morally responsible for their actions. This is surely one of the boundary conditions on a successful general analysis of moral responsibility. And note that it is *not* necessary to posit the absence of causal determinism in order to say that such agents would not be morally responsible for their actions. It is quite well known that invoking the absence of causal determinism is "overkill" here, since what is involved in all of these contexts is some sort (or sorts) of *special* causation. I maintain, then, that it is a goal of theorizing about moral responsibility that it preserve and capture the distinction between these rather *special* contexts and what we take to be the "normal" or "ordinary" contexts of deliberation, practical reflection, and action. But since there is nothing in the "ordinary" contexts that rules out the possibility that causal determinism obtains, there is strong prima facie reason to suppose that the account of moral responsibility (at which we are ultimately aiming) will allow that causal determinism is compatible with moral responsibility.

I have urged that the method of seeking a reflective equilibrium between our general principles and particular judgments will issue in principles that allow for the compatibility of causal determinism and moral responsibility. In making this argument I have suggested that it is a plausible considered judgment that causal determinism *in itself and apart from considerations relevant to alternative possibilities* does not rule out moral responsibility. But someone might object by pointing out that the "ordinary person" – the "man on the Clapham Omnibus" or the student in Philosophy 1 – is likely to recoil at the thought that his actions are causally determined. If such a person is asked whether he would be morally responsible, if his actions are causally determined, he might well insist that this would be impossible.

Of course, an individual might be alarmed by the phrase, "causally determined." It just really sounds bad! But when the underlying issue is presented slightly differently, it is not at all evident that a reasonable and reflective person would have the sort of reaction just described. To begin, the question could be framed as follows, "Assume that moral responsibility need not require freedom to choose or do otherwise. Now if it turned out that there were some scientific theory according to which all truths about human actions could in principle be derived from states of the world in the past, would this fact require us to stop thinking of ourselves and others as *persons*, i.e., as legitimate candidates for love and hatred, gratitude and resentment, and reward and punishment? If such a scientific theory were true, and apart from any issues pertaining to alternative possibilities, would it follow that we ought to give up the distinction between the way we treat certain creatures (persons) and others (non-persons)? Would it follow from the existence of such a scientific theory that *all* sequences issuing in actions are "relevantly similar?" And it is certainly not clear that the answers to *these* questions would be affirmative.

I have already canvassed – and rejected – some possible reasons why someone might be tempted to think that causal determinism in itself would rule out moral responsibility (apart from threatening the existence of alternative possibilities). But suppose now that the reflective individual to whom we are posing our questions says, "Well, I really *do* think that causal determinism would rule out moral responsibility quite apart from threatening my freedom to choose and do otherwise. After all, if causal determinism, as you have presented it, is true, then all my behavior could be *known and predicted in advance*. And if so, how can I be held morally responsible for what I do?"

It is however unclear why predictability in advance would threaten moral responsibility. Of course, I have already considered at some length an argument that if God knows in advance what someone will do, then that person cannot do otherwise; whereas this argument has considerable force, it is not relevant here, since it pertains to alternative possibilities. Why would (human or divine) foreknowledge (and thus the capacity to predict behavior in advance) *in itself and apart from threatening alternative possibilities* vitiate our moral responsibility? After all, in the Frankfurt-type cases the agent's choices and actions are capable of being known and predicted in advance! And yet this does not in any way diminish the idea that the relevant agents in those cases exercise guidance control and are morally responsible for their actions. Thus, upon reflection, I do not see that the possibility of foreknowledge or accurate prediction in itself threatens moral responsibility. And thus this cannot be a reason why causal determinism in itself and apart from considerations relevant to alternative possibilities would rule out moral responsibility.

I am frankly at a loss to see what *other* consideration could be invoked to support the contention that causal determinism would *in itself* rule out moral responsibility. Of course, it does not follow that there are no such reasons! But I think it is at least reasonable to suggest that there is no obvious, strong reason to think that causal determinism threatens moral responsibility apart from calling into question our possession of alternative possibilities. What is relevant to my project is the considered, reflective intuitive judgments of individuals who seek to fit their judgments into a coherent overall picture; no doubt one's first reaction when one hears the phrase, "causally determined," is alarm (or at least anxiety), but I would urge that this initial unreflective response not be considered decisive.[16]

I have then argued that a reliance upon considered and reflective common-sense judgments will support the view that causal determinism *in itself* does not rule out moral responsibility. Against this strategy of relying on common-sense judgments, it might be urged that the same sort of methodology would seem to issue in the claim that we ordinarily have freedom to do otherwise, even if causal determinism were to obtain or God were to exist. Surely, we intuitively *think* we have such freedom, and we intuitively distinguish "ordinary" cases from "special" cases;

common sense has it that we are ordinarily free to do otherwise, and surely we do not need to invoke the absence of causal determination to explain why agents lack such freedom in the *special* cases. But of course I have been at pains to say that we *cannot* legitimately conclude that we have alternative possibilities.

I grant that common sense posits that we normally have alternative possibilities, and that it is only in "special circumstances" that we lack this sort of freedom. But what is crucial here is that there exists a powerful *skeptical challenge* to this common-sense view. I have articulated this challenge in previous chapters, and I have pointed out that it gains its force from appealing precisely to aspects of common sense (such as the fixity of the past and the fixity of the natural laws, and so forth). Thus, when common sense is properly considered *in its totality*, it is indeed impossible straightforwardly to conclude that we sometimes have alternative possibilities.

In contrast, I do not know of any powerful skeptical challenge that has its foothold in common sense to the effect that causal determinism *directly* threatens moral responsibility (i.e., apart from ruling out alternative possibilities).[17] I conclude that the context of the evaluation of the relationship between causal determinism and moral responsibility is crucially different from the context of the evaluation of the relationship between causal determinism and alternative possibilities: in the latter there is a powerful skeptical challenge, whereas in the former there is no such challenge.

5 Frankfurt-type examples and Schizophrenic Situations

Some might worry that I have relied too heavily upon (alleged) insights gained from Frankfurt-type cases. After all, they are somewhat unusual, and frankly, weird. In response, I certainly do not think that the Frankfurt-type cases are "weirder" than, for example, many Gettier-type examples, or Twin Earth thought-experiments. And yet many philosophers have thought that these sorts of examples force radical changes in our accounts of knowledge, belief, and meaning. Although these sorts of examples raise complicated and delicate methodological issues, I do not think Frankfurt-type examples are prima facie any *less* appropriate than these (and many other) prominent and influential philosophical thought-experiments.

Further, I believe Frankfurt-type cases are actually a special case of a rather more general and quite pervasive (at least, in philosophy) set of situations: "Schizophrenic Situations." In a Schizophrenic Situation, important features change (in certain characteristic ways) in various relevant alternative scenarios. In general, Schizophrenic Situations pose problems for subjunctive conditional analyses of various notions; indeed, they appear to decisively defeat *simple* conditional analyses.

Consider, for example, a variant on an example suggested by Alvin Goldman.[18] Suppose there is an ordinary piece of salt, with the typical internal structure of salt. As it sits before us (not placed in water), there is nothing unusual about it. But somehow associated with it is a certain sort of "counterfactual intervener." This is a magician who would cause an impermeable coating to surround the piece of salt, just before it made contact with water, if the piece of salt were to come near water.

Intuitively, the piece of salt is water-soluble. In part this is because its failure to dissolve in water would issue not from its internal structure, but from some external source. And yet it would not dissolve, if it were placed in water. Thus, a simple subjunctive conditional analysis of water-solubility must be false.

This is what I would call a Schizophrenic Situation. It is in many ways similar to Frankfurt-type contexts. Indeed, it is the analogue of a Frankfurt-type case for a *passive power* such as solubility. (Frankfurt-type cases pertain to the active power of freedom.) Note that similar problems arise for the analysis of such passive powers as malleability, fragility, flexibility, and so forth.

Here is another set of Schizophrenic Situations. Many philosophers have been attracted to moral theories according to which one acts rightly insofar as one acts *because* of one's acceptance of some moral rule. On these approaches, it cannot be that one acts *merely* in accordance with the rule, in order for one to be acting rightly; one's acceptance of the rule must in some way motivate one's action. But a problem emerges for such views (in their Kantian and also consequentialist forms). It is surely implausible to suppose that acting rightly requires one in every instance explicitly to think about the principle in question (the Categorical Imperative or the Principle of Utility or whatever); this is surely too stringent a demand. Thus, certain moral philosophers have been tempted to accept some sort of "counterfactual approach" according to which an agent need not actually think about the relevant moral principle before each act, but instead must meet some subjunctive conditional test.[19]

For example, suppose you see an individual drowning, and without *any* explicit thought about moral principles, you jump in and save his life. On the approach we are now considering, this action may have moral value – you may be acting rightly. What must be the case is that, if it had not been the right thing to do, you would not have jumped in to save the individual's life. So, for example, we must ask what you would do, if there had been five people drowning in another part of the lake and only you could save them (with your boat). If under these hypothetical circumstances, you would have acted to save the five, then you are acting rightly in actually saving the one. But if under these hypothetical cirumstances, you still would have jumped in and saved the one, then you are not acting rightly in actually saving the one individual.

But it is evident that this sort of simple subjunctive conditional test cannot be correct. Imagine that you meet this test, and thus you are deemed to act rightly in saving the one. But now imagine someone who does exactly what you do, and has all the same values and long-term dispositions. It's just that this other person has a counterfactual intervener associated with him who would cause him to save the one, even if the five needed help. Now it would turn out, on the approach which accepts the simple subjunctive conditional, that *you* act rightly, but the *other person* does not. But both of you do the same thing, have the same values, and have the same long-term dispositions to act. It would be very implausible to say that you act rightly, whereas the other person does not. It is admittedly too much to ask that agents (who "accept principles" or "act from duty" or "act rightly") think about the relevant principles prior to every action; but it is also evidently too much to ask that they meet some sort of simple, unrefined subjunctive conditional test.

Let me mention one other Schizophrenic Situation. In her intriguing paper, "Asymmetrical Freedom," Susan Wolf says:

> Determination, then, is compatible with an agent's responsibility for a good action, but incompatible with an agent's responsibility for a bad action. The metaphysical conditions required for an agent's responsibility will vary according to the value of the action he performs.[20]

Wolf assumes that the sort of determination in question is incompatible with freedom to do otherwise. She then suggests the following as a way of capturing the sort of freedom required for responsibility:

> He could have done otherwise if there had been good and sufficient reason, where the 'could have done otherwise' in the analysans is not a conditional at all. For presumably an action is morally praiseworthy only

if there are no good and sufficient reasons to do something else. And an action is morally blameworthy only if there are good and sufficient reasons to do something else.[21]

But note that one can easily construct a Schizophrenic Situation which would show that the sort of subjunctive conditional employed by Wolf will not succeed in capturing her point. Imagine, for example, a very ordinary case in which Mary does some good deed: she helps a motorist fix a flat tire. Suppose that this is an entirely ordinary situation, and intuitively Mary could have done otherwise. Here we would want to say that Mary is morally responsible – indeed, praiseworthy – for her action. But imagine that associated with Mary is some sort of counterfactual intervener who would have compelled her to fix the tire anyway, under the circumstance that Mary has a good and sufficient reason not to fix the tire. So, if Mary were rushing to the hospital with a sick child, the counterfactual intervener would render her unable to do anything but fix the tire. Here is an example in which Wolf's condition is *not* met: Mary could not have done otherwise, if there had been a good and sufficient reason not to fix the tire. And nevertheless her action seems to be a clear case of a praiseworthy action: the counterfactual intervener played no role whatsoever in her choice or action.

Frankfurt-type cases are, then, special cases of a rather more general phenomenon: Schizophrenic Situations. In such a situation, crucial features change (in unusual ways) from the actual context to the hypothetical scenario. In general, these situations appear to show that simple analyses which employ subjunctive conditionals or which posit capacities of certain sorts are false. Schizophrenic Situations are a kind of swerve in logical space.

Here I can only gesture at the existence of such situations, and say what I think they suggest. First, they suggest that the Frankfurt-type cases are not so "special" or "unique" as some have supposed: insofar as they are a special case of a more general phenomenon, a phenomenon which arguably poses problems for a wide variety of philosophical analyses, the worry about relying on them can to some degree be defused. Further, whereas they suggest that simple analyses of certain sorts do not work, they surely should not cause us to think that those analyses are not in some way on the right track. And in seeking more refined accounts, they strongly suggest that we should adopt "actual-sequence" approaches; that is, we should look to the properties manifested in the actual sequence and make appropriate use of them in our more sophisticated accounts.

So, for example, if one has the intuition that the piece of salt (described above) is water-soluble, one wants to make use of the fact that it would dissolve in water, if it were placed in water and had its *actual* physical constitution when placed in contact with the water. Similarly in the other cases. For example, if Mary had sufficient reason not to fix the tire *and she retained her actual physical capacities*, then she could do otherwise. I claim that all the Schizophrenic Situations suggest that we somehow need to "reach into the actual sequence" and employ *actual* features to generate our more refined and sophisticated understandings of the phenomena in question. And this is precisely the sort of approach I shall take in the following chapter in giving an "actual-sequence" account of "guidance control."

6 Conclusion

Traditionally it has been supposed that moral responsibility requires control. But our possession of the sort of control that involves alternative possibilities (regulative control) can be called into question. In this chapter I have argued that we can have a very robust and significant sort of control – guidance control – even if we lack regulative control. What is true about the traditional view is that moral responsibility for actions is associated with control; but it need not be the sort of control that involves alternative possibilities.

The Frankfurt-type examples may seem arcane, bizarre, and unusual. But nevertheless they point us to something both remarkably pedestrian and extraordinarily important: moral responsibility for action depends on what actually happens. That is to say, moral responsibility for actions depends on the actual history of an action and not upon the existence or nature of alternative scenarios. This is a simple, powerful insight. Indeed, it is sometimes necessary to employ complex or unusual examples or theoretical structures to bring out clearly some very plain, simple truth. The abstruse nature of the instruments employed to identify and present the point crisply does not in any way threaten the natural appeal of the truth itself.

In this chapter I have developed in some detail the most powerful challenge to the conclusion typically drawn from the Frankfurt-type cases (that alternative possibilities are not required for moral responsibility): the flicker of freedom strategy. I have argued that this strategy fails, in all its various forms. The basic problem is that the flicker of freedom it posits is too weak to ground our moral responsibility ascriptions. The alternative possibilities envisaged are essentially irrelevant to the intuitive view that the agents in the Frankfurt-type cases are morally responsible for their actions. This view is driven by what *actually* occurs in the history of the action, *not* by the existence or nature of alternative possibilities.[22]

Finally, I have argued that guidance control is the freedom-relevant condition sufficient for moral responsibility. That is, guidance control is all the freedom required for moral responsibility. One does *not* have to say that guidance control must be accompanied by (say) the absence of causal determinism. There is simply no good reason to suppose that causal determinism in itself (and apart from considerations pertaining to alternative possibilities) vitiates our moral responsibility. In the following chapter I shall propose a first approximation to an account of guidance control which focuses on the actual sequence issuing in the action and has the implication that such doctrines as causal determinism and God's existence are indeed compatible with moral responsibility.

8

Moral Responsibility and Guidance Control

[Lucky is joined to Pozzo by a rope.]
    POZZO – Stand back! (Vladimir and Estragon move away from Lucky. Pozzo jerks the rope. Lucky looks at Pozzo.) Think, pig! (Pause. Lucky begins to dance.) Stop! (Lucky stops.) Forward! (Lucky advances.) Stop! (Lucky stops.) Think!
Samuel Beckett, Waiting for Godot[1]

[One of the first performances of Waiting for Godot was in San Quentin prison, California.]

1 Introduction

In the previous chapter I argued that guidance control is the freedom-relevant condition sufficient for moral responsibility. Guidance control – the sort of control exhibited when I guide my car to the right, even though I could not have caused it to move in some other direction, and, more generally, a sort of control that does not require alternative possibilities – is all the freedom required for moral responsibility. Further, I argued that such control is compatible with causal determinism (and God's existence). I wish now to begin to give more content to these views by taking the first step toward developing a general theory of moral responsibility.[2] Although I shall not undertake the larger project here, I propose to begin by giving a first approximation to an account of guidance control.

2 Guidance control

As I have suggested above, an account of moral responsibility should capture our intuitive judgments about clear cases. In order to generate a principle that might underlie our reactions to relatively clear cases, it is useful to begin by considering examples in which we are inclined to think that an agent cannot legitimately be held morally responsible for what he does.

Imagine that an individual has been hypnotized. The hypnotist has induced an urge to punch the nearest person after hearing the telephone ring. Insofar as the individual did not consent to this sort of hypnotic suggestion (perhaps he has undergone hypnosis to help him stop smoking), it seems unreasonable to say that he has guidance control of his punching his friend in the nose upon hearing the telephone ring.

Suppose similarly that an evil person has got hold of Smith's television set and has wired it so as to allow him to subject Smith to a sophisticated sort of subliminal advertising. The bad person systematically subjects Smith to subliminal advertising which causes Smith to murder his neighbor. Because of the nature of the causal history of the action, it is apparent that Smith does not control his behavior in the relevant sense.

We feel similarly about actions produced in a wide variety of ways. Agents who perform actions produced by powerful forms of brainwashing and indoctrination, potent drugs, and certain sorts of direct manipulation of the brain are not reasonably to be held morally responsible for their actions insofar as they lack the relevant sort of control. Imagine, for instance, that neurophysiologists of the future can isolate certain key parts of the brain that can be manipulated in order to induce decisions and actions. If scientists electronically stimulate those parts of Jones' brain, thus causing him to help a person who is being mugged, Jones himself cannot reasonably be held morally responsible for his behavior. It is not to Jones' credit that he has prevented a mugging.

Also, if we discover that a piece of behavior is attributable to a significant brain lesion or a neurological disorder, we do not believe that the agent has guidance control of his behavior. Thus, we do not hold him morally responsible for it. Certain sorts of mental disorders – extreme phobias, for instance – may also issue in behavior that the agent does not control in the relevant sense.

Many people believe that there can be genuinely "irresistible" psychological impulses. If so, then these may issue in behavior the agent does not control. Drug addicts may (in certain circumstances) act on literally irresistible urges, and we might not hold them morally responsible for acting on these desires (especially if we believe that they are not morally responsible for acquiring the addiction in the first place).

Also, certain coercive threats (and perhaps offers) rule out moral responsibility. The bank teller who is told that he will be shot unless he hands over the money might have an overwhelming and irresistible desire to comply with the threat. Insofar as he acts from such an impulse, it is plausible to suppose that he does not have guidance control of his action.[3]

Evidently, the causal history of an action matters to us in making moral responsibility attributions. When persons are manipulated in certain ways, they are like marionettes and are not appropriate candidates for praise or blame. Certain factors issuing in behavior are, intuitively, "responsibility-undermining factors."

We can contrast such cases – in which some responsibility-undermining factor actually operates – with cases in which there is the "normal," unimpaired operation of the human deliberative mechanism. When you deliberate about whether to give five percent of your salary to the United Way and consider reasons on both sides, and your decision to give the money is not induced by hypnosis, brainwashing, direct manipulation, psychotic impulses, etc., we think that you can legitimately be praised for your charitable action. Insofar as we can identify no responsibility-undermining factor at work in your decision and action, we are inclined to hold you morally responsible. In such a case, we feel confident in ascribing guidance control to you.

Upon first consideration of this array of cases, it might be thought that there is a fairly obvious way of distinguishing the clear cases of moral responsibility from the clear cases of lack of it. It seems that, in the cases in which an agent is morally responsible for an action, he is free to do otherwise, and in the cases of lack of moral responsibility, the agent is not free to do otherwise. Thus, it appears that the actual operation of what is intuitively a responsibility-undermining factor rules out moral responsibility because it rules out freedom to do otherwise.

The point could be put as follows. When an agent is (for example) hypnotized, he is not sensitive to reasons in the appropriate way. Given the hypnosis, he would still behave in the same way, no matter what the relevant reasons were. Suppose, again, that an individual is hypnotically induced to punch the nearest person after hearing the telephone ring. Now given this sort of hypnosis, he would punch the nearest person after hearing the telephone ring, even if he had extremely strong reasons not to. The agent here is not responsive to reasons – his behavior would be the same, no matter what reasons there were.

In contrast, when there is the normal, unimpaired operation of the human deliberative mechanism, we suppose that the agent is responsive to reasons. So when you decide to give money to the United Way, we think that you nevertheless wouldn't have contributed, had you discovered that there was widespread fraud within the agency. Thus it is very natural and reasonable to think that the difference between morally responsible agents and those who are not consists in the "reasons-responsiveness" of the agents.

But of course we have already seen that there are cases in which an agent can be held morally responsible for performing an action, even though he couldn't have done otherwise (and is not "reasons-responsive"): the Frankfurt-type cases. In a Frankfurt-type case the actual sequence proceeds in a way that grounds moral responsibility attributions, even though the alternative scenario (or perhaps a range of alternative scenarios) proceeds in a way which rules out responsibility. As I have argued above, in a Frankfurt-type case the agent has guidance control of his action, even though he lacks regulative control. We are now in a position to give the beginnings of an account of guidance control.

In a Frankfurt-type case the kind of mechanism that actually operates is reasons-responsive, although the kind of mechanism that would operate in the alternative scenario is not. In the Frankfurt-type case discussed above (in which Jones votes for Clinton on his own and Black does not actually intercede), Jones' action issues from the normal faculty of practical reasoning, which we can reasonably take to be reasons-responsive. But in the alternative scenario, a different kind of mechanism would have operated – one involving direct electronic stimulation of Jones' brain. And this mechanism is not reasons-responsive. Thus, the actual-sequence mechanism can be reasons-responsive, even though the agent is not reasons-responsive. (He couldn't have done otherwise.)

One might then employ the following condition as part of a theory that distinguishes the relatively clear cases of moral responsibility from cases of the lack of it: an agent exhibits guidance control of an action insofar as the mechanism that actually issues in the action is reasons-responsive. (Later I shall revise this kind of condition to take account of temporal considerations, but it is a useful starting point.) Clearly, on such an approach it is crucial to distinguish between the kind of mechanism that operates in the actual sequence and the kind of mechanism that operates in the alternative sequence (or sequences).

I must confess that I do not have any general way of specifying when two kinds of mechanisms are the same. This is a potential problem for my approach; it will have to be considered carefully by the reader. But rather than attempting to say much by way of giving an account of mechanism individuation, I shall simply rely on the fact that we have intuitions about fairly clear cases of "same mechanism" and "different mechanism." For example, I rely on the intuitive judgment that the normal mechanism of practical reasoning is different from deliberations that are induced by significant direct electronic manipulation of the brain. I believe that the development and application of my approach to moral responsibility will rely primarily on relatively clear intuitions about sameness of mechanism. Given these relatively clear intuitive judgments, the approach should be judged by its fruitfulness in sorting through and illuminating the puzzling and difficult problems to which it is applied.

So far I have pointed to some cases in which it is intuitively clear that a person lacks guidance control of his actions and thus cannot be held morally responsible for what he has done and other cases in which it is intuitively clear that an agent has such control and thus can be held responsible for his actions. I have suggested a principle that might help to distinguish the two types of cases. This principle makes use of two ingredients: reasons-responsiveness and the distinction between actual-sequence and alternative-sequence mechanisms. I now wish to explain these ingredients more carefully, beginning with the notion of reasons-responsiveness.

2.1. Reasons-responsiveness

I shall discuss two kinds of reasons-responsiveness: strong and weak. Begin with strong reasons-responsiveness. Strong reasons-responsiveness obtains when a certain kind K of mechanism actually issues in an action and if there were sufficient reason to do otherwise and K were to operate, the agent would recognize the sufficient reason to do otherwise and thus choose to do otherwise and do otherwise. Note that I am here learning from Schizophrenic Situations and focusing on the properties of the *actual* sequence. That is, to test whether a kind of mechanism is strongly reasons-responsive, one asks what would happen if there were sufficient reason for the agent to do otherwise *and the actual-sequence mechanism were to operate.*

Under circumstances in which there are sufficient reasons for the agent to do otherwise and the actual type of mechanism operates, three conditions must be satisfied: the agent must take the reasons to be sufficient, choose in accordance with the sufficient reasons, and act in accordance with the choice. Thus, there can be at least three sorts of "alternative-sequence" failures: failures in the connection between what reasons there are and what reasons the agent recognizes, in the connection between the agent's reasons and his choice, and in the connection between choice and action.

The first kind of failure is a failure to be receptive to reasons. It is the kind of inability which afflicts certain delusional psychotics.[4] The second kind of failure is a failure of reactivity – a failure to be appropriately affected by beliefs. Lack of reactivity afflicts certain compulsive or phobic neurotics.[5] Finally, there is the failure successfully to translate one's choice into action; this failure is a kind of impotence. If none of these failures was to occur in the alternative sequence (and the actual kind of mechanism was to operate), then the actually-operative mechanism would be strongly reasons-responsive. There would be a tight fit between the reasons there are and the reasons the agent has, the agent's reasons and his choice, and choice and action. The agent's actions would fit the contours of reasons closely.[6]

Whereas such a close contouring of actions to reasons is no doubt desirable in many respects, I do not believe that strong reasons-responsiveness is a necessary condition for guidance control and moral responsibility. To see this, imagine that as a result of the unimpaired operation of the normal human faculty of practical reasoning I decide to go (and go) to the basketball game tonight, and that I have sufficient reason to do so. But suppose that I would have been "weak-willed," had there been sufficient reason not to go. That is, imagine that had there been a sufficient reason not to go, it would have been that I had a strict deadline for an important manuscript (which I couldn't meet, if I were to go to the game). I nevertheless would have chosen to go to the game, even though I would have recognized that I had sufficient reason to stay home and work. It seems to me that I actually go to the basketball game freely and can reasonably be held morally responsible for going; and yet the actual-sequence mechanism which results in my action is not reasons-responsive in the strong sense. The failure of strong reasons-responsiveness here stems from my disposition toward weakness of the will.

Going to the basketball game is plausibly thought to be a morally neutral act; on the approach to moral responsibility adopted here, one can be morally responsible for an action, even though the act is neither praiseworthy nor blameworthy. The possibility of weakness of will also poses a problem for intuitively clear cases of moral responsibility for commendable acts. Suppose, for example, that I devote my afternoon to working for the United Way (and my decision and action proceed via an intuitively responsibility-conferring mechanism). And imagine that, if I had a sufficient reason to refrain, it would (again) have been my publication deadline. But imagine that I would have devoted my time to charity, even if I had such a reason not to. Here it seems that I am both morally responsible and praiseworthy for doing what I do, and yet the actual mechanism is not strongly reasons-responsive.

Further, it is quite clear that strong reasons-responsiveness cannot be a necessary condition for moral responsibility for morally blameworthy and/or imprudent acts. Suppose that I steal a book from a store, knowing full well that it is morally wrong for me to do so and that I will be apprehended and thus that it is not prudent of me to do so. Nevertheless, the actual sequence may be responsibility-conferring; no factors that intuitively undermine moral responsibility may actually operate. (Of course, I assume here that there can be genuine cases of weak-willed actions that are free actions for which the agent can be held responsible.) Here, then, is a case in which I am morally responsible for stealing the book, but my actual-sequence mechanism is not strongly reasons-responsive: there actually is sufficient reason (both moral and prudential) to do otherwise, and yet I steal the book.

All three cases presented above provide problems for the claim that strong reasons-responsiveness is necessary for moral responsibility. Strong reasons-responsiveness may be both sufficient and necessary for a certain kind of praiseworthiness – it is a great virtue to connect one's actions with the contours of value in a strongly reasons-responsive way. But of course not all agents who are morally responsible are morally commendable (or even maximally prudent). I believe that moral responsibility requires only a looser kind of fit between reasons and action: "weak reasons-responsiveness."

Under the requirement of strong reasons-responsiveness, we ask what would happen if there were a sufficient reason to do otherwise (holding fixed the actual kind of mechanism). Strong reasons-responsiveness points us to the alternative scenario in which there is a sufficient reason for the agent to do otherwise (and the actual mechanism operates) which is most similar to the actual situation. Put in terms of possible worlds, the non-actual possible worlds which are germane to strong reasons-responsiveness are those in which the agent has a sufficient reason to do otherwise (and in which the actual kind of mechanism operates) which are *most similar* to the actual world. (Perhaps there is just one such world, or perhaps there is a sphere of many such worlds.) In contrast, under weak reasons-responsiveness, there must exist some possible world in which there is a sufficient reason to do otherwise, the agent's actual mechanism operates, and the agent does otherwise. This possible world needn't be the one (or ones) in which the agent has a sufficient reason to do otherwise (and the actual mechanism operates) which is (or are) most similar to the actual world.[7] Clearly, the difference between the possible worlds relevant to strong and weak reasons-responsiveness is parallel to the difference between the worlds relevant to the "can-claims" and the worlds relevant to the backtracking conditionals (described in chapters four and five).

Consider again my decision to go to the basketball game. In this situation, if I were to have a sufficient reason to do otherwise, it would be a publication deadline. And I would under such circumstances be weak-willed and still go to the game. But certainly there exists some scenario in which the actual mechanism operates, I have sufficient reason not to go to the game, and I don't go. Suppose, for instance, that I am told that I will have to pay one thousand dollars for a ticket to the game. Even though I am disposed to be weak-willed under some circumstances, there are some circumstances in which I would respond appropriately to sufficient reasons. These are circumstances in which the reasons are considerably stronger than the reasons which would exist, if I were to have sufficient reason to do otherwise.

Consider, similarly, my commendable act of working this afternoon for the United Way. Even though I would do so anyway, even if I had a publication deadline, I certainly would not work for the United Way, if to do so I would have to sacrifice my job. Thus, the actual mechanism issuing in my action is weakly reasons-responsive. Also, when an agent wrongly (and imprudently) steals a book (i.e., there actually is sufficient reason not to), his actual mechanism might be responsive to at least some possible incentive not to steal. To the extent that it is so responsive, he is properly held morally responsible for stealing the book. Even an agent who acts against good reasons can be responsive to some reasons.

It is reasonable to think that the agent's actual-sequence mechanism must be weakly reasons-responsive, if he is to have the sort of control required for moral responsibility. If (given the operation of the actual kind of mechanism) he would persist in stealing the book even if he knew that by so acting he would cause himself and his family to be killed, then the actual mechanism would seem to be inconsistent with holding him morally responsible for his action. It seems to me that this is because the agent here would not be exhibiting genuine guidance control of his action.

An agent whose act is produced by a strongly reasons-responsive mechanism is commendable; his behavior fits tightly the contours of value. But strong reasons-responsiveness is not necessary for moral responsibility. On my approach, *actual* irrationality is compatible with moral responsibility (as it should be). Perhaps Dostoevsky's Underground Man is an example of an actually irrational and yet morally responsible individual. He allegedly acts against his best reasons, and yet the mechanisms on which he acts are weakly reasons-responsive. Similarly, certain kinds of *hypothetical* irrationality are compatible with moral responsibility; a tendency toward weakness of the will need not point to any defect in the actual mechanism leading to action. Moral responsibility requires *some* connection between reason and action, but the fit can be quite loose.

So far I have placed most emphasis on what I take to be the less controversial claim that the sort of control involved in moral responsibility does not require something as strong as strong reasons-responsiveness. But I have also suggested that weak reasons-responsiveness is *all* that is required for the sort of control involved in moral responsibility. That is, I have claimed that weak reasons-responsiveness is *sufficient* for guidance control. I believe this suggestion has a certain plausibility, at least to a first approximation.[8]

To summarize. In this section I have distinguished two kinds of responsiveness. I have here been concerned to argue that the sort of control involved in moral responsibility for action – guidance control – does *not* require strong reasons-responsiveness, but weak reasons-responsiveness. Further, my suggestion is that weak reasons-responsiveness is *sufficient* for guidance control (at least to a first approximation). That is to say, my suggestion is that weak reasons-responsiveness is a plausible account of guidance control; and guidance control is the freedom-relevant condition necessary and sufficient for moral responsibility.

In the following section, I shall discuss an analogy between this account of moral responsibility and a parallel sort of theory of knowledge. Then I shall further sharpen the formulation of the account by rendering more precise the key idea of a "kind of mechanism issuing in action."

3 Knowledge and responsibility

I have begun to sketch an "actual-sequence" model of moral responsibility by giving at least a preliminary characterization of guidance control. On this approach, an agent can be morally responsible for performing an action, although he is not free to do otherwise. There is an analogy between this sort of theory of moral responsibility and an "actual-sequence" model of knowledge. On this approach to knowledge, an agent may have knowledge of a certain proposition, even though he lacks the pertinent discriminatory capacity. It is sufficient that the actual-sequence mechanism be "sensitive to truth" in the appropriate way.

Already (especially in chapter two) I have discussed some important analogies between arguments about knowledge and freedom. (Indeed, in discussing the Principle of Closure of Knowledge Under Known Implication I began to address some of the issues I touch on here.) Note that the previous discussions pertained primarily to the relationship between knowledge and freedom to do otherwise (and regulative control). Here the issue is the relationship between knowledge and guidance control (and moral responsibility). As before, I believe an exploration of the analogy will be worthwhile and illuminating.

In order for a person to know that p, it is clear that he must believe that p and that p must be true. But this is surely not enough, and there are various different strategies for providing further requirements (the "necessitating" component of knowledge alluded to in chapter two).[9] One "externalist" approach claims that the person's belief that p must be a "reliable indicator" of p's truth, or perhaps, that it must "track" p's truth. Very roughly, one might say that, in order for an agent to have knowledge that p, it must be the case both that: (a) the agent would not believe that p, if p weren't true, and (b) under various conditions in which p were true, the agent would believe that p. One asks here about the agent's beliefs in a sphere of worlds which are relatively similar to the actual world – both worlds in which p is true and worlds in which p is false.[10]

So suppose that as you are driving along you see what you take to be a barn in a field, and you conclude that it is a barn in the field. And it *is* an ordinary barn in a field. Unbeknownst to you, had it not been a barn, a demonic farmer would have installed a papier mâché replica of a barn. In this case you truly believe that it is a normal barn in the field, but your belief does not "track truth": had there been no barn in the field, you still would have believed there to be a barn in the field. In this case you lack a discriminatory capacity which might seem required for knowledge.

Let us contrast this case with another in which you see a banana in a supermarket, and you conclude that there is a banana on the shelf. We suppose here that there is no demonic supermarket manager poised to fool you, and that if there were no banana on the shelf, you would not believe that there is a banana on the shelf. Presumably, in this case your belief tracks truth, and you might be said to know that there is a banana on the shelf. And this is so, even though there exists a logically possible scenario in which a demonic supermarket manager has placed a plastic banana on the shelf and you still conclude that it is a banana. On this account, what is pertinent to knowledge are the scenarios in which p is false which are most similar to the actual world; that there are more remote possibilities in which the proposition p is false is not taken by the approach to be germane to whether the individual has knowledge.[11]

The cases described above might suggest that an agent has knowledge that p only if he has the ability to discriminate the conditions that would obtain if p were true from those that would obtain if p were false. But consider the following examples (due to Nozick):

A grandmother sees her grandson is well when he comes to visit; but if he were sick or dead, others would tell her he was well to spare her upset. Yet this does not mean she doesn't know he is well (or at least ambulatory) when she sees him.[12]

S believes a certain building is a theater and concert hall. He has attended plays and concerts there . . . However, if the building were not a theater, it would have housed a nuclear reactor that would so have altered the air around it (let us suppose) that everyone upon approaching the theater would have become lethargic and nauseous, and given up the attempt to buy a ticket. The government cover story would have been that the building was a theater, a cover story they knew would be safe since no unmedicated person could approach through the nausea field to discover any differently. Everyone, let us suppose, would have believed the cover story; they would have believed that the building they saw (but only from some distance) was a theater.[13]

These examples are epistemological analogues to Frankfurt-type cases (in which an agent is morally responsible for performing an action, although he couldn't have done otherwise). In these cases an agent knows that p, although he lacks the pertinent discriminatory capacity. Just as we switched from demanding agent-responsiveness to demanding mechanism-responsiveness for moral responsibility, it is appropriate to demand only mechanism-sensitivity to truth, in order for an agent to have knowledge.

As Nozick points out, it is possible to believe that p via a truth-sensitive mechanism, and thus know that p, even though an insensitive mechanism would have operated, in the alternative scenario (or scenarios). Thus, we want an actual-sequence theory of knowledge, just as we want an actual-sequence theory of responsibility. We need to distinguish between actual-sequence and alternative-sequence mechanisms and focus only on the properties of the actual-sequence mechanism.

There is, then, a strong analogy between the theories of responsibility and knowledge sketched above: they are both actual-sequence notions of a certain kind.[14] I now wish, however, to point to an important difference between responsibility and knowledge. As I developed the account of responsibility above, if an agent acts on a mechanism of type M, there must be some possible scenario in which M operates, the agent has sufficient reason to do otherwise, and he does otherwise, in order for the agent to be morally responsible for his action. The possible scenario needn't be the one which would have occurred, if M had operated and the agent had sufficient reason to do otherwise. That is, the scenario pertinent to responsibility ascriptions needn't be the scenario (or set of them) in which an M-type mechanism operates and the agent has sufficient reason to do otherwise which are most similar to the actual scenario. In contrast, on the theory of knowledge presented above, if an agent believes that p via an M-type mechanism, then it must be the case that if an M-type mechanism were to operate and p were false, the agent would believe that p is false, if the agent is to know that p.

Roughly speaking, the possibilities that are pertinent to moral responsibility attributions may be more remote than those pertinent to knowledge attributions. I believe, then, that the connection between reasons and action which is necessary for moral responsibility is "looser" than the connection between truth and belief which is necessary for knowledge. Of course, this point is consistent with the claim that both knowledge and moral responsibility are "actual-sequence" notions; it's just that actual-sequence truth-sensitivity is defined more "strictly" (i.e., in terms of "closer" possibilities) than actual-sequence reasons-responsiveness.[15]

Despite the difference just specified, the important point in the analogy between knowledge and moral responsibility is that there is a salient structural similarity between plausible accounts of the two notions: they are both "actual-sequence" notions, and the accounts employ a parallel distinction between actually-operative mechanisms and counterfactually-operative mechanisms. So, just as we found a structural similarity between the modal principles employed in arguments for epistemological and power skepticism, we have found such a similarity in some of the most plausible accounts of knowledge and moral responsibility.[16]

4 A bit about mechanisms

I have suggested that an agent has guidance control of an action insofar as the mechanism that actually issues in the action is reasons-responsive. But given that various different mechanisms may actually operate in a given case, which mechanism is the one that is relevant?

Suppose that I deliberate (in the normal way) about whether to donate five percent of my paycheck to the United Way, and that I decide to make the donation and act on my decision. We might fill in the story so that it is intuitively a paradigmatic case in which I am morally responsible for my action. And yet consider the actually operative mechanism, "deliberation preceeding donating five percent of one's salary to the United Way." If this kind of mechanism were to operate, then I would give five percent of my paycheck to the United Way in any logically possible scenario. Thus, this kind of actually operative mechanism is not reasons-responsive.

But presumably a mechanism such as "deliberating prior to giving five percent of one's salary to the United Way" is not relevant to moral responsibility ascriptions. This is because it is not a "temporally intrinsic" mechanism. The operation of a temporally extrinsic or "relational" mechanism "already includes" the occurrence of the action it is supposed to cause, just as a soft fact or property in some sense already includes (or is at least dependent on) something in the future.

Note that the operation of a mechanism of the kind, "deliberating prior to giving five percent of one's paycheck to the United Way" *entails* that one give five percent of one's paycheck to the United Way. In this sense, then, the mechanism already includes the action: its operation entails that the action occurs. (Of course, this Entailment View of relational mechanisms is parallel to the Entailment View of soft facthood discussed in chapter six.) Thus, it is a necessary condition of a mechanism's relevance to ascriptions of guidance control (and moral responsibility) that it be a "temporally intrinsic" or "non-relational" mechanism in the following sense: if a mechanism M issues in act X, then M is relevant to the agent's guidance control of X only if M's operating does not entail that X occurs. I believe that the requirement that a mechanism be temporally intrinsic is an intuitively natural and unobjectionable one. But of course we have so far only a necessary condition for being a relevant mechanism; there may be various different mechanisms that issue in an action, all of which are temporally intrinsic. Which mechanism is "the" mechanism pertinent to guidance control?

I do not know how to specify in a general way how to determine which mechanism is "the" mechanism that is relevant to assessment of responsibility. It is simply a presupposition of this theory as presented above that for each act, there is an intuitively natural mechanism that is appropriately selected as the mechanism that issues in action, for the purposes of assessing guidance control and moral responsibility.

I do not think that this presupposition is problematic. But if there is a worry, it is useful to note that the basic account can be formulated without such a presupposition. As so far developed, the account says that an agent exhibits guidance control of an action insofar as the (relevant, temporally intrinsic) mechanism issuing in the action is reasons-responsive. Alternatively, one could say that an agent exhibits guidance control of an action insofar as there is no actually-operative (temporally intrinsic) mechanism issuing in the action that is not reasons-responsive. This alternative formulation obviates the need to select one mechanism as the "relevant" one. In what follows, I shall continue to employ the first formulation, but the basic points should apply equally to the alternative formulation.

I wish now to apply the theory to a few cases. We think intuitively that irresistible urges can be "psychologically compulsive" and can rule out guidance control and thus moral responsibility. Imagine that Jim has a literally irresistible urge to take a certain drug, and that he does in fact take the drug. What exactly is the relevant mechanism that issues in Jim's taking the drug? Notice that the mechanism, "deliberation involving an irresistible urge to take the drug," is not temporally intrinsic and thus not admissible as a mechanism pertinent to moral responsibility ascription: its operation entails that Jim take the drug. Consider, then, the mechanism, "deliberation involving an irresistible desire." Whereas this mechanism is temporally intrinsic, it is also reasons-responsive: there is a possible scenario in which Jim acts on this kind of mechanism and refrains from taking the drug. In this scenario, Jim has an irresistible urge to refrain from taking the drug. These considerations show that neither "deliberation involving an irresistible desire for the drug" nor "deliberation involving an irresistible desire" is the relevant mechanism (if the theory of responsibility is to achieve an adequate "fit" with our intuitive judgments).

When Jim acts on an irresistible urge to take the drug, there is some physical process of kind P taking place in his central nervous system. When a person undergoes this kind of physical process, we say that his urge is literally irresistible. And I believe that what underlies our intuitive claim that Jim is not morally responsible for taking the drug is that the relevant kind of mechanism issuing in Jim's taking the drug is of physical kind *P*, and that a mechanism of kind *P* is not reasons-responsive. When an agent acts from a literally irresistible urge, he is undergoing a kind of physical process that is not reasons-responsive, and it is this lack of reasons-responsiveness of the actual physical process that rules out guidance control and moral responsibility.[17] (Of course, I am here assuming that Jim is not morally responsible for having this sort of desire in the first place. If Jim is indeed responsible for having this desire, then the case must be analyzed in accordance with the refinement in the theory developed in the following section.)

Consider again my claim that certain sorts of "direct manipulation of the brain" rule out moral responsibility. It is clear that not all such manipulations would rule out moral responsibility. Suppose, for instance, that a scientist manipulates just one brain cell at the *periphery* of my brain. This kind of manipulation need not rule out responsibility. It is when the scientists intervene and manipulate the brain in a way which is not reasons-responsive that they undermine an agent's moral responsibility for action.[18]

Similarly, not all forms of subliminal advertising, hypnosis, brain-washing, etc. are inconsistent with moral responsibility for an action. It is when these activities yield physical mechanisms that are not reasons-responsive that they rule out moral responsibility. Thus, the theory that associates moral responsibility with actual-sequence reasons-responsiveness can help to explain our intuitive distinctions between causal influences which are consistent with moral responsibility and those which are not.

Consider also the class of legal defenses that might be dubbed "Twinkie-type" defenses. This kind of defense claims that an agent ought not to be punished because he ate too much "junk food" (and that this impaired his capacities, etc.). On the approach presented here, the question of whether an agent ought to be punished is broken into two parts: (1) Is he morally responsible, i.e., rationally accessible to punishment, and (2) if so, to what degree ought he be punished? The theory of moral responsibility I have presented leaves it open to us to respond positively to the first question in the typical "Twinkie-type" case.

Even if an individual has eaten a diet composed only of junk food, it is highly implausible to think that this yields a biological process that is not weakly reasons-responsive. At the very most, such a process might not be strongly reasons-responsive, but strong reasons-responsiveness is not necessary for moral responsibility. And it is implausible to suggest that junk food consumption yields a mechanism that is not weakly reasons-responsive.[19]

Thus the theory of responsibility supports the intuitive idea that "Twinkie-type" defendants are morally responsible for what they do. Of course, the question of the appropriate degree of punishment is a separate question. But it is important to notice that it is not a consequence of the theory of responsibility that an agent who acts on a mechanism that is weakly but not strongly reasons-responsive is properly punished to a lesser degree than an agent who acts on a mechanism that is strongly reasons-responsive. This may but need not be a part of one's full theory of punishment.

5 A refinement: Temporal indexation

I wish now to consider a problem for the sketch of a theory of moral responsibility that I have been developing. This problem will force a refinement in the account. Suppose Max (who enjoys drinking but is not an alcoholic) goes to a party where he drinks so much that he is almost oblivious to his surroundings. In this state of intoxication he gets into his car and tries to drive home. Unfortunately, he runs over a child who is walking in a cross-walk. Although the actual-sequence mechanism issuing in Max's running over the child is plausibly taken to lack reasons-responsiveness, we may nevertheless feel that Max is morally responsible for running over the child.

This is one case in a class of cases in which an agent's act at a time $t1$ issues from a reasons-responsive sequence, and this act causes his act at $t2$ to issue from a mechanism which is not reasons-responsive. Further, Max ought to have known that his getting drunk at the party would lead to his driving in a condition in which he would be unresponsive. Thus, Max can be held morally responsible for his action at $t2$ in virtue of the occurrence of a suitable sort of reasons-responsive mechanism at a prior time $t1$. When one acts from a reasons-responsive mechanism at time $t1$ and one ought to know that so acting will (or may well) lead to acting from an unresponsive mechanism at some later time $t2$, one can be held responsible for so acting at $t2$. Thus, the theory of moral responsibility should be interpreted as claiming that moral responsibility for an act at t requires the actual operation of a reasons-responsive mechanism at t or some suitable earlier time.

An individual might cultivate dispositions to act virtuously in certain circumstances. It might even be the case that when he acts virtuously, his motivation to do so is so strong that the mechanism is not reasons-responsive. But insofar as reasons-responsive sequences issued in his cultivation of the virtue, he can be held morally responsible for his action. It is only when it is true that at no suitable point along the path to the action did a reasons-responsive sequence occur that an agent will not properly be held responsible for his action.

This is a sketchy and incomplete treatment of difficult issues. The basic form of the account I am developing is a "tracing" approach: when an agent is morally responsible for an action which issues from a mechanism that is not weakly reasons-responsive, we must be able to trace back along the history of the action to a point (*suitably related to the action*) where there was indeed a weakly reasons-responsive mechanism. Although I have not filled in all the details of my version of a tracing model, I wish to contrast it with van Inwagen's tracing approach.

As I pointed out in chapter three, van Inwagen argues that we hardly ever have the sort of control that involves freedom to do otherwise ("restrictivism"). More specifically, only in three sorts of cases do we have such freedom: Buridan cases, cases in which duty conflicts with inclination, and situations of conflict between incommensurable values. But van Inwagen also wishes to remain in the "classical tradition" which associates moral responsibility with regulative control. Thus, he develops a tracing principle:

An agent cannot be blamed for a state of affairs unless there was a time at which he could so have arranged matters that that state of affairs not obtain.[20]

Van Inwagen is therefore committed to showing that all states of affairs for which we are responsible can be traced back to one of these three kinds of situations. But why should one think that everything for which we are morally responsible can be traced back to some free choice between equally attractive alternatives, duty and inclination, or incommensurable values?

The most promising strategy for van Inwagen to adopt at this point is to argue that these kinds of conflict situations are precisely the ones through which our characters are formed; hence, we can accept his theory and still be responsible for all states of affairs which come about as a result of actions that are produced by our characters. In the end, however, even this strategy must fail. Much of our character results from the habituation we receive in early life, and these portions of our character don't seem to be necessarily connected with situations of conflict between duty, inclinations, or incommensurable values.

Consider a young woman, call her Betty, who has spent all of her life in a small, rural community. Like most of the citizens of her town, Betty's family is still proud to be American, and over the years Betty has gradually, almost imperceptibly, internalized a certain degree of patriotism. Being raised mostly during the apathy of the Reagan years, Betty has never been in any situation where her mild patriotism has come into conflict with any of her short-term inclinations or other values. Indeed, she has never given the matter much thought – for Betty, being a loyal American has come as naturally as flying the flag on Independence Day. Even though this mild patriotism is a fixed feature of Betty's character, the restrictivist (the proponent of van Inwagen's contention that we rarely have genuine alternative possibilities) must hold that she is not yet responsible for it; he is committed to this view because Betty has not yet been in a conflict situation in which she was able to make a free choice that would have prevented her from having her patriotic disposition. Imagine now that Betty travels abroad for the first time, and through a series of strange coincidences, a singularly incompetent foreign agent mistakes her for a young American soldier who has expressed an interest in selling government secrets. He approaches Betty and asks her, in so many words, to betray her country. Of course, Betty thinks that treason is morally indefensible; she has a strong desire not to do it, and with scarcely a moment's deliberation, she turns down the agent's offer without waiting for any further explanation.

For van Inwagen, Betty clearly was not able to do anything but what she did. Moreover, given that her action resulted from features of her character which in turn could not be traced back to some earlier free decision, it seems that he should say that Betty is not responsible for the ensuing state of affairs that Betty declined to betray her country. But such a conclusion runs directly counter to our actual practices of holding people responsible. Indeed, if Betty is not responsible in this case, then it would appear that van Inwagen's position requires that he severely limit the domain of moral responsibility. This is because a great many of our everyday actions result from other character traits and dispositions which, like Betty's patriotism, are not able to be traced back to one of these rare situations of conflict between duty and inclination or between incommensurable values.

Of course, the restrictive incompatibilist might object that Betty really is responsible for her disposition to patriotism. "Undoubtedly" – the argument goes – "there must have been many more small conflict situations in her life than you have allowed for (or she is even aware of), and these situations taken together account for her present disposition."

However, to make such a concession would prove fatal to the restrictivist's position, for it would undermine his central thesis that rarely if ever are we in one of these situations in which we are free to do otherwise. Thus, the restrictive incompatibilist is faced with a dilemma: either accept a severe restriction on the range of states of affairs for which we can be held morally accountable, or else reject the claim that most of the time we are unable to do otherwise.

Van Inwagen claims that restrictive incompatibilism can be embedded within a traditional approach to moral responsibility via a tracing theory; but his view is in danger of threatening our ordinary views about responsibility as radically as our ordinary views about freedom. I have suggested a different, more plausible kind of tracing theory.

6 Semicompatibilism

I have presented a very sketchy account of guidance control. The basic idea would have to be developed and explained much more carefully, in order to generate a fully adequate theory of responsibility. But enough of the theory has been given to draw out some of its implications. My claim is that the account sketched here leads to compatibilism about moral responsibility and such doctrines as causal determinism and God's foreknowledge.

Let us first consider the relationship between causal determinism and moral responsibility. The account of guidance control presented here helps us to reconcile causal determinism with moral responsibility, even if causal determinism is inconsistent with freedom to do otherwise. The case for the incompatibility of causal determinism and freedom to do otherwise is different from (and stronger than) the case for the incompatibility of causal determinism and moral responsibility.

The approach to moral responsibility developed here says that an agent can be held morally responsible for performing an action insofar as the sequence actually issuing in the action is weakly reasons-responsive; the agent need not be free to do otherwise. And (as I shall explain below) reasons-responsiveness of the actual sequence leading to action is consistent with causal determination. Thus a compatibilist about determinism and moral responsibility need not accept the unappealing claims to which the compatibilist about causal determinism and freedom to do otherwise is committed. If it is the Basic Version of the Argument for Incompatibilism which pushes one to incompatibilism about causal determinism and freedom to do otherwise, this *need not* also push one toward incompatibilism about causal determinism and moral responsibility.

The account of guidance control (and thus responsibility) requires weakly reasons-responsive mechanisms. For a mechanism to be weakly reasons-responsive, there must be a possible scenario in which the same kind of mechanism operates and the agent does otherwise. But of course sameness of kind of mechanism need not require sameness of all details, even down to the "micro-level." Nothing in our intuitive conception of a kind of mechanism leading to action or in our judgments about clear cases of moral responsibility requires us to say that sameness of kind of mechanism implies sameness of micro-details. Thus, the scenarios pertinent to the reasons-responsiveness of an actual-sequence mechanism may differ with respect both to the sort of incentives the agent has to do otherwise and the particular details of the mechanism issuing in action. (Note that if causal determinism obtains and I do X, then one sort of mechanism which actually operates is a "causally determined to do X" type of mechanism. But of course this kind of mechanism is not germane to responsibility ascriptions insofar as it is not temporally intrinsic. And whereas the kind, "causally determined," is temporally intrinsic and thus may be germane, it is reasons-responsive.)

Let me attempt to drive the point home. I am seeking to capture faithfully our considered judgments about clear cases of moral responsibility (and the lack of it). In doing so, I have employed the ingredient, "same kind of mechanism." I claim that the goal of capturing our considered judgments about clear cases requires us *not* to take a stringent view of "same kind of mechanism" (according to which sameness requires sameness down to micro-details). Of course, if one has some *prior commitment* to the view that causal determinism is incompatible with moral responsibility, then one will be inclined to press for such an interpretation. But, apart from such a commitment, I do not see why one would be inclined toward this view of "same kind of mechanism."

If causal determinism is true, then any possible scenario (with the actual natural laws) in which the agent does otherwise at time t must differ in *some* respect from the actual scenario prior to t. The existence of certain possible scenarios of this sort is all that is required by the theory of moral responsibility. It is crucial to my approach that it does *not* require that the agent be able to bring about such a scenario, i.e., that he have it in his power at t so to act that the past (relative to t) would have been different from what it actually was. And the existence of the required kind of scenarios is compatible with causal determinism. Thus, my approach to moral responsibility makes room for responsibility even in a causally deterministic world.[21]

The actual-sequence reasons-responsiveness account of guidance control (and moral responsibility) thus yields "semi-compatibilism": moral responsibility is compatible with causal determinism, even if causal determinism is incompatible with freedom to do otherwise. Compatibilism about determinism and responsibility is compatible with both compatibilism and incompatibilism (as well as agnosticism) about determinism and freedom to do otherwise. The account renders more implausible the doctrine of "hyper-incompatibilism": causal determinism is incompatible with moral responsibility, even if moral responsibility does not require alternative possibilities. (Hyper-incompatibilism is the doctrine, judged unappealing in chapter seven, that causal determinism in itself and apart from considerations relevant to alternative possibilities rules out moral responsibility.)

I believe the same sort of considerations show that moral responsibility is consistent with God's foreknowledge, even if God's foreknowledge is incompatible with freedom to do otherwise. God's existence is surely compatible with the actual occurrence of a weakly reasons-responsive sequence. On one standard view of the nature of God, God's belief is not a part of the mechanism issuing in (say) my action. On this view, His belief is not what causes my action; rather, my action explains His belief. Thus, there are possible scenarios in which the actual kind of mechanism operates and issues in my doing otherwise. (In these scenarios, God believes correctly that I will do other than what I do in the actual world.) Again, the cases for the two sorts of incompatibilism – about divine foreknowledge and responsibility and about divine foreknowledge and freedom to do otherwise – are *different*, and the actual-sequence reasons-responsiveness theory yields semi-compatibilism.

There is another quite prevalent view of God according to which He actually engages in some sort of *causal* activity with regard to human action. Indeed, Alfred Freddoso has been at pains to emphasize that any fully adequate solution to the foreknowledge problem must take this causal dimension into account. In his wonderful introduction to his translation of Molina's *On Divine Foreknowledge*: (Part IV of the *Concordia*), Freddoso says:

> I do not, of course, mean to deny that the reconciliation of freedom and contingency with *any* sort of foreknowledge is extremely problematic. I will call this the problem of *simple* precognition. However, I do mean to affirm that the problem of *divine* precognition runs far deeper than the

problem of simple precognition. To understand exactly why, we must begin by recognizing that the belief in divine foreknowledge is not in itself a foundational tenet of classical Western theism. Instead, it derives its lofty theological status from its intimate connection with the absolutely central doctrine that God is perfectly provident. But the doctrine of providence carries with it a causal dimension . . .[22]

Similarly, Norman Kretzmann has argued that Aquinas' attempted solution of the problem of God's omniscience (which places God outside time) does not fit comfortably with Aquinas' doctrine of God's causal activity.[23] Kretzmann says:

When Aquinas is discussing God's knowledge apart from the temporality problem, however, he makes it clear that in his view God's knowledge is the very opposite of ours in one fundamental respect: 'the thing known is related to human knowledge in one way and to divine knowledge in another way; for human knowledge is caused by the things known, but divine knowledge is the cause of the things known' (*Summa Theologicae* IaIIae, q. 2, a. 3). I think it is clear that this 'mirror-image' theory of God's knowledge is a consequence of Aquinas's view of God as pure actuality (*actus purus*) . . .[24]

I think we can now say at least a bit to assuage the worries of Freddoso and Kretzmann. Even if God causes all human activity, the crucial issue is the *way* He causes it. If God causes human action via a process analogous to causal determination, simply *qua* causal determination (and not *special* causation), then arguably the process itself can be weakly reasons-responsive. And if so, I do not see why human agents cannot be morally responsible for their behavior, even if it is caused in this way by God.

In the first chapter, I argued that, holding fixed the fundamental nature of the process, it does not matter, for the purposes of assessing whether the agent has control, whether the process is initiated by *another person*. I started with examples in which an agent is "at the other end" of a certain process, and I proceeded to argue that the process would equally rule out the relevant sort of control, even if there were no agent. Now I am essentially "going the other way" in making the same point. I am beginning with the claim that causal determination in itself does not rule out moral responsibility insofar as it is consistent with guidance control. Then I am suggesting that, if a process analogous to mere causal determination but initiated by God issues in human action, then the etiology should not in itself rule out moral responsibility either. For it would seem also compatible with guidance control: it could involve the actual operation of a weakly reasons-responsive mechanism.

Notice that it is crucial to this preliminary gesture toward a solution to the problem of God's providential activity that it presupposes a *separation* of regulative control from guidance control. Granted, it is not clear that we have regulative control, if God exists and causes us to behave as we do. But the issue on which I am focusing, and arguably the basic issue, is whether we have guidance control. Note, further, that, just as "same kind of mechanism" does not entail sameness down to the micro-detail in the context of causal determination, so, also, it does not entail sameness of God's mental state, narrowly construed. Indeed, the two contexts are relevantly similar in this respect.

Of course, I have argued that God's mental states are "hard" – temporally non-relational. So, if they are within time, they represent a fixed feature of the past. This is analogous to non-relational physical micro-features of the past, within the context of causal determination. In *neither* case, arguably, can these temporally genuine features of the past be "altered" or "affected" – the past is fixed.[25] But guidance control does *not* require alternative possibilities; the approach I have suggested, according to which guidance control is all the freedom required for moral responsibility, thus achieves the same effect as Aquinas' placement of God outside time. Further, there is no reason stemming from the goal of preserving common-sense considered judgments about moral responsibility to require sameness of micro-detail in *either* context: "standard" causal determination or God's providential causation. A theorist such as Kretzmann worries that Aquinas loses the good effects of placing God outside of time by requiring that God cause human actions. But I have argued that God's causal activity in itself need not vitiate moral responsibility, and thus this feature of Aquinas' theory does not necessarily undermine the atemporality feature.[26]

Also, I wish (very briefly) to sketch a potential application of my approach to issues relevant to the problem of evil (the problem of how the existence of a perfectly good, omnipotent, and omniscient God is compatible with the sort of evil that exists in our world). One important response to the problem is the "free-will defense"; on this approach, one claims that a perfect God must have created the best of all possible worlds, which in turn must contain human beings who act freely. If the proponent of the problem of evil as casting doubt on the existence of God responds that God could have created agents who always freely do the right thing, the typical response is to deny that this is possible. That is, the response by the proponent of the free will defense is that God could not possibly *cause* agents to freely do the right thing (causation being incompatible with acting freely), and absent causation God could not *ensure* that agents always do the right thing.

Now it might be that the proponent of the free will defense thinks that acting freely requires freedom to do otherwise (or, in my terms, that guidance control requires regulative control). But I have severed this connection. And, given the separation of acting freely from freedom to do otherwise, I do not see why God could not have set things up so that human beings always choose the right thing as a result of a weakly reasons-responsive mechanism. That is, I do not see why God could not have ensured in advance that agents have guidance control of their actions and yet always choose and do the right thing.[27] Of course, a world in which there is no evil caused by humans acting freely may not be the best of all possible worlds for some reason apart from considerations of free will, but I do not see how one could argue for this conclusion based upon considerations relevant to free will. This admittedly sketchy presentation at least casts some doubt on the free will defense. As with the puzzle about God's providential activity, the free will defense can be addressed more effectively, given the separation of acting freely (guidance control) and freedom to do otherwise (regulative control).[28]

7 Return of the bogeymen

With the analysis of the previous sections in hand, I now wish to return to some of the examples with which this book began. I believe I am now in a position to address the challenges set by these examples.

Recall the nice metaphor articulated by Joel Feinberg:

> We can think of life as a kind of maze of railroad tracks connected and disjoined, here and there, by switches. Wherever there is an unlocked switch which can be pulled one way or the other, there is an 'open option;' wherever the switch is locked in one position the option is 'closed.' As we chug along our various tracks in the maze, other persons are busily locking and unlocking, opening and closing switches, thereby enlarging and restricting our various possibilities of movement.[29]

Feinberg's metaphor gives expression to the natural belief in an open future. But, unfortunately,

Martin Chuzzlewit finds himself on a trunk line with all of its switches closed and locked, and with other 'trains' moving in the same track at his rear, so that he has no choice at all but to continue moving straight ahead to destination D.[30]

Note now what Feinberg concludes:

... all of [Chuzzlewit's] options are closed, there are not alternative possibilities, he is forced to move to D. But now let us suppose that getting to D is Chuzzlewit's highest ambition in life and his most intensely felt desire. . . . According to the theory that one is at liberty to the extent that one can do what one wants . . . , Chuzzlewit enjoys perfect liberty . . . But . . . this theory blurs the distinction between liberty and compulsion . . . If Chuzzlewit is allowed no alternative to D, it follows that he is forced willy-nilly to go to D.[31]

It can now be seen why this final passage is problematic. From the lack of alternative possibilities, it does *not* follow that the agent in question does what he does as a result of *force* or *compulsion*. Of course, it may be the case that such an agent *has* to do what he does; but it does not follow from this that he is "forced" to do what he does in a sense that rules out his being accountable for what he does.[32]

As I have argued above, there can be two sorts of explanations for the lack of alternative possibilities. In one sort of case, a factor that plays some role in the actual sequence implies that an agent has no alternative possibilities. In another sort of case (the Frankfurt-type scenario), a factor or set of factors in the alternative sequence implies that the agent does not have (robust) alternative possibilities. In the latter sort of case there may be no responsibility-undermining factor in the actual sequence. Thus, it is simply *false* that

If human beings had no alternative possibilities at all, if all their actions at all times were the *only* actions permitted them, they . . . could take no credit or blame for any of their achievements, and they could no more be responsible for their lives, in prospect or retrospect, than are robots, or the trains in our fertile metaphor that must run on 'predestined grooves.' They could have dignity neither in their own eyes nor in the eyes of their fellows, and both esteem for others and self-esteem would dwindle.[33]

Similarly, Swinburne's view, articulated in chapter one, can be seen to be false:

... an agent would not be morally responsible at all (he would never be praiseworthy or blameworthy) if he was caused necessarily, predetermined, to try to do what he did, by his brain state, and that in turn by some prior state, until we come to causes outside the agent's body and ultimately to causes long before his birth. For in that case in a crucial sense the agent could not have done other than he did do. ... [34]

Recall, also, that weird and disturbing amusement park ride described by Carl Ginet. In the fanciful version of the example, although one has the illusion of choice and control, someone else is really controlling the path of the car (and inducing the illusions of choice and control). In chapter one I assimilated the examples of Feinberg and Ginet to the extent that they both stand in contrast to the intuitive picture of the future as open – as a garden of forking paths. But now it is crucial to distinguish them. For the rider in Ginet's example lacks alternative possibilities because of a certain sort of *actual-sequence* intervention by external factors. More specifically, the external controller both induces an illusion of choice in the rider and also controls the movements of the car by a certain sort of process involving gears, pulleys, wheels, and so forth. Thus, the car's movements (and the rider's actions) do *not* issue from an *appropriate actual sequence*: they do not issue from a weakly reasons-responsive mechanism.

Although both Martin Chuzzlewit and Ginet's rider lack regulative control, they are crucially different insofar as Ginet's rider (but not Chuzzlewit) also lacks guidance control. The examples nicely illustrate the difference between the two ways in which it can be true that an agent lacks alternative possibilities. In the case of Ginet's rider, some set of factors which play a role in the actual sequence explains his lack of alternative possibilities.[35] In contrast, in the case of Martin Chuzzlewit a set of factors in the alternative scenario (or range of alternative scenarios) explains his lack of alternative possibilities.[36]

In chapter one I posed a challenge (or perhaps set of challenges) to which I now wish to return. Recall the array of Dennett's "Bogeymen": the Invisible Jailer, the Nefarious Neurosurgeon, the Hideous Hypnotist, the Peremptory Puppeteer, the Cosmic Child Whose Dolls We Are, and the Malevolent Mindreader. I said these examples constitute an invitation and a challenge. First, they invite us to notice what is common to them: some feature is present in each case and is both quite external to the agent and is sufficient for the agent's behavior. Thus, in this range of examples an application of the Principle of the Transfer of

Powerlessness yields the result that the agents lack freedom to do otherwise. Second, they invite us to note that what is common to them is also shared by the contexts of God's existence and causal determinism. Finally, in light of these facts, the challenge is to say how we can be morally responsible for our actions, if God exists or causal determinism obtains.

By now the answer should be clear. Although the obvious cases of lack of responsibility share with the contexts of God's existence and causal determinism features in virtue of which it is plausible to say that the relevant agent lacks regulative control, it does not follow that in the contexts of God's existence and causal determinism the agent lacks *guidance control*. Indeed, I have argued that these contexts *differ* from the cases in many of the thought-experiments precisely in this respect: there is no factor present in the actual sequence that is plausibly taken to be a responsibility-undermining factor.

Failure to distinguish between actual-sequence and alternative-sequence explanations for the lack of alternative possibilities can blur one's metaphysical vision. Indeed, consider again Dennett's characterization of my example of the Nefarious Neurosurgeon:

> How would you like to have someone strap you down and insert electrodes in your brain, and then control your every thought and deed by pushing buttons on the 'master' console? Consider, for instance, the entirely typical invocation of this chap by Fischer ["Responsibility and Control," 1982, p. 26]; the ominous Dr. Black, who arranges things in poor Jones' brain so that Black can 'control Jones' activities. Jones, meanwhile, knows nothing of this.'[37]

Evidently, in Dennett's version of the example, the neurologist actually exercises control over Jones, which clearly rules out his moral responsibility. But in my version of the example Black did *not* engage in such intervention: he simply monitored Jones' brain activity. (My version of the example was a Frankfurt-type case.)

Note that the difference between the two versions of the example is crucial. Of course, they both possess the features in virtue of which Jones is plausibly taken to lack regulative control. (The Transfer Principle yields the same result in both versions of the case.) And they both possess the same sorts of factors that Dennett alleges may "scare" us inappropriately and thus distort our analysis. But whereas in Dennett's version of the case Jones does not exercise guidance control, in my version he does. And there is no reason to suppose that the contexts of

God's existence and causal determinism are not relevantly similar to my version of the case.

I do not wish to claim that in *all* of Dennett's thought-experiments the relevant agent would not be morally responsible. Rather, my claim is that the analysis developed above can help us to sort through the cases in a more fine-grained and accurate fashion (and to see that the contexts of causal determinism and God's existence are quite different from the paradigmatic cases of lack of moral responsibility). Consider what Dennett says about the Invisible Jailer:

> Are you *sure* you're not in some sort of prison? Here one is invited to consider a chain of transformations, taking us from obvious prisons to unobvious (but still dreadful) prisons, to utterly invisible and undetectable (but still dreadful?) prisons. Consider a deer in Magdalen College park. Is it imprisoned? Yes, but not much. The enclosure is quite large. Suppose we moved the deer to a larger enclosure – the New Forest with a fence around it. Would the deer still be imprisoned? In the State of Maine, I am told, deer almost never travel more than five miles from their birthplace during their lives. If an enclosure were located outside the normal unimpeded limits of a deer's lifetime wanderings would the deer enclosed be imprisoned? Perhaps, but note that it makes a difference to our intuitions whether some*one* installs the enclosure. Do you feel imprisoned on Planet Earth – the way Napoleon was stuck on Elba? It is one thing to be born and live on Elba, and another to be put and kept on Elba *by someone*. A jail without a jailer is not a jail. Whether or not it is an undesirable abode depends on other features; it depends on just how (if at all) it cramps the style of its inhabitants.[38]

Dennett is correct to say that if the existence of a jail does not "cramp one's style," then its mere existence is relatively unproblematic. As the jail gets bigger and bigger, it is more likely that it would not cramp the style of its inhabitants. Thus, Dennett in effect develops a *spatial analogue* of a Frankfurt-type example; in the spatial analogue, as in the Frankfurt-type cases, the lack of alternative possibilities *plays no role* in the relevant behavior. Indeed, in the example from John Locke after which Frankfurt's examples are patterned, the analogy with a prison is unmistakable; in Locke's example, it is alleged that a man may voluntarily stay in a room which, unbeknownst to him, is locked.[39]

But it is unclear whether "it makes a difference to our intuitions whether some*one* installs the enclosure." Which intuitions? As argued in chapter one, whether one is put in the jail by someone else or one simply stumbles into it surely cannot make any difference as to the existence of alternative possibilities – one is in any case in prison. And if one does not wish to call a "jail without a jailer" a jail, nevertheless this sort of arrangement rules out alternative possibilities as effectively as a jail. The kernel of truth in Dennett's remarks about other agents does not have to do with alternative possibilities; rather, I would suggest it has to do with guidance control. When one is "put and kept" in jail by someone, this suggests the absence even of *guidance control*. Thus, I claim that the introduction of the agent (the jailer) in Dennett's thought-experiment is relevant *not* because it is pertinent to the existence of regulative control, but because it suggests the absence of what I have identified as the crucial freedom-relevant ingredient in moral responsibility: guidance control.

More specifically, when one is forcibly taken, handcuffed, and put in jail by a police officer, one does not have guidance control of one's behavior. I am reminded of Bertrand Russell's critique of Schopenhauer's view of freedom as the "freedom to obey the police." But, as I have argued above, the actual sequences issuing in actions need not be assimilated to *this sort* of police action and *this sort* of obedience to police, if causal determinism obtains or God exists. Isaiah Berlin says that determinism, "for all that its chains are decked out with flowers, and despite its parade of noble stoicism and the splendour and vastness of its cosmic design, nevertheless represents the universe as a prison."[40] The prison is the lack of regulative control. The flowers are the presence of guidance control.

8 Conclusion

In previous chapters I have developed a set of arguments which call into question the natural view that we (at least sometimes) have alternative possibilities. Thus, it is pressing to consider whether moral responsibility requires the sort of control which involves alternative possibilities: regulative control. In chapter seven I argued that it does *not*; rather, the sort of control required for moral responsibility is guidance control. Further, I argued that guidance control is the freedom-relevant condition sufficient for moral responsibility. That is to say, it is not *also* required for moral responsibility that God does not exist and that causal determinism does not obtain. Thus, guidance control is the freedom-relevant condition necessary and sufficient for moral responsibility.

In this chapter I have given a first approximation to an account of guidance control in terms of weak reasons-responsiveness. This account goes some distance toward establishing semicompatibilism: the doctrine that causal determinism (or God's existence) is compatible with moral responsibility, even if causal determinism (or God's existence) rules out freedom to do otherwise.

There are two importantly different ways in which one could lack regulative control. In one way some factor which plays a role in the actual sequence both renders it true that one lacks regulative control *and also* that one lacks guidance control. In such cases one is not morally responsible. But in another way the factor which renders it true that one lacks regulative control does *not* also make it the case that one lacks guidance control. In such cases one can be morally responsible. Failure to distinguish the different ways in which one might lack regulative control can vitiate one's ability to classify the full range of examples frequently discussed in the debates about free will and moral responsibility. Having made this distinction, we can help to protect our intuitive picture of ourselves as morally responsible agents (and, indeed, as persons) from the threats posed by causal determinism and God's existence.

9

Putting it Together

And now the end is near and so I face the final curtain;
My friend, I'll say it clear, I'll state my case, of which I'm certain;
I've lived a life that's full, I traveled each and every highway;
And more, much more than this, I did it my way . . .
From "My Way," by P. Anka, J. Revaux, and C. François, as
sung by Frank Sinatra

1 Recapitulation

We naturally think of the future as open. We think of the future as
containing various paths that branch off one past; although we know we
will travel along just one of these paths, we take it that some of the other
paths are (at least sometimes) genuinely accessible to us. In deliberating
and deciding on a course of action, we intuitively think of ourselves (at
least sometimes) as determining which path to take, among various
paths we *could* take. Thus, we think of ourselves as having control over
which path we take: we conceive of ourselves (at least sometimes) as
having regulative control.

It can seem that the possession of regulative control is precisely what
distinguishes us from non-persons. After all, the behavior of an animal
appears to be the product of strong instinctual urges, and a heat-seeking
missile simply moves and "reacts" in accordance with its program. Non-
human animals and mechanical devices such as missiles are not *persons*;
they do not have strong rights to continue to exist, and they are not
appropriate candidates for the reactive attitudes. It is a quite powerful
and plausible idea that the possession of regulative control is required for
personhood (and moral responsibility).

But, upon reflection, our confidence that we possess this sort of control can be shaken. After all, most of us do not feel absolutely confident that causal determinism is false or that God does not exist. For example, I am not certain that I will not pick up the *Los Angeles Times* tomorrow morning and read about a brilliant new theory announced by a consortium of prominent physicists at Stanford and Berkeley according to which the universe is at a deep level causally deterministic. And a powerful challenge to our confidence in our possession of regulative control can be generated, given the assumption of causal determinism or God's existence.

The reason this challenge is powerful is that it latches onto important elements of common sense, such as the fixity of the past and the fixity of the laws of nature. It is precisely for this sort of reason – its strong grounding in common sense – that the skeptical challenge to our natural and intuitive belief that we can know various things about the empirical world is powerful. Of course, this is not to say that the parallel skeptical challenges (in epistemology and action theory) are *decisive*, but it does indicate why they are not easy to dismiss without serious consideration.

Frequently the challenges (to our possession of regulative control) from God's existence and causal determinism are treated entirely separately. Indeed, there are quite separate literatures dealing with the issues arising from these challenges. The separateness of the discussions may simply reflect the different interests of the participants in the debates, and this is, of course, entirely unobjectionable. But I believe it can be useful to treat the two challenges as versions of the same argument. Throughout this book I have done this, in the hopes that the underlying similarities in the issues can be highlighted.

I begin in chapter one by presenting a set of ingredients which can generate a version of the skeptical worry about our control. These include plausible intuitive formulations of the ideas that the past and the laws of nature are "fixed" and beyond our control. Further, I discuss the Principle of the Transfer of Powerlessness. The Transfer Principle acts as a sort of "slingshot," projecting the modal property of powerlessness (or lack of regulative control) from one place to another. Application of the Transfer Principle yields the correct results over a broad range of clear cases of lack of regulative control. For example, if you have no control over the fact that someone has slipped a powerful tranquilizer into your drink, and you have no control over the fact that given that you have taken this tranquilizer, fine movements are ruled out, it certainly seems to follow that you have no control over fine movements of your hands.

The Principle of the Fixity of the Past, the Principle of the Fixity of the Natural Laws, and the Transfer Principle can be combined to yield the Transfer Version of the skeptical challenge to our control. (It is interesting to note that an epistemological principle structurally similar to the Transfer Principle – the Principle of Closure of Knowledge Under Known Entailment – is typically employed to generate the parallel challenge in epistemology.)

In chapter two I seek to gain a better understanding of the Principle of the Transfer of Powerlessness. I begin by setting out some principles discussed by Anthony Kenny. Kenny claims that these "transfer-like" principles underlie the incompatibilist's argument (i.e., the skeptical challenge to our possession of regulative control). Further, Kenny claims that these principles are subject to counterexamples and thus that the incompatibilist's argument can be refuted. I dub Kenny's view, "Scotism."

It will be useful to recall the Transfer Principle:

If: (a) $N_{S,t}$ (p)
and (b) $N_{S,t}$ (If p, then q),
then (c) $N_{S,t}$ (q).

The interpretation of the doubly indexed (to an agent and time) modal operator is "power necessity." That is to say, when "$N_{S,t}$ (p)," then p obtains and S cannot at t prevent p from obtaining. When p is power necessary for S at t, S lacks regulative control over p at t.

Kenny sets out a version of the skeptic's challenge to our view of ourselves as having regulative control. On Kenny's version, the skeptic relies upon a principle like (but not identical to) Transfer. I call this principle Transfer*:

S can (cannot) do X.
In the circumstances, doing X is (would be) doing Y.
Therefore, S can (cannot) do Y.

It is useful to distinguish two versions of Kenny's Transfer* (depending upon whether the modal notion in question is "ability" or "inability"). Thus, Transfer* I:

S can do X.
In the circumstances, doing X is (would be) doing Y.
Therefore, S can do Y.

And Transfer* II:

> S cannot do X.
> In the circumstances, doing X is (would be) doing Y.
> Therefore, S cannot do Y.

Note first that Kenny's Transfer* is different from Transfer. Further, clearly Transfer* I and Transfer* II are importantly different. I argue that the putative counterexample to Transfer* I offered by Kenny is not convincing, when the principle is interpreted appropriately. Further, whereas I offer reason to reject Transfer* II, this in no way vitiates the skeptic's argument: even as developed by Kenny, the argument depends on Transfer* I and *not* Transfer* II. Further, the problems with Transfer* II do not threaten Transfer. Scotism is doubly defective. First, the principle attributed to the incompatibilist by Kenny – suitably interpreted – is *not* vulnerable to the alleged counterexample. And, second, the counterexample does not even purport to address the principle employed in chapter one to generate the skeptical worry: Transfer.

Michael Slote uses a different strategy for calling into question the basic modal principle upon which the incompatibilistic skeptic's challenge appears to rest. Slote begins by pointing out that if the relevant modal operator expresses certain kinds of necessity – epistemic, deontic, and "causal alethic," the analogues of the Transfer Principle for the modality in question arguably fail. Slote suggests that the failures can be explained in virtue of the "selectivity" of the pertinent forms of necessity. Finally, Slote claims that this same explanation can be invoked in the case of power necessity. That is, he claims that a certain sort of selectivity can be found in power necessity, and that this underlies the failure of Transfer.

There is a structural similarity between the modal "engines" of the parallel skeptical arguments (in epistemology and action theory). Slote suggests that it is obvious that the Principle of Closure of Knowledge Under Known Implication is invalid, but this is a very contentious matter. It is hard to see how to argue for its invalidity without begging the question against the epistemic skeptic. In the context of certain kinds of epistemic "fragmentation" and "irresponsibility," however, it does appear that the Principle of Closure of Knowledge Under Known Implication is invalid. But it is not straightforward to proceed from this to the invalidity of the Transfer Principle. I argue that it is not at all plausible to suppose that the particular kind of selectivity found in contexts of epistemic fragmentation, or an analogue of this sort of fragmentation, is also present in the context of action theory (and power necessity). In general, there is *no* reason to think that whatever forms of selectivity are present in the *other* modal contexts (and allegedly explain the failure of the analogues of Transfer) are *also* present in the context of action.

Peter van Inwagen has argued that acceptance of the Transfer Principle is *sufficient* in itself for the lack of regulative control in a wide range of situations – quite apart from any *special* assumptions such as causal determinism or God's existence. If van Inwagen is correct, then a radically counterintuitive conclusion can be drawn *simply* from the Transfer Principle, and we could be quite sure that we lack regulative control in almost all contexts. Van Inwagen attempts to mitigate the force of this point by developing a "tracing" theory of moral responsibility according to which we could still be morally responsible, even while lacking regulative control in most contexts.

In chapter three, I argue that van Inwagen is *not* correct: the Transfer Principle does *not* in itself imply the lack of regulative control in most situations. And it is a good thing, since the tracing theory sketched by van Inwagen would *not* protect our status as morally responsible in a world in which we (most of the time) lacked regulative control.

Thus, the Transfer Principle is not *sufficient* to generate the conclusion that, despite the appearances, we lack alternative possibilities. It is important to see that it is also not *necessary*. The basic ingredients of the Fixity of the Past and the Fixity of the Natural Laws can be combined in another way – *not* employing the Transfer Principle (or any closely related modal principle) – to generate precisely the same skeptical conclusion. One way of combining these ingredients is crystallized in the Conditional Version of the Argument for Incompatibilism. Just as in the context of knowledge, in the context of action the modal principle is not necessary to generate the problematic conclusion.

The Conditional Version of the Argument for Incompatibilism makes use of the following interpretations of the intuitive ideas of the fixity of the natural laws and past:

(FL) For any action Y, and agent S, if it is true that if S were to do Y, some natural law which actually obtains would not obtain, then S cannot do Y.

(FP) For any action Y, agent S, and time t, if it is true that if S were to do Y at t, some fact about the past relative to t would not have been a fact, then S cannot at t do Y at t.

Employing these principles one can get to the incompatibilist's conclusion without the use of a Transfer-like principle.

In chapter four I point out that these principles are not uncontroversially valid. In the case of each principle, the compatibilist
argues that various *versions* must be distinguished. Then the compatibilist wishes to argue that the plausible versions of the principles do
not generate the skeptical conclusion, and the versions that do generate
this conclusion are implausible.

Let us briefly recall the considerations pertinent to (FP). The
incompatibilist claims that the truth of a certain backtracking counterfactual conditional *rules out* the associated "can-claim." The view here is
that if it is a necessary condition of one's performing a certain action that
the past be different from what it actually was, then it follows that one
cannot perform the action in question. In response, the compatibilist
adduces a range of examples in which, he alleges, an agent has it in his
power to perform some action which is such that, were he to perform it,
the past would have been different from what it actually was. If the
compatibilist is correct about this range of examples, (FP) must be
rejected.

Now it is not at all evident that the backtrackers are true in these
examples. But suppose they are. We appear to be at an impasse. The
incompatibilist will say that the can-claims in the examples are thus false,
and the compatibilist will tenaciously cling to the can-claims. This, I
suggest, is just one of many Dialectical Stalemates in the cluster of issues
relevant to free will and moral responsibility. What I suggest here is that
we notice that (FP) is not the *only* plausible way of capturing the
intuitive idea of the fixity of the past. There is another way of representing the fixity of the past. Accepting this, one can even *give up* (FP) but
still generate the worrisome skeptical result. This alternative formulation
of the fixity of the past (and also the fixity of the laws) yields the Basic
Version of the Argument for Incompatibilism (developed in chapter
five).

On the Basic Version of the Principle of the Fixity of the Past, all
accessible future paths must be *extensions* of the actual past; more
explicitly, an agent can do X only if his doing X can be an extension of
the actual past, holding the laws fixed. Accepting this Basic Version of
the Principle of the Fixity of the Past allows one perspicuously to analyze
a spectrum of puzzling examples, including the vexatious Newcomb's
Problem. Indeed, it gives us a clear way of avoiding the impasse between
Lewis and Horgan in which the issue of the truth of the relevant
backtracking conditionals is paramount. Further, it yields a simple,

lucid, and natural argument for the two-box solution in the case of the inerrancy of the predictor, and the one-box solution in the case of the infallibility of the predictor. Lewis is an "invariant two-boxer" (a two-boxer for both the cases of inerrancy and infallibility). Horgan is an invariant one-boxer. Levi is a one-boxer for infallibility, but he argues for a variable solution for the case of an inerrant predictor, depending on the relevant probabilities. Further, Levi has argued that the two-box solution for inerrancy conjoined with the one-box solution for infallibility is *incoherent*. In contrast, I have employed the Basic Version of the Principle of the Fixity of the Past to argue for precisely this sort of solution; I am a two-boxer for the case of an inerrant predictor, and a one-boxer for the case of an infallible predictor. The Basic Version of the Principle of the Fixity of the Past provides a nice explanation of this seemingly puzzling solution (originally suggested by Nozick).

But of course even the Basic Version of the Principle of the Fixity of the Past is *not* uncontroversial. I do not have a knockdown argument for it, but I do think that it is quite plausible. Note that a proponent of this version of the principle (or any of the other versions) views freedom ascriptions as based at least in part on purely *relational* facts. That is to say, the relationship between the present and the past itself helps to determine the truth of freedom ascriptions quite apart from the effects the past has on the present. In contrast, the compatibilist tends to think that the past can only affect freedom ascriptions via producing certain conditions in the present.

Most compatibilists believe that one is free to do otherwise unless certain "special" circumstances obtain, and mere causal determination is not deemed to be such a circumstance. Thus, the compatibilist holds that the past can limit our current alternatives only by creating one of a range of *special* circumstances in the present. On this view, the past must cast a certain sort of *shadow* on the present, in order for it to constrain one. Consider these remarks by Keith Lehrer:

> . . . a condition C is an advantage at t S needs to do A at t *only if* C is a condition occurring entirely at t. Sartre once remarked that the past can impose no limits on what a person can do in the present. There is, I suggest, some element of truth in this admittedly exaggerated statement. The past may, I propose, limit what a person can do now, but only if the past has brought about some present condition that limits what the person can do now. Thus, the past can only prevent me from taking some course of action *indirectly*. It can do so only by what it has wrought in the present, by producing some result in the present that *directly* prevents me from taking that course of action now. . . . It is only the

causal *shadow* that the past casts upon the present, and not the past itself, that deprives me of an advantage I require, and directly prevents me from performing the action. I refer to the principle as the *shadow principle*.[1]

But whereas the compatibilist holds that only contemporaneous conditions can rule out alternative possibilities, the incompatibilist believes that constraints on one's freedom to do otherwise can arise from the *relationship* between the present and past *in itself*. Thus, the incompatibilist rejects the Shadow Principle. In contrast, he accepts something like the *Dog's Tail Principle*: the past is viewed as like a dog's tail, which follows the dog wherever it goes. Indeed, one is tempted to dub the Basic Version of the Principle of the Fixity of the Past the "Dog's Tail Principle."

The compatibilist replies that, on this view, the tail is wagging the dog. But, despite the manifest attractions of the Shadow Principle, I do not ultimately think it is tenable. Admittedly, it is natural to suppose that the only constraining conditions are contemporaneous, and that only "special circumstances" rule out alternative possibilities. Of course, I *do* wish to argue that only "special circumstances" rule out moral responsibility – but this is in part because moral responsibility does not require alternative possibilities. And, upon reflection, I believe the Shadow Principle can be seen to be less natural than the Dog's Tail Principle.

The Dog's Tail Principle requires that any genuinely accessible future pathway must be an *extension* of the actual past, and the proponent of the Shadow Principle must deny this. This is the fundamental problem with the Shadow Principle. Although a picture is not an argument, a picture can be an enormously helpful heuristic device. And it seems that the Dog's Tail Principle corresponds to the very natural, intuitive picture of the future as a garden of forking paths. That is, the picture is of a branching, tree-like structure: at various nodes, there are several pathways that represent genuinely accessible futures, but there is *just one single path* that can be traced *backward* in time. Although various paths branch off the current node into the future, there is no mirror-image of branching forks back into the past. Surely, this is the common-sense, intuitive picture. More specifically, this is how we picture the structure of time and possibility, when we conceive of ourselves as having regulative control.

Another metaphor. Imagine a path that represents some allegedly possible future pathway. Is it genuinely possible, in the sense of being a pathway that one has it in one's power to make part of the actual world? The answer is "yes" *only if* one could in principle "draw a line" that *connects* this possible future pathway with the pathway that represents the actual past. If there is no possibility for such a connection, then "one can't get there from here." And it seems overwhelmingly natural to think that one must be able to get there from here, if a possible pathway is to represent a genuinely accessible future.

And consider what the contrasting picture must be like, given the Shadow Principle. Here one can have access to possible future pathways that have *no connection* to the actual past. These future pathways are associated with "pasts" which are different from the actual past "all the way back." The picture here is of future pathways branching off the present, and associated with each of these possible futures is *its own* pathway into the past. In my view, this picture is as unintuitive as it is unlovely.

Perhaps there is an explanation for the cluttered, awkward picture that corresponds to the Shadow Principle. The Shadow Theorist concedes that an agent cannot do something, insofar as there is some contemporaneous *obstacle* to the agent's doing it. These obstacles are construed as conditions that render the performance of the action unreasonably difficult or "practically impossible." But the Shadow Theorist *also* must allow that an agent may be able to perform some action that is *causally impossible, given the past.* But if one is willing to say that conditions that make it unreasonably difficult or "practically impossible" to do something rule out the claim that the agent has it in his power to do that thing, then surely one should also say that one does not have it in one's power to do something that is *causally impossible, given the past.* The view that it cannot be in one's power to perform an action that is causally impossible, given the past, is crystallized by the Basic Version of the Principle of the Fixity of the Past – the Dog's Tail Principle – and denied by the Shadow Principle. Perhaps the failure of the Shadow Theorist to accommodate this extremely natural point results in the complicated, unnatural picture associated with the view.[2]

Ultimately, then, I accept the Basic Version of the Principle of the Fixity of the Past. This principle says that genuinely open futures must be extensions of the actual past; in Ginet's words, our freedom is the *freedom to add to the given past.* This point can appear to be so obvious as to be entirely pedestrian. But I have sought to show that, although it is simple, it is a powerful insight. It can help to structure and illuminate a variety of puzzles, as well as to suggest a natural, basic version of the Argument for Incompatibilism. For example, together with the heuristic device of possible worlds semantics, it can explain in a perspicuous fashion the following very puzzling contexts. There can be situations (such as that of the Salty Old Seadog) in which the only way an agent can do something is by adding to a given past, the agent can do the thing, and (arguably, at least) if he were to do it, the past would have been different from what it actually was!

Also, I can now say a bit more about the *point* of the restructuring of the free will problem I have offered. Recall the evidently intractable set of Dialectical Stalemates involved in an evaluation of the Conditional Version of the Argument for Incompatibilism. Shifting to the Basic Version allows us to avoid these Stalemates, but issues in disagreements of its own. What then is the point of the restructuring?

First, it is important to emphasize that it is unreasonable to suppose that the only sort of restructuring that can be useful is the kind that issues in a relatively straightforward decisive resolution of the underlying problem. Admittedly, the shift to the Basic Version does not achieve this effect. But I believe it still has considerable advantages. The Basic Version really is "more basic": it presents the issues in a more basic and natural way. This allows one to see what is at stake in the debates in a clearer way. This is in part achieved by linking the different positions to different intuitive views and their associated "pictures." Insofar as a philosophical position can be stated in a natural way – in a way that is associated with a clear picture – it can emerge more forcefully what precisely the commitments of that position are. In this way it can become easier to choose among the positions and to grade their plausibility. And this is so even if one is not *forced* to accept any given position. The restructuring I have offered allows us to associate clear pictures with the compatibilist and incompatibilist positions, and in the process I believe it helps to render the incompatibilist position considerably more plausible. Further, it can help us to see the structure of the issues – the logical terrain – more clearly.

Allow me again to employ a version of a simple example in order to bring out the idea more explicitly. Imagine (again) that we are climbing up a path toward a peak (which is our goal). Suddenly, we are confronted with a huge boulder in our path, and it is clear that we cannot go around it and continue upward. There is however another path that happens to branch off our path at a point just before the boulder. We know that this other path continues up the mountain toward the peak. But we also know that there is a boulder on this path, somewhat farther up the mountain. Given this, what possible reason is there for taking this second path?

Even if we are quite sure that the boulder on the second path cannot be dislodged or circumambulated, there still might be a point to our continuing: the path might itself be lovely, we might enjoy the climb, and we might gain a better view of the terrain from our position farther up the mountain. But it can also be the case that, although we know it won't be straightforward or easy, the boulder on the second path may be possible to move or somehow to walk around. In taking this second path there are no guarantees; but there is considerable hope that we will be able not only to see more of the terrain (and to see it more clearly), but also to overcome the obstacle and proceed to the mountain peak.

Our freedom, then, is the freedom to extend the actual past. But which facts exactly are part of the past, in the relevant sense? In chapter six I explore this set of issues. The fatalist points out that (arguably, at least) it follows from S's doing X at $t2$ that it was true at $t1$ that S would do X at $t2$. Is the fact that it was true at $t1$ that S would do X at $t2$ part of the actual past relative to $t2$? If so, then it would seem to follow that S is unable at $t2$ to refrain from doing X at $t2$.

There is an important difference between a fact such as that Condition C (some intrinsic, non-relational state of the universe) obtained at $t1$ and a fact such as that it was true at $t1$ that S would do X at $t2$. The first fact is a hard fact about $t1$, whereas the second fact is a soft fact about $t1$. Hard facts are temporally non-relational (as regards the future), whereas soft facts are temporally relational (as regards the future). A hard fact about t is "fully accomplished and over-and-done-with at t," whereas a soft fact about t is not. The intuitive idea of the fixity of the past applies only to the set of all hard facts about the past, not to the soft facts as well. Thus, the Basic Version of the Principle of the Fixity of the Past must be interpreted so as to require that genuinely open future paths must be extensions of the set of all *hard* facts about the past.

But now consider the fact that God believes at $t1$ that S will do X at $t2$. Is this a hard or a soft fact about $t1$? The answer is not straightforward. On the one hand, the fact about God's belief appears to be like the fact that it was true at $t1$ that S will do X at $t2$. More specifically, the facts are alike in that they both entail that S will do X at $t2$. Thus, on the Entailment View of Soft Facthood, the fact about God's belief would be deemed a soft fact about $t1$. And yet the fact about God's belief does not seem to be in all important respects like the "prior truth fact." We might think of a hard fact about a time as "genuinely and solely" about that time. It seems that the prior truth fact is not even genuinely about $t1$: it does not appear to entail that anything "really happen" at $t1$. But whereas the fact about God's belief may not be *solely* about $t1$, it does seem to be *genuinely* about $t1$: it appears to entail that something "really happen" at $t1$ (i.e., that God's mind be in a certain state at $t1$). Thus, the fact about God's belief is in some sense "in between" the prior truth fact and the fact that Condition C obtained at $t1$ (which is plausibly taken to be *both* genuinely and solely about $t1$).

I attempt to provide an analysis which exhibits the precise sense in which the fact about God's belief is "in between" the other two. The fact about God's belief may be construed or interpreted in various ways, but I argue that, no matter how it is construed, it is plausible to think that it is a *special* sort of soft fact – a soft fact that carries with it *excess baggage*. The fact about God's belief is like the prior truth fact insofar as they are both soft facts. But the fact about God's belief is like the fact about the temporally non-relational state of the universe at t insofar as the relevant agent's falsifying the fact about God's belief would require his so acting that *some* temporally genuine feature of the past would not have been a feature of the past. In other words, in the case of both facts – the fact about God's belief and the fact about Condition C – any path extending into the future which does not contain them (in the past) must lack *some* genuine feature of the past and thus cannot be an extension of the actual past. Thus, at a deep level – the level relevant to the skeptical challenge to our possession of regulative control – the latter two facts (the fact about God's belief and the fact about Condition C) are *relevantly similar*.

I have essentially advocated that we take a "higher magnification" look at the class of soft facts. Relative to particular contexts, certain of these facts will be "hard-core soft facts"; in order to falsify these facts, the relevant agent must falsify some *component* hard facts. And relative to particular contexts, other soft facts will be "hard-type soft facts"; in order to falsify these facts, the relevant agent must so act that some individual who had some temporally non-relational property in the past would not have had that *property*. Taking this more nuanced and subtle approach, we can resist the inappropriate assimilation of all soft facts.

Some have been unfriendly to the complexity I have sought to introduce into the analysis of soft facts. William Lane Craig says:

> Now it seems to me that in Fischer's analysis the distinction between so-called 'hard facts' and 'soft facts', which was originally introduced by Saunders and Pike, has gone out of control, so that we are now confronted with 'hard-type soft facts' and 'soft-type soft facts', which makes such terminology of questionable value. . . . And the end is not yet in sight: for while on Fischer's analysis, all hard-type soft facts are fixed, it is not the case that all soft-type [soft] facts lack fixity, so that futher distinctions may be anticipated. . . . One thus arrives at the following unwieldy classification . . .[3]

A colleague of William Hasker might be driven (in part) by a similar concern, although he presents it rather more gently. Hasker says:

> A colleague suggested to me that besides hard facts and soft facts, there may also be facts sunny-side-up. But why stop there? Why not scrambled facts, poached facts, and even facts Benedict?[4]

Is the relative complexity of my analysis a bit of a dog's breakfast? I do not believe so. Indeed, it is not clear exactly what the objection is. The objection might be that the taxonomical scheme I have sketched is arbitrary, *ad hoc*, or somehow adventitious. Or perhaps the objection is to the complexity *per se*.

To the first objection it is difficult to know how to respond. I can simply commend my analysis to the consideration of the reader and respectfully suggest that it is at least less problematic than the scheme Borges describes in a (supposed) Chinese encyclopedia

> [o]n [w]hose remote pages it is written that animals are divided into (a) those that belong to the Emperor, (b) embalmed ones, (c) those that are trained, (d) suckling pigs, (e) mermaids, (f) fabulous ones, (g) stray dogs, (h) those that are included in this classification, (i) those that tremble as if they were mad, (j) innumerable ones, (k) those drawn with a very fine camel's hair brush, (l) others, (m) those that have just broken a flower vase, (n) those that resemble flies from a distance.[5]

Further, the complexity is introduced to solve a set of apparently intractable puzzles. I believe the test of the analysis should be whether it is fruitful – whether it can help to illuminate and perhaps ultimately resolve these problems. A tremendous amount of ink has been spilt by proponents of the thesis that God's beliefs are soft facts. Against this assault stands the resilient view that such facts are hard facts, or at least that they are not relevantly similar to certain paradigmatic soft facts. Operating solely with the simple and crude distinction between hard and soft facts, it is difficult to make any progress toward resolving this dispute. But given a more refined and articulated structure, progress can be made.

To illustrate. Recently, Nelson Pike has produced a thoughtful review of the issues that have emerged in the literature on the problem of God's foreknowledge and human freedom since the publication of his seminal paper, "Divine Foreknowledge and Voluntary Action."[6] In the original paper Pike articulated a version of the skeptic's challenge to our possession of regulative control, given the existence of God. In the review piece, he points out that John Turk Saunders challenged Pike's argument on precisely the ground that it is not clear that God's beliefs are hard facts about the past; that is, it is not clear that they are "fully accomplished and over-and-done-with" at the times at which they are held.[7]

At this point Marilyn McCord Adams made an important contribution to the debate.[8] She suggested a "proto-version" of the Entailment View of Soft Facthood, and argued that relative to this criterion it can be seen that God's beliefs are *soft* facts about the times at which they are held. After all, if a fact about *t1* entails that something "really" happens at some later time *t2*, how can the first fact be considered "fully accomplished and over-and-done-with" at *t1*?

Adams' point has considerable force. But Pike also acknowledges the force of the intuition behind the view that any "belief-event" must be temporally genuine and non-relational. Recall that this intuition can be specified roughly as follows: one and the same state of mind at *t1* cannot count as one belief if something occurs at *t2* and quite another belief (or no belief at all) if something else occurs at *t2*. About this sort of specification of the intuitive idea, Pike says, "Here, I think, is as clear a statement as one could have of the intuition underpinning . . . the conviction that past belief-events (including divine belief-events) must be counted as full fledged consituents of the 'hard' past."[9]

Now Pike says:

> Fischer is focused on the fact that the foreknowledge argument postulates a divine *belief* stationed in the past relative to a human action. Fischer thus thinks that the argument is rooted in a 'hard' fact about the past and, accordingly, that the Ockhamist approach . . . cannot succeed. On the other hand, Adams is focused on the fact that in the context of the foreknowledge problem, divine beliefs are qualified in such a way that they *entail* the performance of future human actions. . . . What we have here, I think, are two fully respectable positions poised in head-on conflict.[10]

In light of the above reflections, Pike now believes that it is more promising to look for a *dissolution* of the "foreknowledge problem" than a solution. (He suggests that perhaps God should be construed as omniscient but not *essentially* omniscient, although he concedes that a defense of this sort of dissolution will be "a long, hard story.")[11]

But given the nuanced analysis I have sketched above, I can give a more penetrating account of the phenomena to which Pike adverts. And

I can seek a solution rather than a dissolution of the problem of foreknowledge. It can be *granted* that God's beliefs are soft facts insofar as
they satisfy the Entailment Criterion of Soft Facthood. But, depending
upon how these facts are interpreted, it is plausible to think they are
either hard-core or hard-type soft facts. In either case they have a feature
– a component or aspect – that is hard. Whereas Adams' Entailment
View gives the truth about the *facts'* status, the considerations about the
hardness of "belief-events" give the truth about the status of their
components or features. Thus, at a deeper level, the situation is *not* an
impasse: the two sets of considerations address *different issues* and are
entirely compatible. Further, they can be combined to yield the conclusion that God's beliefs, although soft, are nevertheless plausibly
construed as *fixed*. At a fundamental level, the argument for skepticism
about our possession of regulative control from God's existence is on a
par with the argument for such skepticism from causal determinism.

The different versions of the argument for skepticism about our
possession of regulative control can be construed as different ways of
combining some of the same ingredients. The Transfer Version and the
Conditional Version can be seen as first approximations to the Basic
Version. I contend that these versions are not equivalent; certain objections to the first two versions are not also objections to the Basic
Version.[12] Also, it emerges that certain ingredients (such as the Transfer
Principle and the Conditional Version of the Fixity of the Past) are not
necessary in order to generate the skeptical conclusion.

The Basic Version of the Argument for Incompatibilism is a simple,
natural, and powerful argument. Thus, given that we cannot be certain
that causal determinism is false and that God does not exist, our status
as persons (and thus morally responsible agents) is called into question.
In order to protect our firm sense of ourselves as persons, it is prudent
to seek an account of moral responsibility that does *not* require the
possession of regulative control.

This sort of account of moral responsibility is precisely what I have
begun to sketch. I begin (in chapter seven) by distinguishing between
two kinds of control: regulative control and guidance control. (Two
notions of freedom correspond to the two kinds of control: "freedom to
do otherwise" corresponds to regulative control, and "acting freely"
corresponds to guidance control.) Whereas we intuitively associate
moral responsibility with control, I suggest that the sort of control
relevant to moral responsibility for action is guidance control. This kind
of control does not involve alternative possibilities. A class of examples

– "Frankfurt-type examples" – renders plausible what we should in any case welcome, given the skeptic's argument: guidance control is the freedom-relevant condition necessary and sufficient for moral responsibility.

In chapter eight, I give a first approximation to an account of guidance control. On this approach, an agent exercises guidance control insofar as his action issues from a mechanism that is weakly responsive to reasons. Further, I argue that weak reasons-responsiveness is compatible with such conditions as God's existence and causal determination. Thus, on this account, guidance control – and hence moral responsibility – are compatible with God's existence and causal determinism.

There are strong reasons to accept this semicompatibilistic view. These reasons consist in part in a set of considerations designed to show that it is implausible that causal determinism *in itself and apart from considerations relevant to alternative possibilities* rules out moral responsibility. The general strategy of argument is as follows. Apart from the existence of alternative possibilities, there are various possible desiderata of moral responsibility: the capacity to originate or initiate actions, the capacity to be active, to be creative, and so forth. But there are compatibilist and incompatibilist accounts of each of these notions, and it is unclear – apart from considerations relevant to alternative possibilities – why one should prefer the incompatibilist accounts. Indeed, Frankfurt-type examples are not only useful in motivating the thesis that regulative control is not required for moral responsibility; they also are helpful in arguing that guidance control is *all* the freedom required for moral responsibility (and it is *not* also required that causal determinism fail to obtain).

Although the Frankfurt-type cases are admittedly quite fanciful, I wish to emphasize that they point us to something extraordinarily simple: moral responsibility for an action depends on the actual sequence that leads to the action, and not on the existence (and properties) of alternative scenarios. Moral responsibility for an action depends on the way it comes about – its history. This view about responsibility, conjoined with my view about freedom, constitutes a pair of extremely simple and natural views: our freedom is the freedom to extend the actual past, and moral responsibility for our actions depends on that actual past (and not other scenarios). But the simplicity of this picture does not diminish its potency. The apparently rather mundane view about responsibility can help us to respond to the very disturbing skeptical challenge to our moral responsibility.

2 Some future projects

I wish to point to two particularly salient places where the approach I have been sketching needs to be filled in. First, I have given a first approximation to an account of moral responsibility for actions. But of course we hold agents morally responsible for more than merely their actions. We hold agents morally responsible for omissions and consequences of their actions and omissions. Also, perhaps we hold individuals morally responsible for their character, or at least aspects of their character. (This may include momentary emotional responses as well as long-term dispositions.)

The sketch of an account of moral responsibility for actions developed above needs to be elaborated and also embedded within a more *general* theory which applies to character, omissions, and consequences (in addition to actions). Ideally, such a general theory will exhibit the relationship between moral responsibility for these various different kinds of thing; more specifically, I believe it will employ the association of moral responsibility with *control* to display the deep connections between moral responsibility for character, actions, omissions, and consequences.[13] Thus, the beginning of a theory adumbrated here gives a promising direction to future work on moral responsibility.

Second, moral responsibility is surely only one aspect of a complete understanding of agency. Another dimension of agency pertains to our view of ourselves as *practical reasoners*. That is, we deliberate about the future and form intentions and more general plans for the future. And in this deliberation and practical reasoning, we typically take ourselves to have genuine alternative possibilities. The view of the future as a garden of forking paths is a central feature of the natural, intuitive picture of ourselves as agents who deliberate about and plan for the future.

Above I sought to give an account of moral responsibility according to which moral responsibility does not require alternative possibilities. Further, I attempted to make this view attractive by connecting it to a fairly natural and intuitive view about control. Thus, I tried to give at least part of a *picture* of morally responsible agency to go along with the beginnings of an account. But it is not a straightforward task to give a picture of deliberation and practical reasoning according to which we may not have alternative possibilities. I believe this aspect of agency – the deliberative aspect – can be reconciled with the possibility that we lack regulative control, but this project must await future work. A more complete "actual-sequence" approach to agency will not only encompass the full *content* of moral responsibility (including character, actions, omissions, and consequences). It will also include *both* the forward-looking aspect of agency (the deliberative aspect) and the backward-looking aspect of agency (moral responsibility).

3 Some advantages

In this section I shall highlight some of the advantages of the general approach I have begun to develop. First, it insulates our most basic and important attitudes toward ourselves and others from assault in the light of the possible truth of causal determinism (or the possible existence of God). Our view of ourselves as persons and morally responsible agents could not be called into question by (say) a sophisticated new scientific theory (of the sort envisaged in chapter one). Note, further, that the account of guidance control (in terms of weak reasons-responsiveness) is consistent with *both* causal determinism and indeterminism. This account does not *require* the falsity of causal determinism; neither does it require its truth. Thus, our conception of ourselves and others as persons is maximally protected.

And this protection of our most fundamental beliefs about human beings does *not* require one to give up the strong intuitive beliefs in the fixity of the past, the fixity of the natural laws, or the Transfer Principle. I have argued that if one believes that we do indeed sometimes have regulative control even if (say) causal determinism obtains, then one *must* give up either the fixity of the past or the fixity of the natural laws. *But I need not give up either*, on *any* plausible interpretation.

Although Michael Slote and, evidently, Daniel Dennett are willing to deny the Transfer Principle, I pointed out that this is *not enough* to secure protection of our personhood. In any case, I do not know whether the Transfer Principle is valid. Thus, it is a good thing that I need not deny its validity; I can simply remain neutral about it, while conceding its intuitive plausibility. And I need not say (as van Inwagen does) that this intuitively attractive principle in itself forces one to think that we rarely possess regulative control and that our personhood depends on a certain sort of tracing principle (which is in any case highly implausible).

And whereas I am not *forced* by the Transfer Principle to say that we rarely possess regulative control, I can nevertheless accommodate the kernel of truth in the Frankfurt-type examples: moral responsibility does not require regulative control. Indeed, I can say that our personhood and moral responsibility does not depend upon the existence of *any* sort of alternative possibilities. In my opinion, this is the natural, straightforward lesson of the Frankfurt-type cases. These cases point us to what in any case should have been an appealing view: that moral responsibility depends upon what happens in the course of events leading to an action, and *not* on the existence of alternative scenarios.

Although I have presented only the barest skeleton of a theory, it is clearly preferable to other accounts of moral responsibility. In particular, it is preferable to theories which simply focus on selected arrangements of elements internal to an agent's motivational systems. Elsewhere I have called these approaches "mesh" theories of moral responsibility.[14]

A mesh theory isolates some *harmony* within the internal psychological economy of the agent and posits that this is the freedom-relevant condition sufficient for moral responsibility. Consider, as an example, Harry Frankfurt's "hierarchical" model of moral responsibility. On this model, a person is morally responsible for an action (roughly) insofar as there is a mesh between a higher-order preference and the first-order preference that actually moves him to action. In Frankfurt's terms, the selected mesh is between the agent's "second-order volition" (a preference about which first-order preference should issue in action) and his "will" (the first-order preference that moves the individual to action).[15]

Of course, the obvious problem with such an approach is that the selected mesh can be produced by intuitively responsibility-undermining processes. And the same general sort of problem afflicts even the refined versions of Frankfurt's theory. On the more refined approach, moral responsibility for an action is associated with conformity between "identification" and will.[16] According to Frankfurt, one way of identifying with a first-order desire would be to formulate an unopposed second-order volition to act on it, together with a judgment that no further reflection would cause one to change one's mind. Presumably, however, this second-order volition and the associated judgment could *also* be produced in a responsibility-undermining way – say, by direct electronic stimulation of the brain, subliminal advertising, and so forth.[17]

It seems to me that *any* hierarchical mesh theory is subject to similar worries. The problem is a general one: the theory posits a harmonious arrangement of internal elements of the psyche as sufficient for moral responsibility, and yet this arrangement can be induced by processes that are incompatible with moral responsibility. The general problem with such theories then is that they are purely *structural* (focusing on internal relationships rather than the relationship between the agent and the external world) and *ahistorical* (focusing on the current time-slice rather than the process which issues in the action).[18]

The "multiple-source" mesh theories are also purely structural and evidently ahistorical (at least on a natural interpretation). Rather than positing a hierarchy of preferences, these theories posit different *sources* of preferences. Gary Watson has sketched such a theory, according to which there are "valuational preferences" (which are endorsed in some sense by "Reason") and "motivational preferences" (the preferences which actually move one to action).[19] Employing these resources, one might say that an agent is morally responsible for an action insofar as there is a mesh between the valuational and motivational preference to perform the action.

Again, the problem is that such a theory is ahistorical (and purely structural). The mesh between elements of different preference systems may be induced by electronic stimulation, hypnosis, brainwashing, and so on. The moral I draw from these considerations is that an adequate theory of moral responsibility will attend to the *history* of an action, and not simply to its current time-slice characteristics. Further, it will require more than simply some internal arrangement of elements of an agent's mental economy: it will attend to the relationship between the agent and the external world.

I believe the first approximation to an account of moral responsibility for action which I have sketched is attractive in part because it begins to consider the history of an action and the relationship between the reasons the world presents and the agent. But clearly the account needs to be filled in and refined substantially. Indeed, as it is presented it would seem vulnerable to an objection similar to the one I have levelled at the mesh theories. More specifically, I have suggested that an agent is morally responsible for an action insofar as the action issues from a mechanism which is weakly reasons-responsive. But it may be that the actual operation of this sort of mechanism occurs as a result of a responsibility-undermining process – direct stimulation of the brain, hypnosis, and so forth. So whereas my approach suggests that we look to the past rather than solely the current time-slice, it may be that it does not look sufficiently *far* into the past. That is, it may only be "locally historical," whereas what is needed (arguably) is a more globally historical theory of moral responsibility. I concede this point, and I intend to develop a more globally historical theory in future work. Whereas the approach I have sketched here is incomplete, it does point us, however provisionally, in the right direction.

Some philosophers have claimed that the notion of free will is "incoherent."[20] I cannot here go into their arguments in detail. But I do wish to suggest that some of the appearance of incoherence may disappear when different notions of freedom (or control) are distinguished. "Free will" is surely an umbrella term which denotes a family of related but *distinct* notions. Arguably, these notions cannot all be combined into a unitary, coherent phenomenon. But perhaps the problem comes precisely from attempting to do this. The crucial distinctions having been made, it is not so evident that we will find incoherence.

In the first part of his book (which presents an "incoherentist" position), Richard Double argues for the plausibility of what he calls an "internalistic" view of free will and moral responsibility. To support this, he says:

> Imagine that on Earth and on its molecule-for-molecule replica, Twin Earth, there are two persons who are likewise qualitatively identical (including the states of their Cartesian minds, if they have them), call them 'Jim' and 'Twin Jim'. Imagine also that (i) all of Jim's and Twin Jim's choices are qualitatively identical, as are their entire psychological histories, and (ii) some of Jim's choices satisfy the libertarian notion of freedom (that is, there are other causally possible Earths where Jim's choices are different given the conditions that hold on Earth), whereas all of Twin Jim's choices are determined. Now, if the dignity objection to determinism is sound, it seems that Jim, but not Twin Jim, is sometimes worthy of dignity. But how can that be? They have done all the same things for the same reasons – they are qualitatively indistinguishable physically, intellectually, emotionally, and so on.[21]

Double goes on to argue that, although the internalistic view of such notions as free will and moral responsibility (favored by the compatibilist) has considerable plausibility, it ultimately cannot be *combined* with other more *externalistic* considerations (favored by the incompatibilist) to get plausible and coherent concepts.

But where Double finds incoherence, I find the need to make a distinction. The thought-experiment supports the idea that causal determinism in itself does not appear to threaten *acting freely* (and guidance control). Thus, it does not in itself appear to threaten personhood and responsibility (and hence dignity). Of course, if the relevant notions of freedom (and control) are distinguished, it is evident that it would not follow from the thought-experiment that causal determinism poses no threat to freedom to do otherwise (and regulative control). It may be that Jim is free to do otherwise, whereas Twin Jim is never free to do otherwise, and yet they are equivalent with regard to moral responsibility ascriptions. A more articulated view of "free will" – in which different notions of freedom are distinguished – can help to make at least some of the apparent tensions and inconsistencies disappear.

To highlight the importance of the more articulated view, I return, finally, to Peter Strawson's landmark essay, "Freedom and Resentment."[22] At the beginning of this book, I pointed out that Strawson identifies a set of attitudes – the "reactive attitudes" – and associated activities which are distinctive of personhood. It is important to emphasize, as Strawson does, that treating ourselves as persons and as morally responsible agents involves *more* than merely seeking to influence behavior by applying configurations of negative and positive reinforcement. It involves a set of attitudes such as indignation and resentment, love and gratitude – as well as associated practices of punishment and reward. Indeed, Strawson begins his argument by noting "the very great importance we attach to the attitudes and intentions towards us of other human beings, and the extent to which our personal feelings and reactions depend upon, or involve, our beliefs about these attitudes and intentions."[23]

Strawson is at pains to show that we cannot deracinate this set of attitudes without considerable distortion of our conceptions of ourselves as persons and morally responsible agents. To attempt to do so is, in my view, to go some distance toward opting for a version of what Herbert Morris calls "therapy world":

> In this world we are now to imagine when an individual harms another his conduct is to be regarded as a symptom of a cold. Actions diverging from some conception of the normal are viewed as manifestations of a disease in the way in which we might today regard the arm and leg movements of an epileptic during a seizure.[24]

But how can we protect our status as individuals subject to the reactive attitudes, given the possibility that the world is causally deterministic? I shall now reconstruct what I take to be Strawson's answer to this sort of question. If one seeks to *ground* the having of *these* attitudes (rather than engaging in mere conditioning or therapy), one would look for the satisfaction of some "theoretical requirement." And it is plausible that the theoretical requirement in question will be that the agents are "metaphysically free." But such freedom must be "libertarian" or "contra-causal" freedom, which is mysterious and unappealing. Thus, it is more attractive to say that *no* theoretical requirement needs to be satisfied in order for an agent to be morally responsible. Rather, the propensity of the community to hold the reactive attitudes toward the agent itself *constitutes* the agent's moral responsibility. Strawson emphasizes that it is a *mistake* to seek some theoretical grounding for moral responsibility and personhood.

But the approach I have sketched in this book offers an alternative path through the thicket articulated by Strawson. Perhaps Strawson is correct to suppose that the most salient possible theoretical grounding for the reactive attitudes is that agents must be construed as *free*. And Strawson is also correct in presupposing that if the freedom in question is freedom to do otherwise, then it must be contra-causal freedom. (This point is motivated by the kinds of considerations that flow from the Argument for Incompatibilism.) But if *acting freely* is distinguished from freedom to do otherwise, it emerges that there may well be a kind of freedom which is robust enough to ground the reactive attitudes but need not be understood as libertarian or contra-causal freedom. This sort of freedom, I have argued, is not essentially mysterious. Thus, it is not necessarily a mistake to seek a theoretical grounding for personhood and moral responsibility. It is only a mistake to seek it in the context of an insufficiently nuanced map of the contours of freedom.

Strawson's theory holds that being morally responsible is nothing other than being a recipient of the reactive attitudes and a participant in the associated practices. As Watson writes,

> In Strawson's view, there is no such independent notion of responsibility that explains the propriety of the reactive attitudes. The explanatory priority is the other way around: It is not that we hold people responsible because they *are* responsible; rather, the idea (*our* idea) that we are responsible is to be understood by the practice, which itself is not a matter of holding some propositions to be true, but of expressing our concerns and demands about our treatment of one another.[25]

The close connection Strawson draws between being responsible and actually being the recipient of the reactive attitudes raises questions about the ability of his theory to criticize and revise existing practices. After all, once the actual application of the reactive attitudes is taken to be constitutive of moral responsibility, one wonders what should be said about situations in which communities hold people responsible who intuitively are not. Does the mere fact that certain attitudes are taken toward an agent establish that he is an appropriate candidate for this treatment? Imagine, for example, a society in which severely retarded or mentally disturbed individuals are resented, blamed, and harshly punished for their failure to adhere to the norms of the community. (Perhaps the society attributes their failure to poor character or an evil nature.) Even though all the members of this community strongly feel moral outrage, resentment, and indignation, should the mere fact of their commitment to these feelings preclude further worry that the adoption of such attitudes toward these agents is not justified? Similarly, imagine a society in which some members of a particular class of citizens (perhaps those of a certain race or sex) are systematically treated only as objects to be used in the interest of social utility, and all reactive attitudes are withheld from the group. Would this fact alone suffice to warrant that these persons are not morally responsible?

The problem here is that Strawson's theory may reasonably be said to give an account of what it is for agents to be held responsible, but there seems to be a difference between being *held* responsible and actually *being* responsible. Surely it seems possible that one can be held responsible even though one in fact is not responsible, and conversely that one can be responsible even though one is not actually treated as a responsible agent. By understanding responsibility primarily in terms of our actual practices of adopting or not adopting certain attitudes toward agents, Strawson's theory runs the danger of blurring the difference between these two issues. In contrast, I avoid this danger by construing moral responsibility as *rational accessibility* to the reactive attitudes.

4 A new paradigm

The two parallel sorts of skepticism discussed in this book – in epistemology and action theory – are strikingly similar in many respects. They both can naturally be formulated by employing a structurally similar modal principle grounded in common sense. In action theory the argument leads to the conclusion that we do not have regulative control. In epistemology the argument leads to the conclusion that we do not have knowledge of the empirical world.

But I believe the *importance* of the skeptical results is radically different in the two cases. In epistemology the skeptical conclusion implies that I can't know that I am not a "brain in a vat" artificially stimulated to have my beliefs about the empirical world. (Further, we may suppose that these empirical beliefs are systematically false.) If I were to wake up one morning and find out that I am a brain in a vat who has substantially false beliefs about the world, I would feel horribly cheated. I place great value on not being deceived – and not having incorrect beliefs – about basic and important features of the world, such as my family and friends, my work, and so forth. Thus, although my "internal life" may have been

quite fine, I would still react to the discovery that I am (or had been) a
brain in a vat with great disappointment – and resentment.

In action theory the conclusion of the skeptical argument is that I do
not have regulative control (given the truth of causal determinism or
God's existence). But this *in itself* need not be worrisome. After all, I
suppose it is possible that I have *always* been subject to "counterfactual
interveners" of the sort envisaged in the Frankfurt-type cases. Indeed,
my whole life could be one long string of Frankfurt-type situations. If so,
it may be that I have never had regulative control. But this would not
disturb me in a deep way. Granted, I would have been incorrect about
a rather basic belief: that I frequently have genuinely open alternative
paths into the future. But apart from my irritation about the falsity of
this belief, I would not have the sort of profound disappointment
and resentment that would accompany the discovery that I am a brain
in a vat. Thus, the two skeptical conclusions would be greeted very
differently.

Galen Strawson usefully distinguishes two versions of the "brain in a
vat story."[26] According to the first version

> one's brain is a brain in a vat with all its afferent and efferent nerve
> pathways linked up to a supercomputer, and *all* one's mental goings-on
> are computer-produced; not only all the *inputs* to one's brain, all one's
> sensory experiences, and so on, but also all one's thoughts, decisions,
> intention-formations, and attempted initiations of physical actions.[27]

According to a second version

> the computer simply plays the experience-providing role we ordinarily
> suppose the external world to play in providing our actual experiences. It
> provides all the sensory inputs, it sends all the afferent neural impulses,
> and so on, but it does not control all the workings of the brain, which
> responds to the afferent signals in just the way that your or my brain does
> in fact . . .[28]

Galen Strawson argues that in the second version of the story the brain
in a vat can indeed be a free agent. Of course, the brain in a vat still is
systematically deceived, but Strawson claims it can nevertheless be free.

What is of more interest to me is what Strawson says about the first
version:

> . . . it could be argued that if determinism is true then even the person
> who exists in the first version of the story is at least as free as we are. It

could be argued that if determinism is true it cannot possibly make a deep difference to the question of freedom whether everything that happens in a brain is directly produced and controlled by an external computer, or whether it happens in the way it actually happens in our actual brains (assuming that we are indeed fully embodied physical things).[29]

But again it is crucial to distinguish *different* "questions of freedom." As to the question of freedom to do otherwise, I do not disagree with Strawson's assimilation of determinism to the computer's control. But there is also the quite different question of acting freely. Here the assimilation is not so unproblematic. Indeed, I have argued that there *is* a deep difference between the case of causal determination and control by an external computer. In the case of the computer, the agent (who is subject to the stimulation) lacks *both* regulative and guidance control, but in the case of mere causal determination the agent may have guidance control. That is, even under causal determinism the agent's action may issue from a weakly reasons-responsive mechanism, whereas it is plausible to think that the manipulated agent's action does *not* issue from such a sequence.

Here, again, it is useful to distinguish different notions of freedom (and control). Having made the appropriate distinction, it emerges that we would *not* necessarily be relevantly like the first brain in a vat, even if causal determinism were to obtain. Even if, under determinism, we lacked alternative possibilities, this need not in itself be alarming, and it need not imply that we do not act freely.

Return, briefly, to the haunting quotation with which I began this book. Recall that Michael Ross says, "Sometimes I feel that I am slipping away and I'm afraid of losing control. If you are in control you can handle anything but if you lose control you are nothing . . . ." It has been precisely the connection between control and personhood that I have been exploring in this book. I have argued that it is indeed true that if one lacks *one* sort of control (guidance control), one is "nothing" – one's personhood is eliminated. But I have insisted that one can indeed lack *another* sort of control (regulative control) without *eo ipso* losing one's personhood or in any sense "slipping away."

Borges describes a fictional labyrinth or garden of forking paths:

> . . . *The Garden of Forking Paths* is a picture, incomplete yet not false, of the universe such as Ts'ui Pen conceived it to be. Differing from Newton and Schopenhauer, your ancestor did not think of time as absolute and uniform. He believed in an infinite series of times, in a dizzily growing,

ever spreading network of diverging, converging and parallel times. This web of time – the strands of which approach one another, bifurcate, intersect or ignore each other through the centuries – embraces *every* possibility.[30]

On the view depicted by Borges, each path into the future is equally concrete and equally real.[31] In contrast, the traditional (and common-sense) view has it that there is just one concrete and real path into the future, together with many genuinely open alternative pathways. On the view I have suggested, there may (for all we know) be *only* one genuinely accessible path into the future – our actual path.

The future may – or may not – contain more than one genuinely open path; I do not know. It is quite natural to think of the future as open, but it may turn out that the various paths I picture in my mind are mere tantalizing chimeras. Employing a slightly different metaphor, there is just one line extending from the present into the past, and the future may indeed be symmetric – there may be just one line extending into the future. But even so – even if there is just one available path into the future – I may be held accountable for *how I walk down this path*.[32] I can be blamed for taking the path of cruelty, negligence, or cowardice. And I can be praised for walking with sensitivity, attentiveness, and courage. Even if I somehow discovered there is but one path into the future, I would still care deeply how I walk down this path. I would aspire to walk with grace and dignity. I would want to have a sense of humor. Most of all, I would want to do it my way.

Notes

1 Karen Clarke, "Life on Death Row," *Connecticut Magazine* 53 (1990), pp. 51–5; and 63–7.
2 Peter F. Strawson, "Freedom and Resentment," *Proceedings of the British Academy* 48 (1962), pp. 1–25. Strawson's essay, along with various discussions of it, are reprinted in John Martin Fischer and Mark Ravizza, eds, *Perspectives on Moral Responsibility* (Ithaca: Cornell University Press, 1993).
3 For a discussion of this account of moral responsibility, see the introductory essay in Fischer and Ravizza, eds, 1993; and chapter 9 below.
4 For arguments that suggest that we could (in principle) do away with the reactive attitudes without losing a way of life that is recognizably human (and in certain respects attractive), see Galen Stawson, *Freedom and Belief* (Oxford: Clarendon Press, 1986), esp. pp. 84–120; and Gary Watson, "Responsibility and the Limits of Evil," in F. Schoeman, ed., *Responsibility, Character, and the Emotions: New Essays on Moral Psychology* (Cambridge: Cambridge University Press, 1987), pp. 256–86. Both are reprinted in Fischer and Ravizza, eds, 1993.
5 I will be giving a particular interpretation to Borges' phrase. I shall use it to mean that various possible futures branch off the present. In his short story, "The Garden of Forking Paths," Borges describes a fictional labyrinth or garden which is alleged to represent the idea that all future times are equally real. (Jorge Luis Borges, *Fictions* [London: Calder and Boyars, 1974], pp. 81–92.)
6 Here I speak of following a path, as I wish to allow for actions and omissions. Also, I should say that the relevant notion of "can" is the "all-in" sense of can, rather than the "can" of general ability. One may of course possess a general ability without having the opportunity to exercise it in particular circumstances. Here, the relevant notion of "can" expresses the idea that one is genuinely free to perform an action in the particular circumstances: one has both the general ability and the opportunity to

exercise it. Regrettably, I do not know of an adequate reductive analysis of this notion, and thus I shall have to rely upon the intuitive idea of a genuinely open possibility. (For a useful discussion of the various notions of possibility relevant to freedom of the will, see Peter van Inwagen, *An Essay on Free Will* [Oxford: Clarendon Press, 1983], pp. 8–13.)

The terms, "free will" and "freedom of the will," are used in different ways. Sometimes they are used to highlight a power of the will more narrowly construed; that is, they are sometimes employed to refer to a power of choice or decision, rather than the power to translate these choices or decisions into actions. Further, the terms are often employed to denote different particular conceptions of freedom (which will be articulated and distinguished later in this book). In a given context, if one needs to be more precise, one can sharpen one's terminology. For my purposes it will be unproblematic to use "free will" in a fairly general and imprecise way, and to give rather more precise accounts of different specific notions of freedom (and control) as I go along.

7   Joel Feinberg, "The Interest in Liberty on the Scales," in *Rights, Justice, and the Bounds of Liberty: Essays in Social Philosophy* (Princeton: Princeton University Press, 1980), pp. 30–44, esp. 36–40.

8   Jeffrie Murphy asks: "Does not each person want to believe of himself, as a part of his pride in his human dignity, that he is *capable* of performing, freely and responsibly performing, evil acts that would quite properly earn for him the retributive hatred of others? And shouldn't he at least sometimes extend this compliment to others?" (See Jeffrie G. Murphy and Jean Hampton, *Forgiveness and Mercy* [New York: Cambridge University Press, 1988], p. 102.) Presumably, part of the intuition here is that our respect for others stems from seeing them as responsible agents who, even though they are able to do the bad, refrain from doing so and choose instead to act in accord with morality. Indeed, Gary Watson suggests that a Kantian conception of moral agency which emphasizes an ability to set ends requires this type of freedom: Gary Watson, "Free Action and Free Will," *Mind* 96 (1987a), pp. 145–72.

9   Richard Swinburne, *Responsibility and Atonement* (Oxford: Clarendon Press, 1989), p. 51.

10 Although I shall be presenting a particular version of the challenge, it is a member of a family of arguments that are similar in important ways. Some other members of the family (with regard to causal determinism) are presented in: Carl Ginet, "Might We Have No Choice?", in K. Lehrer, ed., *Freedom and Determinism* (New York: Random House, 1966), pp. 87–104; and "The Conditional Analysis of Freedom," in P. van Inwagen, ed., *Time and Cause: Essays Presented to Richard Taylor* (Dordrecht: D. Reidel, 1980), pp. 171–86; David Wiggins, "Towards a Reasonable Libertarianism," in T. Honderich, ed., *Essays on Freedom of Action* (Boston: Routledge and Kegan Paul, 1973), pp. 31–62; Peter van Inwagen, "The

Incompatibility of Free Will and Determinism," *Philosophical Studies* 27, (1975), pp. 185–99; and van Inwagen (1983), pp. 55–105; and John Martin Fischer, "Incompatibilism," *Philosophical Studies* 43 (1983b), pp. 127–37; and "Freedom and Miracles," *Noûs* 22 (1988b), pp. 235–52. There is a classic distillation of a member of the family of arguments (with regard to God's existence) in Nelson Pike, "Divine Omniscience and Voluntary Action," *Philosophical Review* 74 (1965), pp. 27–46; reprinted in Fischer, ed., 1989. For alternative versions, see John Martin Fischer, "Introduction: God and Freedom," in John Martin Fischer, ed., *God, Foreknowledge, and Freedom* (Stanford: Stanford University Press, 1989), pp. 1–56; and "Recent Work on God and Freedom," *American Philosophical Quarterly* 29 (1992b), pp. 91–109.

11 The notion of "power necessity" is introduced in Ginet (1980). For discussions of some of its elements, see Fischer (1983b) and (1988b); and Carl Ginet, "In Defense of Incompatibilism," *Philosophical Studies* 44 (1983), pp. 391–400.

12 Note that this is "one-way" causal determinism (going forward in time). There is also a two-way version, but the one-way version is all that is needed for the argument.

13 I am putting the point in a stark way. A less dramatic, but still worrisome, formulation is that we don't know whether we are persons in the way we ordinarily suppose ourselves to be. Perhaps the truth of determinism would entail, not that we are not persons in *any* recognizable sense, but that our personhood does not come to nearly as much as we ordinarily suppose. It would at least undermine the *extent* of our personhood. (I owe this point to correspondence with Tim O'Connor.)

14 Don Delillo, *White Noise* (New York: Penguin Books, 1986). For this quote I am indebted to the introduction to Scott M. Christensen and Dale R. Turner, eds, *Folk Psychology and the Philosophy of Mind* (Hillsdale, New Jersey: Lawrence Erlbaum Associates, 1993), p. xv.

15 Of course, this assumption can be called into question.

16 Ginet (1966), pp. 102–3. Peter van Inwagen presents a similar hypothetical example:

> (M) When any human being is born, the Martians implant in his brain a tiny device – one that is undetectable by any observational technique we have at our disposal, though it is not *in principle* undetectable – which contains a 'program' for that person's entire life: whenever that person must make a decision, the device *causes* him to decide one way or the other according to the requirements of a table of instructions that were incorporated into the structure of the device before that person was conceived.
>
> Now someone might object that (M) is not in fact consistent with our observations, since we can normally 'feel' our decisions 'flowing' naturally from our desires and our beliefs; but if (M) were true (so the objection runs), we should 'feel' ourselves being interfered with. But to meet this

objection we need only suppose that the Martian device causes us to have
desires and beliefs appropriate to the decisions it will cause us to make. (van
Inwagen, [1983], p. 109)

17 Daniel C. Dennett, *Elbow Room: The Varieties of Free Will Worth Wanting*
(Cambridge, Mass.: MIT Press, 1984), p. 72.
18 In his discussion of the relationship between causal determinism and
control, Dennett argues that there is a kind of control which is compatible
with causal determinism: "self-control." I do not wish to deny that there
is a kind of control arguably consistent with causal determinism. Rather,
I wish to emphasize that it is not as simple as Dennett leads one to believe
to dismiss the challenge from causal determinism to the idea that we have
control in the sense that involves alternative possibilities.
19 Dennett (1984), pp. 4 and 6–7.
20 Dennett (1984), p. 7.
21 Dennett (1984), pp. 8 and 10.
22 Dennett (1984), pp. 6–7.
23 Dennett (1984), p. 16.
24 Dennett (1984), p. 18.
25 Alan Abrahamson, "Lyle Menendez Admits Lies, Insists He Killed in
Fear," *Los Angeles Times*, September 22, 1993, p. A19.

Chapter 2 *The Transfer Principle: Its Plausibility*

1 I shall briefly discuss below an approach which denies that the form of
argument under discussion,

If: (a) (p)
and (b) $N_{S,t}$ (If p, then q),
then: (c) $N_{S,t}$ (q).

is always problematic. Although he does not wish to defend fatalism,
Bernard Berofsky does wish to defend certain instantiations of this argu-
ment-form: Bernard Berofsky, *Freedom from Necessity: The Metaphysical
Basis of Responsibility* (New York: Routledge and Kegan Paul, 1987).
2 Anthony Kenny, "Freedom, Spontaneity, and Indifference," in T.
Honderich, ed., 1973, pp. 87–104; *Will, Freedom, and Power* (Oxford:
Basil Blackwell, 1975), pp. 155–7; and *The God of the Philosophers*
(Oxford: Clarendon Press, 1979), pp. 55–8.
3 Until otherwise specified, I shall use "control" to mean that sort of control
which involves genuinely open alternative possibilities.
4 Kenny (1975), p. 156. I discuss the full range of Kenny's examples in John
Martin Fischer, "Scotism," *Mind* 94 (1985b), pp. 231–43.

5 Kenny (1975), p. 156.

6 Kenny says, "So far as I know the first philosopher to point out the fallaciousness of this pattern of argument [employing Transfer*] was Duns Scotus, discussing the problem of divine foreknowledge." (Kenny [1975], p. 156.)

7 It might be thought that, properly speaking, one cannot be said to be able to perform act-particulars, but only acts of certain types. If so, the Scotist's Transfer* I can be reformulated as follows:

> S can perform an X-type act.
>
> In the circumstances, performing an X-type act would be to perform some particular act which is (would be) truly describable as D.
>
> Therefore, S can perform some particular act which is (would be) truly describable as D.

8 This sort of example was suggested to me by Jonathan Kvanvig and Christopher Menzel.

9 Recall Transfer:

> $N_{S,t} (p)$
>
> $N_{S,t} (\text{If } p, \text{ then } q)$
>
> Therefore, $N_{S,t} (q)$

Understanding p to say that S does X and q to say that S does Y, an instantiation of the principle would imply:

> S does X and S cannot do otherwise
>
> If S does X, then S does Y, and S cannot prevent this fact from obtaining
>
> Therefore, S does Y, and S cannot do otherwise.

Note that the counterexample to Transfer* II (developed in the text) cannot be applied to Transfer. This is in part due to the fact that the connection (the identity claim) posited by Transfer* II is between the thing the agent *cannot* do and something else, whereas Transfer posits a connection between something the agent *does* and something else. Given this difference, it does not appear to be possible to generate counterexamples to Transfer along the lines of the counterexamples to Transfer* II (such as the example of dancing the jig).

10 Michael Slote, "Selective Necessity and the Free-Will Problem," *Journal of Philosophy* 79 (1982), pp. 5–24. My discussion of Slote relies heavily upon John Martin Fischer, "Power Necessity," *Philosophical Topics* 14 (1986c), pp. 77–91.

11 Slote (1982), p. 5.

12 Dennett (1984), pp. 148–9.
13 Michael Slote, "Review of Peter van Inwagen's *An Essay on Free Will*," *Journal of Philosophy* 82 (1985), p. 328.
14 Slote (1982), p. 10.
15 For this suggestion, see Anthony Brueckner, "Skepticism and Epistemic Closure," *Philosophical Topics* 13 (1985), pp. 89–118.
16 Fred Dretske, "Epistemic Operators," *Journal of Philosophy* 67 (1970), pp. 1007–23.
17 Jonathan Vogel, "Are There Counterexamples to the Closure Principle?" in M. D. Roth and G. Ross, eds, *Doubting: Contemporary Perspectives on Skepticism* (Norwell: Kluwer, 1990), pp. 13–27.
18 For a detailed and useful discussion, see Brueckner (1985); also, see Vogel (1990).
19 Two theorists who have adopted relevant alternatives approaches that do not in themselves entail that skeptical scenarios are relevant alternatives are Alvin Goldman and Robert Audi: Alvin Goldman, "Discrimination and Perceptual Knowledge," *Journal of Philosophy* 73 (1976), pp. 771–91; and Robert Audi, "Defeated Knowledge, Reliability, and Justification," in Peter A. French, Theodore E. Uehling, Jr., and Howard K. Wettstein, eds, *Midwest Studies in Philosophy* V (Minneapolis: University of Minnesota Press, 1980), pp. 75–95.
20 See especially the "tracking" approach developed by Robert Nozick in *Philosophical Explanations* (Cambridge, Mass.: Harvard University Press, 1981).
21 For this sort of argument, see Brueckner (1985).
22 Alternatively, on the basis of this sort of intuition, the skeptic may simply deny the relevant alternatives approach to analyzing knowledge.
23 Slote (1982), pp. 11–15.
24 I am not absolutely certain Slote is correct here. Indeed, Paul Hoffman reports (in conversation) that his intuition is that I do indeed have an obligation to bring champagne – an obligation to Smith. Here, the issues pertain to obligations arising from promises. There is a fascinating discussion of analogous issues concerning consent, including whether consent (and the moral reasons stemming from it) is governed by an analogue of the Transfer Principle, in Judith Jarvis Thomson, "Imposing Risks," in Mary Gibson, ed., *To Breathe Freely* (Totowa, N.J.: Rowman and Allanheld, 1983), pp. 124–40.
25 Slote (1982), p. 13.
26 Slote (1982), p. 16.
27 Slote (1982), p. 17.
28 Slote (1982), p. 19.
29 Slote (1982), p. 19.
30 It seems to me that the moral "ought" (in contrast to "obligation"), under any plausible analysis, is not selective. If this is correct, then we could solve

a surprisingly persistent puzzle. It is natural to suppose that an agent ought to do what he believes to be right. This seems to entail that if an agent believes that something is right, then he ought to do it. But then it would seem to follow that someone who believes it is right to torture, rape, and murder (and so forth) *ought* to behave in this manner. But whereas it is indeed appropriate to "let your conscience be your guide" (the "Jiminy Cricket Principle"), the conditional statement does not adequately capture this ideal. In contrast, it is better to understand this ideal as saying that it morally ought to be the case that one does what one believes right: i.e., it morally ought to be the case that (if one believes something is right, one does it). Here, the conditional is embedded within an operator which captures the force of the moral ought. Now if the analogue of Transfer holds for ought, we could infer from the facts that an agent ought to believe that X is right and that it ought to be the case that an agent does what he believes is right the conclusion that the agent ought to do X. But in the puzzling case described above, it is presumably true that the agent ought *not* believe that it is right to rape, torture, murder, and so forth. Thus, we need not conclude that the agent ought to behave in these horrible ways, and the puzzle is resolved. For an alternative solution to the puzzle, see Oliver A. Johnson, "'Is' and 'Ought': A Different Connection," *Journal of Value Inquiry* 25 (1991), pp. 147–60.

The case of the moral ought is also instructive because it seems to obey the analogue of Transfer although in fact it arguably fails to be agglomerative or closed under logical implication. Some philosophers have denied that the moral ought is agglomerative. For instance, Ruth Barcan Marcus argues from the existence of genuine moral dilemmas and the principle that "ought implies can" that ought is non-agglomerative: Ruth Barcan Marcus, "Moral Dilemmas and Consistency," *Journal of Philosophy* 77 (1980), pp. 121–36, esp. pp. 133–4. Further, it seems that "ought p" is clearly not closed under logical implication (at least where "ought" is construed as an operator on propositions or sentences). Suppose, for example, that it ought to be the case that I help the person being mugged. That I help a person being mugged implies that a person is being mugged. But it surely does *not* follow that it ought to be the case that a person is being mugged. Of course, if (as Slote seemed to suggest) such conditions as agglomerativity and closure under implication were considered *necessary* for the validity of the relevant modal principle, then there would be pressure to reject the principle for "ought." But I have urged us to resist this kind of pressure, since there is no reason to think the conditions are necessary for the relevant modal principle.

31 There is an interesting putative counterexample to Transfer in David Widerker, "On An Argument for Incompatibilism," *Analysis* 47 (1987), pp. 37–41. This example appears to require the assumption of indeterminism; thus, it might be possible for a proponent of the argument for

incompatibilism to employ a version of Transfer that is restricted to deterministic contexts. For useful discussions of this (and other) apparent counterexamples to Transfer, see Carl Ginet, *On Action* (Cambridge: Cambridge University Press, 1990), p. 104; and Timothy O'Connor, "On the Transfer of Necessity," *Noûs* 27 (1993), pp. 204–18. If the Transfer Principle is appropriately construed as a kind of modal slingshot, then O'Connor considers an example in which Transfer is a slingshot *back* in time.

Chapter 3 The Transfer Principle: Its Role

1   Also, as I pointed out in chapter two, there are interesting putative counterexamples to Transfer that I did not treat in any detail.
2   Peter van Inwagen, "When is the Will Free?" in James Tomberlin, ed., *Philosophical Perspectives IV: Action Theory and Philosophy of Mind* (Atascadero, Ca.: Ridgeview Publishing Co., 1990), pp. 399–422. My discussion here relies heavily upon John Martin Fischer and Mark Ravizza, "When the Will is Free," in James E. Tomberlin, ed., *Philosophical Perspectives VI: Ethics* (Atascadero, Ca.: Ridgeview Publishing Co., 1992), pp. 423–51.
3   Van Inwagen (1990), p. 405.
4   Van Inwagen (1990), p. 405.
5   Van Inwagen (1990), p. 406.
6   Van Inwagen (1990), p. 406.
7   Van Inwagen uses this term broadly to include both standard Buridan cases in which "one wants each of two or more incompatible things and it isn't clear which one he should (try to) get, and the things are interchangeable" (p. 415), and cases which he calls "vanilla/chocolate cases." These are situations in which "the alternatives are not really interchangeable (as two identical and equally accessible piles of hay) but in which the properties of the alternatives that constitute the whole difference between them are precisely the objects of the conflicting desires" (p. 415).
8   Paul Hoffman has reminded me (in conversation) that van Inwagen's view here is precisely the opposite of that of many philosophers, including Descartes. Descartes believes we are maximally free when it is clear what we ought to do, and minimally free when it is not.
9   Van Inwagen (1990), p. 409. I shall simply follow van Inwagen in suppressing the temporal index.
10 Van Inwagen (1990), p. 405.
11 Van Inwagen (1990), p. 406.
12 Van Inwagen (1990), p. 412.
13 Van Inwagen (1990), p. 415.
14 Van Inwagen (1990), p. 407. Although van Inwagen calls this conditional,

"(C)," it will be useful for my purposes to call it, "(C1)."

15 It is of course not clear that this conceptual claim is true. A Kantian theorist of action might argue that actions can be motivated by reason alone and that desire is not a necessary precursor of genuine action. Thus, I do not wish to suggest that the (Humean) conceptual claim is obviously true; rather, I only suggest that it has a certain plausibility. Further, it is clear that if the Humean conceptual point is indeed false, then van Inwagen's argument is even in worse shape: in this case even the weaker interpretation would issue in a falsehood and thus no support for (2).

16 In *De Fato* Alexander suggests that when one's freedom is called into question it can be reasonable to do something (that might on other occasions be seen as irrational) simply in order to demonstrate one's ability to do otherwise: "Next it is not by compulsion that the wise man does any one of the things which he chooses, but as himself having control also over not doing any one of them. For it might also sometimes seem reasonable to the wise man *not* to do on some occasion what would reasonably have been brought about by him – in order to show the freedom of his actions, if some prophet predicted to him that he would of necessity do this very thing." (Alexander of Aphrodisias, *De Fato ad Imperatores*, in R. W. Sharples, ed. and trans., *Alexander of Aphrodisias on Fate* (London: Duckworth, 1983), p. 79).

17 The notion of successfully acting on a desire is ambiguous between being moved by the desire and actually succeeding in getting the object of one's desire. I mean to adopt the latter interpretation.

18 Of course, a critic might object that this scenario presupposes that we always do have the ability to call such a worry to mind. However, nothing the restrictivist has said suggests that an incompatibilist must deny that we have *this* ability, and until such an argument is given it seems reasonable to adhere to the common wisdom that we are free to think as we will. And one cannot here point out that *if* causal determinism were true – together with incompatibilism – it would follow that we would not have the power in question. This is because the restrictivist's argument is supposed to show that Transfer implies that we are rarely free to do otherwise, even if determinism were false (i.e., that Transfer in itself is sufficient for the result).

19 Admittedly van Inwagen does want to construe his example in such a way that the incompatibilist must agree that the person is unable to call to mind any reason for not answering the phone. To ensure this condition, he writes: "But we might also imagine that there exists no basis either in my psyche or my environment (at the moment the telephone rings) for any of these things [i.e., things that would give me a reason not to answer the phone or that would keep me from answering it]. We may even, if you like, suppose that at the moment the telephone rings it is causally determined that no reason for not answering the phone will pop into my mind in the

next few seconds . . ." (p. 413). I will agree that if a person's motivational set is such that he has no reason to answer the phone or pro-attitude toward answering the phone, then he will not answer the phone. This is simply an instance of the sort of consideration which supports the alleged Humean conceptual point. However, what is at issue is whether a person with such a motivational set *can* answer the phone. As far as I can tell, the restrictivist has not presented any argument to show that a person with this motivational set lacks the power to call to mind the worry that he might be unable to refrain from answering the phone. If a person has this power, then (even if he actually has no reason to or desire to refrain from answering the phone) he does have the power to call to mind a reason not to answer the phone. Given that certain other conditions are satisfied, it is plausible to suppose that he has the power to refrain from answering the phone.

Of course, if it is supposed that causal determinism obtains, then the incompatibilist must say that the agent does not have the power to generate the relevant reasons and thus lacks the power to refrain from answering the phone. But in the context of an assessment of restrictivism, it is not fair to assume causal determinism; after all, the restrictivist's claim is that, even if causal determinism were false, we would rarely be free to do otherwise.

20   I am grateful to Sarah Buss, Nancy Schauber and Eleonore Stump for each calling this objection to my attention.
21   Van Inwagen (1990), p. 407.
22   Van Inwagen (1990), pp. 406–7.
23   Dennett (1984), pp. 133ff.
24   Harry Frankfurt uses the term "unthinkable" to describe actions which an agent cannot bring himself to will to perform. According to Frankfurt, some acts will be unthinkable for an agent because of his moral inhibitions, but "on the other hand, the considerations on account of which something is unthinkable may be entirely self-regarding and without any moral significance." See Harry G. Frankfurt, "Rationality and the Unthinkable," in *The Importance of What We Care About: Philosophical Essays* (New York: Cambridge University Press, 1988), p. 182. Another reason why an agent may be unable to will something is given by Lehrer's examples of agents who cannot bring themselves to choose to do something because they suffer from a pathological aversion. See Keith Lehrer, "Cans Without Ifs," *Analysis* 29 (1968), pp. 29–32; and " 'Can' in Theory and Practice: A Possible Worlds Analysis," in Myles Brand and Douglas Walton, eds, *Action Theory: Proceedings of the Winnipeg Conference on Human Action* (Dordrecht: D. Reidel, 1976), pp. 241–70.
25   Van Inwagen (1990), p. 405.
26   St Augustine, *Confessions*, trans. by R. S. Pine-Coffin (Baltimore: Penguin Books, 400/1961), p. 49.

27 Augustine (400/1961), p. 47.

28 Augustine (400/1961), p. 52.

29 Augustine (400/1961), pp. 50–1.

30 Feodor Dostoevsky, *Crime and Punishment*, trans. by Jessie Coulson. (Oxford: Oxford University Press, 1866/1980), p. 7.

31 Dostoevsky (1866/1980), p. 104.

32 Dostoevsky (1866/1980), pp. 400–2.

33 It is a bit more accurate to say that van Inwagen contends that Transfer, in conjunction with very weak and plausible assumptions (and apart from the assumption of causal determinism or God's existence), entails that we rarely have the sort of control that involves alternative possibilities. My argument then shows that van Inwagen's assumptions are neither weak nor plausible.

34 Susan Wolf, "Asymmetrical Freedom," *Journal of Philosophy* 77 (1980), pp. 152–3; this essay is reprinted in John Martin Fischer, ed., *Moral Responsibility* (Ithaca: Cornell University Press, 1986) [emphasis added].

35 Dennett (1984), p. 133.

36 It is interesting to note that Wolf, like van Inwagen, begins with an example – that of allowing one's children to be incinerated – which is an action most people would find both indefensible and unthinkable, and then moves to an example – that of punching one's neighbor – which most people would just find indefensible. Since I want to focus on the question of whether the mere ability to do indefensible things does indeed make one crazy, I will concentrate on her second example.

37 For example, Descartes in his Fourth Meditation claims: "It is free will alone or liberty of choice which I find to be so great in me that I can conceive no other idea to be more great; it is indeed the case that it is for the most part this will that causes me to know that in some manner I bear the image and similitude of God." For contemporary defenses of the view that the idea of an unfree will is inconceivable see Brian O'Shaugnessy, *The Will: A Dual Aspect Theory* (Cambridge: Cambridge University Press, 1980); and Rogers Albritton, "Freedom of the Will and Freedom of Action," Presidential Address, *Proceedings and Addresses of the American Philosophical Association* 59 (1985), pp. 239–51. As Watson points out, the truth behind such claims seems to be that "our concept of the will is such that there is no such thing as failing to will; willing is necessarily successful"; from this point, however, "it does not follow that one cannot be prevented from willing, not by having obstacles placed in the path, but by having one's will pushed as it were toward one path or another." (Watson [1987a], p. 163.) Also, there is an excellent discussion of these issues in Paul Hoffman, "Freedom and Strength of Will: Descartes and Albritton," unpublished manuscript, University of California, Riverside.

38 Watson raises this worry in Watson (1987a), p. 164.

39 I have suggested that examples like those of Augustine challenge even this intuition: for if we take Augustine at his word, he seems to be a case of someone who did act against his best interests, in a manner he believed to be indefensible, and still was not crazy.

40 Wolf puts this latter point well when she asks: "Why would one want the ability to pass up the apple when to do so would merely be unpleasant or arbitrary? Why would one want the ability to stay planted on the sand when to do so would be cowardly and callous? . . . To want autonomy is to want not only the ability to act rationally, but also the ability to act *ir*rationally – but this latter is a very strange ability to want, if it is an ability at all." Susan Wolf, *Freedom Within Reason* (New York: Oxford University Press, 1990), pp. 55, 56.

41 I am reminded of the following story. A family is at a restaurant. Well after they have had enough food, the waiter continues to bring them more and more. Finally, quite exasperated, the parents plead to the waiter to stop bringing food. At this point the waiter responds, "Oh, you must have misunderstood. This is not an "all-you-*wish*-to-eat" restaurant, it is an "all-you-*can*-eat" restaurant.

42 For this sort of argument, see John Martin Fischer, "Ockhamism," *Philosophical Review* 94 (1985a), pp. 81–100. More specifically, here is the Assumption of Counterfactual Independence (CI):

> (CI) If God exists, then no human agent can act in such a way that God would not exist.

This kind of assumption appears to be defensible in light of God's perfection or supremacy, but perhaps its defense is not a straightforward matter. (See Nelson Pike, "Fischer on Freedom and Foreknowledge," *Philosophical Review* 93 (1984), pp. 599–614.)

43 I do not claim that the Conditional Version of the Argument for Incompatibilism is "formally valid"; that is, I do not claim it instantiates some structure which is valid simply in virtue of its form. Rather, I believe that it is reasonable to accept its conclusion, given both its formal structure and the *content* of its premises.

44 Van Inwagen (1983), p. 57.

45 Van Inwagen (1983), p. 57.

46 Slote (1982), p. 9.

47 *Pace* van Inwagen and Slote, I want to argue that a "finer-grained" approach to the various arguments for incompatibilism is needed which recognizes that not all formulations make use of the same inference rules or involve the incompatibilist in the same commitments.

48 Berofsky (1987).

49 Indeed, recognizing that the incompatibilist's argument can be formulated without either Transfer or Berofsky's principle calls into question

much of the motivation for developing such a system of contingent necessity.

50 This should surely put to rest the accusation – repeated almost like a mantra – that incompatibilism rests on some kind of modal fallacy.

51 It is interesting to note that the structurally parallel principle – the Principle of Closure of Knowledge Under Known Implication – is *also* not necessary (even in its revised form) to generate the parallel skeptical conclusion (that we do not know ordinary things about the world external to us). There is a notion of justification that does not require actual belief. On this notion of justification, one can have justification for believing p without actually believing it: here one is envisaged as having an *entitlement* or *right* to believe p even if one does not actually have this belief. For a development of this notion, see Robert Audi, "Foundationalism, Epistemic Dependence, and Defeasibility," *Synthese* 55 [1983], pp. 119–38.

Employing this notion of justification, one could reason as follows. If an agent has justification for believing that p, and p entails q, then the agent has justification for believing that q. That is, for this notion of justification, it is plausible that there is closure under implication and not merely closure under known implication. Thus, the failure of integration discussed in the text does not even arise.

One could then run the skeptical argument employing this alternative principle (or principle of closure which employs an alternative notion of justification). Thus, it seems that the Principle of Closure of Knowledge Under Known Implication is not necessary in order to generate the skeptical result. Ironically, in this respect the two principles – Transfer and the Closure of Knowledge Under Known Implication – are indeed similar. (I am indebted here to conversations with Anthony Brueckner.)

Chapter 4 The Laws and the Past: The Conditional Version of the Argument

1 Van Inwagen (1975), p. 193.

2 Van Inwagen (1983), p. 62.

3 Peter van Inwagen, "Laws and Counterfactuals," *Noûs* 13 (1979), p. 446.

4 Ginet (1983), p. 398.

5 For this sort of strategy for denying (FL), see David Lewis, "Are We Free to Break the Laws?" *Theoria* 47 (1981a), pp. 113–21. Also, see Fischer (1983b) and (1988b).

6 David Lewis, "Counterfactual Dependence and Time's Arrow," *Noûs* 13 (1979a), p. 473.

7 Lewis (1979a), p. 465.

8 Kit Fine, "Critical Notice: *Counterfactuals*," *Mind* 84 (1975), p. 452.

9 Lewis (1979a), pp. 467ff.

10 Lewis (1979a), p. 468.

11 Lewis (1979a), pp. 470–1.

12 Lewis (1979a), p. 471.
13 Frank Jackson, "A Causal Theory of Counterfactuals," *Australasian Journal of Philosophy* 55 (1977), pp. 3–21.
14 Of course, the LAWS of a world must hold true at all times in that world; but the laws of one world may obtain at some but not all times in *another* world. (They are thus not laws in that other world.)
15 That is, if one construed the sentence, "You can build a spaceship that would travel faster than the speed of light," as involving an unanalyzable "can-operator" (suitably agent-indexed) prefixed to the sentence, "build a spaceship that would travel faster than the speed of light," it would be hard to understand why this sentence would be false in virtue of the fact that the prefixed statement (the statement contained within the scope of the operator) describes a violation of a law *after* the time of the relevant action, whereas a prefixed statement that describes a violation of a law *before* the time of the relevant action would not *eo ipso* be false. How could one explain this difference?
16 For this sort of view, see Jonathan Bennett, "Counterfactuals and Temporal Direction," *Philosophical Review* 93 (1984), pp. 57–91.
17 Ginet (1990), pp. 113–14.
18 Some philosophers have cast doubt upon the distinction between a causal and non-causal interpretation of "bringing about the past." For this sort of argument, see William Hasker, "Foreknowledge and Necessity," *Faith and Philosophy* 2 (1985), pp. 121–57; and *God, Time, and Knowledge* (Ithaca: Cornell University Press, 1989), esp. pp. 96–115. In Hasker's words, ". . . the distinction between counterfactual power over the past and power to bring about the past collapses: it is a distinction that fails to distinguish" (Hasker [1989], p. 111). But I have argued at length in the introductory essay to Fischer, ed., 1989, pp. 18–23, that Hasker's arguments do not imply that there is no difference between (FPnc) and (FPc).
    The following is a reason why one might accept Hasker's No Difference claim. Such locutions as "bringing it about that *p*," and "causing it to be the case that *p*" are "causal" locutions. Both imply, in my view, that the agent causes *something*. Seeing this, one might fail to notice that there are (at least) two interestingly different interpretations of the locutions, depending on exactly *what* is supposed to be caused. If *p* is the proposition that some event *e* occurs, then on the causal interpretation, one is required to cause *e*. In contrast, on the non-causal interpretation, one is required to cause *something else*, which is such that were it to occur, *e* would have occurred. Hiding behind a causal locution, then, are two different ideas. (For more discussion, see Fischer [1988b], esp. footnote 5.)
19 John Turk Saunders, "The Temptations of 'Powerlessness'," *American Philosophical Quarterly* 5 (1968), pp. 100–8.
20 Saunders (1968).
21 Saunders (1968), p. 105.

22 John Martin Fischer, "Power Over the Past," *Pacific Philosophical Quarterly* 65 (1984), pp. 335–50.

23 In personal correspondence, Anthony Kenny has embraced this claim.

24 For a more detailed discussion, see Fischer (1984).

25 I say "simply" presupposes the falsity of skepticism for the following reason. If one has very strong independent warrant for the rejection of skepticism, and Closure is the most plausible candidate for rejection, then perhaps it is appropriate to reject it.

26 I describe a classic Dialectical Stalemate in the context of the discussions of whether – and how – death can be a bad thing for the individual who dies, in the introduction to John Martin Fischer, ed., *The Metaphysics of Death* (Stanford: Stanford University Press, 1993), esp. pp. 14–27.

27 For a recent attempt to substantially restructure some of the traditional problems relevant to free will, see Wolf (1990). There is a discussion of Wolf's attempt in John Martin Fischer and Mark Ravizza, "Responsibility, Freedom, and Reason," *Ethics* 102 (1992a), pp. 368–89. One might usefully distinguish between relatively "global" efforts at reconstruction and relatively "local" efforts. In contrast to Wolf's effort, the suggestion I develop in the following chapter is a relatively local effort toward restructuring.

28 Nozick (1981), p. 7.

Chapter 5 The Basic Version and Newcomb's Problem

1 For the sake of simplicity, I shall speak in terms of the "actual past"; strictly speaking, the point is that an agent can in world w do X only if his doing X can be an extension of the past in w holding the natural laws of w fixed.

2 Carl Ginet independently has developed the same basic idea. He puts it very nicely as follows:

> If I have it open to me now to make the world contain a certain event after now, then I have it open to me now to make the world contain everything that has happened before now plus that event after now. We might call this the principle that *freedom is freedom to add to the given past* . . . (Ginet [1990], pp. 102–3)

3 The assumption that God's beliefs are genuine features of the past will be explored at length in the following chapter.

4 For a possible-worlds analysis of freedom, see Lehrer (1976). For discussions of Lehrer's analysis, see: Terence Horgan, "Lehrer on 'Could'-Statements," *Philosophical Studies* 32 (1977), pp. 403–11; Robert Audi, "Avoidability and Possible Worlds," *Philosophical Studies* 33 (1978), pp.

413–21; and John Martin Fischer, "Lehrer's New Move: 'Can' in Theory and Practice," *Theoria* 45 (1979), pp. 49–62.

5 Robert Stalnaker, "A Theory of Conditionals," in N. Rescher, ed., *Studies in Logical Theory* (Oxford: Basil Blackwell, 1968), pp. 98–112; David Lewis, *Counterfactuals* (Cambridge, Mass.: Harvard University Press, 1973); and John Pollock, *Subjunctive Reasoning* (Dordrecht: D. Reidel, 1976).

6 This is actually a slightly different version of the semantics for conditionals I attributed to David Lewis in the previous chapter. I find this version a bit simpler and more natural to work with, and nothing in my discussion depends on adopting this version rather than the previous one.

7 I have not *argued* that in analyzing the "can" of freedom (as opposed to the subjunctive conditional) one looks at worlds that are merely suitably related to the actual world but not necessarily in the set of most similar possible worlds. I am not sure how exactly to argue for this; it *does* seem to me to emerge from a consideration of examples and the possible-worlds framework for analyzing the examples that the worlds relevant to the can-claim need not be among the most similar possible worlds. I ask the reader to take it as a plausible supposition, and in part to test it by its fruitfulness in illuminating the cases to which I apply it.

8 James Joyce, *Ulysses* (New York: Random House, 1961), p. 34.

9 For a nice development of this sort of picture of the possible-worlds apparatus, see Robert Stalnaker, *Inquiry* (Cambridge, Mass.: MIT Press, 1984).

10 Robert Nozick, "Newcomb's Problem and Two Principles of Choice," in N. Rescher, ed., *Essays in Honor of Carl G. Hempel* (Dordrecht: D. Reidel, 1969), pp. 114–46. For a useful collection of pieces on Newcomb's Problem, see Richmond Campbell and Lanning Sowden, eds, *Paradoxes of Rationality and Cooperation: Prisoner's Dilemma and Newcomb's Problem* (Vancouver: University of British Columbia Press, 1985).

11 Lewis (1979a), "Prisoner's Dilemma is a Newcomb Problem," *Philosophy and Public Affairs* 8 (1979b), pp. 235–40; and "Why Ain'cha Rich?" *Noûs* 15 (1981b), pp. 377–80.

12 Terence Horgan, "Counterfactuals and Newcomb's Problem," *Journal of Philosophy* 78 (1981), pp. 331–56.

13 Terence Horgan, "Newcomb's Problem: A Stalemate," in Campbell and Sowden, eds, 1985, pp. 223–34, esp. 234.

14 For this sort of approach, see, e.g., Robert Stalnaker, "A Letter to David Lewis," in W. L. Harper, R. Stalnaker, and G. Pearce, eds., *Ifs* (Dordrecht: D. Reidel, 1981 [1972]), pp. 151–2; Isaac Levi, "Newcomb's Many Problems," *Theory and Decision* 6 (1975), pp. 161–75; and Alan Gibbard and W. L. Harper, "Counterfactuals and Two Kinds of Expected Utility," in C. A. Hooker, J. J. Leach, and E. F. McClennen, eds, *Foundations and Applications of Decision Theory* (Dordrecht: D. Reidel,

1978), pp. 125–62.

15 Alan Gibbard, "Decision Matrices and Instrumental Expected Utility," unpublished paper presented to a conference at the University of Pittsburgh, as quoted in Horgan (1981), p. 353.

16 Gregory S. Kavka, "What is Newcomb's Problem About?" *American Philosophical Quarterly* 17 (1980), p. 279.

17 In his paper, "'Could', Possible Worlds, and Moral Responsibility," *Southern Journal of Philosophy* 17 (1979), pp. 345–58, Horgan in effect rejects the fixed-past requirement on possible worlds relevant to can-claims.

18 Alvin Plantinga has presented a set of examples that are structurally similar to Newcomb's Problem. Consider the example of Paul and the ant colony:

> Let us suppose that a colony of carpenter ants moved into Paul's yard last Saturday. Since this colony has not yet had a chance to get properly established, its new home is still a bit fragile. In particular, if the ants were to remain and Paul were to mow his lawn this afternoon, the colony would be destroyed. Although nothing remarkable about these ants is visible to the naked eye, God, for reasons of his own, intends that it be preserved. Now as a matter of fact, Paul will not mow his lawn this afternoon. God, who is essentially omniscient, knew in advance, of course, that Paul will not mow his lawn this afternoon; but if he had foreknown instead that Paul *would* mow this afternoon, then he would have prevented the ants from moving in. The facts of the matter, therefore, are these: if Paul were to mow his lawn this afternoon, then God would have prevented the ants from moving in. So if Paul were to mow his lawn this afternoon, then the ants would not have moved in last Saturday. But it is within Paul's power to mow this afternoon. There is therefore an action he can perform such that if he were to perform it, then the proposition . . . "That colony of carpenter ants moved into Paul's yard last Saturday," would have been false. (Alvin Plantinga, "On Ockham's Way Out," *Faith and Philosophy* 3 (1986), p. 254; this piece is reprinted in Fischer, ed., 1989.)

Of course, within the context of a discussion of whether God's foreknowledge is compatible with human freedom, it cannot legitimately be assumed that God has foreknowledge of Paul's not mowing this afternoon and nevertheless that Paul has it in his power to mow this afternoon. Unfortunately, Edward Wierenga appears to make precisely this assumption: Edward Wierenga, *The Nature of God: An Inquiry into Divine Attributes* (Ithaca: Cornell University Press, 1989). Wierenga says:

> . . . is there really some action *A* which someone now or later could do such that if *A* were done this proposition [*Socrates drank hemlock*] would have been false? Incredible as it may seem, for all anyone knows, there is such an action. Perhaps this point will be clear if we appeal to an example Alvin

Plantinga employs in this connection [the example of Paul and the ant colony] . . . (p. 99)

Plantinga's own presentation of this example is part of his attempt to analyze Ockham's notion of "accidental necessity" in terms of the powers of human agents. Clearly, however, if accidental necessity is itself analyzed in terms of human powers, and it is further assumed that a human can have it in his power to do other than what God foreknew he would do, then accidental necessity (so analyzed) cannot be employed to help to solve the foreknowledge problem. (William Hasker makes this point in Hasker [1989].)

19 Isaac Levi has argued that the two-box solution for inerrancy conjoined with the one-box solution for infallibility is incoherent: Levi (1975). He argues that this position presupposes that dominance reasoning should be appropriate whenever there is causal independence (of my choice and the predictor's prediction). Since the assumption of causal independence remains even when the predictor is infallible, Levi suggests that consistency demands that dominance reasoning applies here as well: there is no difference as regards causal independence between the case of inerrancy and infallibility. My analysis provides a response to Levi; it shows how the asymmetry of inerrancy and infallibility I have defended can be maintained without inconsistency. Interestingly, Levi also holds that there is an asymmetry between inerrancy and infallibility, but of a different sort. He argues for the one-box solution for infallibility, but for a variable solution for inerrancy, depending on the probabilities.

20 Of course, I do not in general wish to defend Calvinism, but only this particular feature of it. With respect to this feature, one is reminded of what Mark Twain said about Wagner's music: "It's not as bad as it sounds."

21 William Lane Craig, "'Nice Soft Facts': Fischer on Foreknowledge," *Religious Studies* 25 (1989), 235–46. For similar arguments, see also his "Divine Foreknowledge and Newcomb's Paradox," *Philosophia* 17 (1987a), pp. 331–50; *The Only Wise God* (Grand Rapids, Michigan: Baker Book House, 1987b); and *Divine Foreknowledge and Human Freedom: The Coherence of Theism: Omniscience* (Leiden: E. J. Brill, 1991).

22 Wolf (1990), p. 107.

23 Wolf (1990), p. 108.

24 Wolf (1990), p. 110.

25 Wolf (1990), pp. 110–11.

26 Wolf (1990), p. 151.

27 Wolf (1990), pp. 151–2.

28 In chapter three I argued that the Conditional Version of the Argument for Incompatibilism is highly plausible, even if not formally valid. The lack of formal validity produces the dialectical space to claim that the Transfer

Principle really is required for the Argument for Incompatibilism: in his paper, "When the Will is Not Free" (forthcoming, *Philosophical Studies*), Peter van Inwagen occupies precisely this space. But even if one finds reason to reject the Conditional Version, I hardly think this shows that Transfer is necessary for the Argument for Incompatibilism. Indeed, the Basic Version does not explicitly use Transfer, and it seems to me impossible to say that the Basic Version of the argument somehow implicitly employs Transfer. Similarly, Carl Ginet rejects Transfer but embraces something quite similar to the Basic Version of the Argument for Incompatibilism: Ginet (1990).

Chapter 6 The Facts

1 William P. Alston, "Divine Foreknowledge and Alternative Conceptions of Human Freedom," *International Journal for Philosophy of Religion*, 18 (1985), footnote 3, p. 31; reprinted in Fischer, ed., 1989.
2 Nelson Pike introduces the distinction in this fashion in, "Of God and Freedom: A Rejoinder," *Philosophical Review* 75 (1966), p. 370.
3 I am here simplifying and assuming that time cannot stop. David Widerker has pointed out that this is a contentious assumption. (See David Widerker, "Two Fallacious Objections to Adams' Hard/Soft Fact Distinction," *Philosophical Studies* 57 (1989a), pp. 103–7; for an extended discussion, see John Martin Fischer, "Snapshot Ockhamism," in James E. Tomberlin, ed., *Philosophical Perspectives V: Philosophy of Religion* (Atascadero, Ca.: Ridgeview Publishing Co., 1991a), pp. 355–71.) Given the contingency of time's continuation, the fact that the alarm clock rings at seven does not entail any fact about any later times, since it does not entail that time continue after seven. I do not wish here to assume that time's continuation is a contingent matter. But, if one makes that assumption, one can employ a different sort of Entailment View of Soft Facthood: one can say that a soft fact about a given time entails that time continue after that time. Note that the analysis I develop in this chapter will also apply, given this alternative version of the Entailment View.
4 See, for example, Joshua Hoffman and Gary Rosenkrantz, "Hard and Soft Facts," *Philosophical Review* 93 (1984), pp. 433–42; reprinted in Fischer, ed., 1989. Also see Marilyn McCord Adams, "Is the Existence of God a 'Hard' Fact?" *Philosophical Review* 76 (1967), pp. 492–503; reprinted in Fischer, ed., 1989; David Widerker (1989a); and John Martin Fischer, "Freedom and Foreknowledge," *Philosophical Review* 92 (1983a), pp. 67–79; reprinted in Fischer, ed., 1989; and Fischer (1991a).
5 Plantinga (1986).
6 Plantinga (1986), p. 248.
7 See William of Ockham, *Predestination, God's Foreknowledge and Future*

Contingents, trans. by Marilyn McCord Adams and Norman Kretzmann (New York: Appleton-Century-Crofts, 1969), pp. 46–7. For a nice treatment of Ockham's view, and its historical precedents, see Alvin Plantinga (1986). In calling the view in the text, "Ockhamism," my goal is not exegetical; rather, my main purpose is to stake out a certain position.

8 The reasoning here is parallel to a form of argumentation developed by William Hasker (Hasker [1989], esp. pp. 75–95). Hasker reasons as follows. Clearly, the fact that Yahweh believes at *t1* that *S* will do *X* at *t2* is a hard fact about *t1* and thus fixed at *t2*. Further, Hasker assumes that the fact, "If Yahweh exists, Yahweh is God," is metaphysically necessary and thus fixed at *t2*. Now because it is reasonable to think that fixity is closed under entailment and the two facts entail the fact that God believes at *t1* that *S* will do *X* at *t2*, it follows that this latter fact is fixed at *t2*. The basic ideas that drive Hasker's argument and mine are the same. We differ insofar as I do not (in the text here) assume that it is metaphysically necessary that the individual who actually is God be God, and I need not assume that fixity is closed under entailment.

9 Similarly, if "God" is a title term and "Yahweh" names an individual who actually occupies the role of God and possesses the divine attributes essentially, then one cannot divide the fact about God's belief into parts, one of which is a kernel element (relative to *S* at *t2*) which is a hard fact about *t1*. On this view, "Yahweh believes at *t1* that *S* does *X* at *t2*," is a soft fact about *t1*; since omniscience is an essential feature of Yahweh, the fact entails that *S* does *X* at *t2*.

10 For a stab, see John Martin Fischer, "Hard-Type Soft Facts," *Philosophical Review* 95 (1986a), pp. 591–601. There are critical discussions in: David Widerker, "Two Forms of Fatalism," in Fischer, ed., 1989, pp. 97–110; and "Troubles With Ockhamism," *Journal of Philosophy* 87 (1990), pp. 462–80. For a response to Widerker, including an attempt at an improved specification of the distinction, see John Martin Fischer, "Hard Properties," *Faith and Philosophy* 10 (1993a), pp. 161–9. For important thoughts about the more general issue of distinguishing genuine from nongenuine properties, see David Lewis, "New Work for a Theory of Universals," *Australasian Journal of Philosophy* 61 (1983), pp. 343–77.

11 J. A. Fodor, "Methodological Solipsism Considered as a Research Strategy in Cognitive Psychology," *Behavioral and Brain Sciences* 3 (1980), pp. 63–109.

12 Fodor (1980), p. 64.

13 Eddy Zemach and David Widerker, "Facts, Freedom, and Foreknowledge," *Religious Studies* 23 (1988), pp. 19–28; reprinted in Fischer, ed., 1989, esp. p. 119.

14 Hilary Putnam, "The Meaning of 'Meaning,'" reprinted in Hilary Putnam, *Mind, Language, and Reality* (Cambridge: Cambridge University Press, 1975), pp. 215–71, esp. pp. 223–7. See also Tyler Burge, "Indi-

vidualism and the Mental," in French, Uehling, and Wettstein, eds, *Midwest Studies in Philosophy* IV (1979), pp. 73–121.

15 Zemach and Widerker (1988), p. 118.

16 Fodor (1980); and "Cognitive Science and the Twin-Earth Problem," *Notre Dame Journal of Formal Logic* 23 (1982), pp. 98–118; Burge (1979); and "Two Thought Experiments Reviewed," *Notre Dame Journal of Formal Logic* 23 (1982), pp. 284–93.

17 For this sort of argument, see Fodor (1980). In particular, Fodor says:

> We are on the verge of a bland and ecumenical conclusion: that there is room both for a computational psychology – viewed as a theory of formal processes defined over mental representations – *and* a naturalistic psychology, viewed as a theory of the (presumably causal) relations between representations and the world which fix the semantic interpretations of the former. . . . The first move . . . is to give reasons for believing that at least *some* part of psychology should honor the formality condition. Here too the argument proceeds in two steps. I'll argue first that it is typically under an *opaque* construal that attributions of propositional attitudes to organisms enter into explanations of their behavior; and second that the formality condition is intimately involved with the explanation of propositional attitudes so construed. (p. 66)

Later, in more plain English, Fodor says:

> My claim has been that, in doing our psychology, we want to attribute mental states fully opaquely because it's the fully opaque reading which tells us what the agent has in mind, and it's what the agent has in mind that causes his behavior. (p. 67)

18 In his early writings, Nelson Pike conceded that if God's beliefs are construed so they are fundamentally different in nature from human beliefs, then his incompatibilistic argument would not be sound. He pointed out that the argument gets its bite at least in part from the assumption that God's beliefs and human beliefs are similar in their essence (although clearly different, for example, in their manner of instantiation). My point in the text suggests a specification of precisely what the similarity must be, if the incompatibilist's argument is to be sound: God's beliefs, like human beliefs, must conform to something like the formality condition.

19 Wierenga (1989), pp. 107–8.

20 I do not mean to suggest that God's mental states must have some phenomenological quality. But it at least seems necessary that these states make information accessible to God; features of His belief states must give God access to the relevant information.

21 Fodor (1980), p. 67.

22 Jonathan L. Kvanvig, *The Possibility of an All-Knowing God* (New York: St Martin's Press, 1986), esp. pp. 110–14.

23 I am translating some of Kvanvig's language into mine, but I do not believe this translation distorts his fundamental points.

24 It is a complex and controversial matter whether the "present" is fixed. Whereas some philosophers hold that S may at $t2$ be able to refrain from doing X at $t2$, even though S does in fact do X at $t2$, others would deny this claim. I wish to avoid taking a stand on this issue here; thus, I shall adopt the convention of speaking of what the agent can at the relevant time *or just prior to that time* do. Thus, if one holds that the present is fixed, then the pertinent time, for the purposes of my analysis, is just prior to the present.

25 Of course, the fixity in question here is relativized to human agents (given ordinary powers and current technology). Clearly, if God is omnipotent, He should be able to cause the sun to flicker out.

26 Plantinga provides the resources in Plantinga (1986). But although he suggests these arguments, it is not evident that Plantinga would accept them.

Chapter 7 Responsibility and Alternative Possibilities

1 This sort of example, and the associated philosophical point, is presented in Harry Frankfurt, "Alternate Possibilities and Moral Responsibility," *Journal of Philosophy* 66 (1969), pp. 829–39; and "Freedom of the Will and the Concept of a Person," *Journal of Philosophy* 68 (1971), pp. 5–20; both pieces are reprinted in Fischer, ed., 1986.

2 For a parallel distinction between two kinds of control, see Michael J. Zimmerman, *An Essay on Moral Responsibility* (Totowa, New Jersey: Roman and Littlefield, 1988), pp. 32–4.

3 Note that the example would have precisely the same implications if alternative possibilities were ruled out by virtue of the existence of *another agent*. So imagine that the car is a "driver instruction" automobile with dual controls. Although I actually guide the car to the right, we can imagine that the instructor could have intervened and caused the car to go to the right, if I had shown any inclination to cause it to go in some other direction.

4 Aristotle argued that there are two conditions that rule out the voluntariness of an action: ignorance and force. Following Aristotle, I shall suppose that there are at least two sorts of conditions relevant to moral responsibility: epistemic conditions and freedom-relevant conditions. In this book, I shall focus primarily upon the freedom-relevant condition. In conversation, Gary Watson has convinced me that there are (arguably) other conditions – perhaps pertaining to psychological complexity or "norma-

tive competence" – that are not naturally subsumed under the epistemic or freedom-relevant categories. A full theory of moral responsibility would need to say something about these further conditions.

5   David Blumenfeld develops this kind of Frankfurt-type example in, "The Principle of Alternate Possibilities," *Journal of Philosophy* 67 (1971), pp. 339–44.

6   It is not absolutely clear to me that this is so. This is because it seems to me at least conceivable that a Frankfurt-type case could be constructed in which the counterfactual intervention would not be triggered by any specific event but would by an extraordinary *cosmic accident* occur at just the right time. I do not know why this sort of example is impossible, but I will not press the point.

7   This strategy is developed by Peter van Inwagen: van Inwagen (1983), pp. 166–71.

8   For a development of this sort of view, see van Inwagen (1983), pp. 166–80. Van Inwagen's elegant approach is basically as follows. When one thinks about a Frankfurt-type example, it may at first appear that it is a situation in which both of the following are true: the agent cannot avoid bringing an event about and he is morally responsible for bringing it about. But this appearance is misleading; it is not clear that both claims are true *of the same thing*. More specifically, it can be granted that the agent is morally responsible for *something*, but this is the event-particular (which he *can* in fact avoid bringing about). Also, it can be granted that the agent cannot avoid bringing about *something*. But this is the event-universal, and he is *not* responsible for bringing *this* about.

9   William Rowe attributes this sort of libertarian view to Thomas Reid in William L. Rowe, *Thomas Reid on Freedom and Morality* (Ithaca: Cornell University Press, 1991). He applies the view in the way suggested to the analysis of the Frankfurt-type cases; see especially pp. 75–93. For a discussion of Rowe's book, see John Martin Fischer, "Review of Rowe's *Thomas Reid on Freedom and Morality*," *Faith and Philosophy* 10 (1993b), pp. 266–71.

10 Margery Bedford Naylor suggests this sort of approach in "Frankfurt on the Principle of Alternate Possibilities," *Philosophical Studies* 46 (1984), pp. 249–58.

11 I believe that the argument presented in the text exhibits the flaw in van Inwagen's defense of the second version of the flicker of freedom strategy. Van Inwagen considers

> PPP1 (Principle of Possible Prevention 1): A person is morally responsible for a certain event-particular only if he could have prevented it.

Van Inwagen wonders if a Frankfurt-type counterexample to this principle can be constructed. He tries, as follows:

Gunnar shoots and kills Ridley (intentionally), thereby bringing about Ridley's death, a certain event. But there is some factor, F, which (i) played no causal role in Ridley's death, and (ii) would have caused Ridley's death if Gunnar had not shot him – or, since factor F might have caused Ridley's death *by* causing Gunnar to shoot him, perhaps we should say, 'if Gunnar had decided not to shoot him' – and (iii) is such that Gunnar could not have prevented it from causing Ridley's death except by killing, or by deciding to kill, Ridley himself. So it would seem that Gunnar is responsible for Ridley's death, though he could not have prevented Ridley's death.

It is easy to see that this story is simply inconsistent. What is in fact denoted by 'Ridley's death' is not, according to the story, caused by factor F. Therefore, if Gunnar had not shot Ridley, and, as a result, factor F had caused Ridley to die, then there would have been an event denoted by 'Ridley's death' which had factor F as (one of) its cause(s). But then this event would have been an event other than the event in fact denoted by 'Ridley's death'; the event in fact denoted by 'Ridley's death' would not have happened at all. But if this story is inconsistent it is not a counter-example to PPP1. And I am unable to see how to construct a putative Frankfurt-style counter-example to PPP1 that cannot be shown to be inconsistent by an argument of this sort.(Van Inwagen [1983], p. 170)

In my view, van Inwagen's mistake here is to assume that the *only* way in which a Frankfurt-type example could threaten the principle would be by presenting an alternative sequence in which the same event-particular (as the actual event) occurs. But I have in effect argued that this is false; I have shown how one could concede that the event-particular in the alternative sequence is different from that in the actual sequence and *still* conclude from the Frankfurt-type examples that (PPP1) is false.

To drive home the point, note that if one adopts (PPP1), one should also adopt

(PPP1*): A person is responsible for event e only if there exists some property F such that $F(e)$ and an alternative sequence open to the person in which he brings about $\sim F(e')$ [$e \neq e'$] as a result of an intention to do so.

On (PPP1*), Jones is not morally responsible for voting for Clinton, and yet intuitively Jones *is* morally responsible for voting for Clinton. Since one who accepts (PPP1) should also accept (PPP1*), and Frankfurt-type examples exhibit the unacceptability of (PPP1*), they also call (PPP1) into question. Thus, it is *false* that the *only* way in which such examples could threaten (PPP1) would be by presenting an alternative sequence in which the same event-particular (as the actual event) occurs.

12 Nozick (1981), p. 312.
13 Nozick (1981), p. 312.

14   I do not deny that if causal determinism were true, we would share a
     certain feature – the lack of originative value (as defined by Nozick) – with
     puppets and marionettes. But I still would maintain that it does not follow
     that the causal histories of our actions are *relevantly similar* (all things
     considered) to those of puppets and marionettes: I explain this sort of
     point in chapter eight.

15   John Rawls, *A Theory of Justice* (Cambridge, Mass.: Harvard University
     Press, 1973). Also, for an application of this sort of methodology to the
     realm of freedom, see Christine Swanton, *Freedom: A Coherence Theory*
     (Indianapolis: Hackett Publishing Company, Inc., 1992).

16   In correspondence, Tim O'Connor reminds me that it need not be solely
     an untutored, unreflective intuition that supports incompatibilism. Con-
     sider, for example, Clarence Darrow's masterful use of an environmental
     determinism thesis in numerous successful legal defenses. Or the effect of
     Freudian psychology on some people's conception of themselves and
     others. I certainly confess that I have not offered a knockdown argument
     against the view that causal determinism in itself rules out moral responsi-
     bility. But my sense is that the force of Darrow's arguments (and Freud's
     insights, if they are indeed insights) derives not from causal determinism
     per se, but adverting to *certain special sorts of determination*. I develop this
     point more fully in chapter eight.

17   I know of only one "direct" argument. It is presented in Peter van
     Inwagen's, "The Incompatibility of Responsibility and Determinism," in
     M. Brady and M. Brand, eds, *Bowling Green Studies in Applied Philosophy*
     2 (1980), pp. 30–7; this essay is reprinted in Fischer, ed., 1986. See also
     van Inwagen (1983), pp. 182–8. Van Inwagen here employs a principle
     structurally parallel to the Transfer Principle, but with a slightly different
     interpretation of the modality. This issues in what might be called the
     Principle of Transfer of Non-responsibility: if you are not morally respon-
     sible for one thing, and you are not morally responsible for that thing's
     leading to another, you are not morally responsible for the other. Now, an
     argument clearly parallel to the arguments discussed above can be gener-
     ated to show that causal determinism rules out moral responsibility. Given
     that you are not morally responsible for the past, and you are not morally
     responsible for the laws of nature, and assuming the Principle of Transfer
     of Non-responsibility, causal determinism seems to rule out moral
     responsibility *directly*.

     But it seems to me that this argument *clearly* does not work. And it is
     the Frankfurt-type cases that show this by exhibiting the invalidity of the
     Principle of Transfer of Non-responsibility. For example, Jones is not
     morally responsible for the fact that Black is ready to intervene, and he is
     not responsible for the fact that, if Black is so ready, Jones will indeed vote
     for Clinton. But Jones *is* morally responsible for voting for Clinton. Thus,
     whereas it is not straightforward to provide a counterexample to the

Principle of the Transfer of Powerlessness, Frankfurt-type examples do indeed provide counterexamples to the Principle of the Transfer of Non-responsibility. Powerlessness is in this respect different from non-responsibility. For an excellent and very careful discussion of these issues, see Mark Ravizza, "Semicompatibilism and the Transfer of Non-responsibility," *Philosophical Studies* (forthcoming).

18   Alvin Goldman, *A Theory of Human Action* (Englewood Cliffs: Prentice Hall, 1970), pp. 199–200.

19   For roughly this kind of move (with refinements), see Barbara Herman, "On the Value of Acting from the Motive of Duty," *Philosophical Review* 90 (1981), pp. 359–82; and Peter Railton, "Alienation, Consequentialism, and the Demands of Morality," *Philosophy and Public Affairs* 13 (1984), pp. 134–71.

20   Wolf (1980).

21   Wolf (1980).

22   Some months ago, I was at the local supermarket. When I got to the checkout counter, the checker asked, "Would you like a paper bag or plastic?" I thought for a moment and replied, "Plastic is fine." Then the checker smiled and said, "It's a good thing – I see we only have plastic!" We both laughed. (On the way home, I turned right at the usual place, not even noticing the sign, which reads, "Right lane must turn right . . .")

Chapter 8 Moral Responsibility and Guidance Control

1   Samuel Beckett, *Waiting for Godot: tragicomedy in 2 acts* (New York: Grove Press, 1954), p. 28.

2   Here I borrow heavily from John Martin Fischer, "Responsiveness and Moral Responsibility," in F. Schoeman, ed., *Responsibility, Character, and the Emotions: New Essays on Moral Psychology* (Cambridge: Cambridge University Press, 1987), pp. 81–106. My approach will be similar to various contemporary efforts at explicating moral responsibility, for example: Alasdair MacIntyre, "Determinism," *Mind* 66 (1957), pp. 28–41; Jonathan Glover, *Responsibility* (New York: Humanities Press, 1970); Herbert Fingarette, *The Meaning of Criminal Insanity* (Berkeley: University of California Press, 1972); Wright Neely, "Freedom and Desire," *Philosophical Review* 83, 1974, pp. 32–54; Timothy Duggan and Bernard Gert, "Free Will as the Ability to Will," *Noûs* 13 (1979), pp. 197–217 (reprinted in Fischer, 1986); Lawrence Davis, *A Theory of Action* (Englewood Cliffs: Prentice-Hall, 1979); Michael Levin, *Metaphysics and the Mind–Body Problem* (Oxford: Clarendon Press, 1979); Nozick (1981), and Dennett (1984). For an excellent survey of some aspects of these approaches, see: David Shatz, "Free Will and the Structure of Motivation," in Peter A. French, Theodore E. Uehling, and Howard K. Wettstein, eds, *Midwest*

Studies in Philosophy X (Minneapolis: University of Minnesota Press, 1985), pp. 451–82.

3 I contrast this kind of bank teller with one who, in exactly the same circumstances, does not have an irresistible impulse to comply with the threat. Such a teller might be morally responsible (though not necessarily blameworthy) for handing over the money.

4 Here I am indebted to Duggan and Gert (1979).

5 Duggan and Gert (1979).

6 Robert Nozick requires this sort of close contouring of action to value for his notion of "tracking value": Nozick (1981), pp. 317–62. In this respect, then, Nozick's notion of tracking value corresponds to strong reasons-responsiveness. Nozick claims that an agent who tracks value displays a kind of moral virtue, but he does not claim that tracking value is a necessary condition for moral responsibility.

7 I shall adopt the constraint that the possible worlds pertinent to the weak reasons-responsiveness of the actual-sequence mechanism must have the same natural laws as the actual world.

8 Originally, Ferdinand Schoeman kindly brought to my attention a sort of example that threatens my claim that weak reasons-responsiveness is sufficient for guidance control. Imagine someone who is, by any ordinary criterion, insane. This person commits a barbarous act, such as killing a number of persons on the Staten Island Ferry with a saber. And suppose that this individual would have killed the persons under all possible circumstances except one: he would have refrained if he believed that it was Friday and thus a religious holiday. Intuitively, the individual is highly irrational and should not be considered morally responsible, and yet he seems to satisfy the condition of acting from a reason-responsive mechanism. Weak reasons-responsiveness obtains by virtue of the agent's responsiveness to a "bizarre" reason, even though the agent is not responsive to a wide array of "relevant" reasons. For excellent discussions of the issues raised by such examples, see David Shatz, "Compatibilism, Values, and 'Could Have Done Otherwise'," *Philosophical Topics* 16 (1988), pp. 151–200; and Mark Ravizza, "Is Responsiveness Sufficient for Moral Responsibility?" (unpublished manuscript).

I now think the account of guidance control in terms of weak reasons-responsiveness needs to be refined in part to accommodate such examples. But I do not think the revision will be radical; most importantly, I do not see any reason to think it will alter the fundamental nature of the account of moral responsibility as *not* requiring alternative possibilities. For some preliminary suggestions about a suitable revision, see Ravizza, "Is Responsiveness Sufficient for Moral Responsibility?", and his dissertation at Yale University, *Moral Responsibility and Control: An Actual-Sequence Approach.*

9 One might distinguish between "internalist" and "externalist" accounts of

knowledge. An internalist proceeds by requiring that the agent have a certain sort of justification for his belief. Typically, this sort of justification involves a distinctive sort of "access" or ability to articulate reasons. The externalist abandons the search for this sort of justification and requires certain kinds of causal connections between the fact known and the agent's belief.

10   I am obviously presenting only a sketch of a theory of knowledge here. Further, I do not here suppose that this is obviously the correct account of · knowledge. I am merely pointing to an analogy between my approach to moral responsibility and the externalist conception of knowledge. The approach to knowledge presented here follows those of (among others) Dretske and Nozick: F. Dretske, "Conclusive Reasons," *Australasian Journal of Philosophy* 49 (1971), pp. 1–22; and Nozick (1981), pp. 167–98.

11   Nozick claims that this fact helps to refute a certain kind of epistemological skeptic: Nozick (1981), pp. 197–247. Of course, this is the sort of skeptic we discussed in chapter two who relies upon the Principle of Closure of Knowledge Under Known Implication. If Nozick's account of knowledge is correct, then this principle must be false.

12   Nozick (1981), pp. 197–247.

13   Nozick (1981), pp. 180–1. Nozick attributes this example to Avishai Margalit.

14   Let me say a few words about the notion of an "actual-sequence" approach. By this I mean that only the properties of the actual sequence are relevant to the phenomenon in question. But notice that these "actual-sequence" properties may indeed be dispositional properties; as such, their proper analysis may involve (for example) other possible worlds. In the context of an actual-sequence approach to moral responsibility, I have argued that it is required that a weakly reasons-responsive mechanism actually operates; then, I have analyzed weak reasons-responsiveness in terms of other possible worlds. Whereas other possible worlds are relevant to ascertaining whether there is some actually operative dispositional feature (such as weak reasons-responsiveness), such worlds are *not* relevant in virtue of bearing on the question of whether some alternative sequence is genuinely accessible to the agent.

15   It is an interesting question exactly *why* this should be so.

16   As above, I am leaving extremely vague the crucial notion of "same mechanism." There are certainly very deep problems with this notion in epistemology. For discussions of some of these, see Robert Shope, "Cognitive Abilities, Conditionals, and Knowledge: A Response to Nozick," *Journal of Philosophy* 81 (1984), pp. 29–48; and Richard Foley, "What's Wrong with Reliabilism?" *The Monist* 68 (1985), pp. 188–202.

17   The claim, as stated, relies on the intuition that the physical process *P* is the relevant mechanism. Alternatively, one could simply point out that in Jim's case there exists an actually-operative mechanism (of kind *P*) that is

temporally intrinsic and not reasons-responsive.

18   Daniel Dennett says, "The possibility of short-circuiting or otherwise tampering with an intentional system gives rise to an interesting group of perplexities about the extent of responsibility in cases where there has been manipulation. We are generally absolved of responsibility where we have been manipulated by others, but there is no one principle of innocence by reason of manipulation." (Daniel Dennett, "Mechanism and Responsibility," in Honderich, ed. [1973], p. 175.) In contrast to Dennett's suggestion, my approach provides a *general* way of distinguishing responsibility-undermining manipulation from manipulation which is consistent with responsibility.

19   I believe that the reasons-responsiveness approach can be fruitful in analyzing insanity pleas such as that of the Menendez brothers (referred to in chapter one). A detailed treatment of these issues will have to await another occasion.

20   Van Inwagen (1990), p. 419.

21   Harry Frankfurt also wishes to argue that causal determinism does not rule out moral responsibility. In light of the Frankfurt-type examples, Frankfurt points out that one might be tempted to assert that

> a person is not morally responsible for what he has done if he did it because he could not have done otherwise. . . . if it was causally determined that a person perform a certain action, then it will be true that the person performed it because of those causal determinants. And if the fact that it was causally determined that a person perform a certain action means that the person could not have done otherwise, as philosophers who argue for the incompatibility thesis characteristically suppose, then the fact that it was causally determined that a person perform a certain action will mean that the person performed it because he could not have done otherwise. The revised principle . . . will entail . . . that a person is not morally responsible for what he has done if it was causally determined that he do it. I do not believe, however, that this revision of the principle is acceptable. (Frankfurt [1969], p. 838)

In light of this sort of problem Frankfurt suggests that the principle of alternative possibilities should be replaced by a principle which states that a person is not morally responsible for what he has done if he did it *only* because he could not have done otherwise. Frankfurt says, "This principle does not appear to conflict with the view that moral responsibility is compatible with determinism." (Frankfurt [1969], pp. 838–9)

But Frankfurt's strategy here is puzzling to me. It is somewhat unclear what it would be for an agent to do something "only because he could not have done otherwise." Presumably, as I have suggested above, what distinguishes *action* from mere movements or mere events is that an action is preceded by and performed because of *some* appropriate pro-attitude (or perhaps volition). Whatever one's precise account of the antecedents of action, surely it must include the presence of some pro-attitude. But then it will follow that *no* action is performed *solely* because the agent could not have done otherwise; all actions, as opposed to mere events, will occur at least in part because of the pro-attitude. And if this is so, then Frankfurt's proposed exculpating condition will not rule out holding an agent morally responsible for performing *any* action. In seeking to make room for moral responsibility in a causally deterministic world, it would seem that Frankfurt has made *too much* room.

22   Alfred J. Freddoso, in his "Introduction"; Luis De Molina, *On Divine Foreknowledge* (Part IV of the *Concordia*), trans. A. Freddoso (Ithaca: Cornell University Press, 1988), p. 2.

23   Norman Kretzmann, "Goodness, Knowledge, and Indeterminacy in the Philosophy of Thomas Aquinas," *Journal of Philosophy* 80 (1983), pp. 631–49.

24   Kretzmann (1983), pp. 644–5.

25   The issue of the fixity of these features does not arise in Aquinas' approach, since he places God outside the human temporal framework.

26   Admittedly, this is the barest sketch of a solution to a very complicated set of problems. But I hope my preliminary and provisional thoughts suggest fruitful lines of inquiry.

27   Since God would have set things up in advance so that agents would be caused to behave as they actually do, He could *ensure* that they so behave. And yet the causation would not be of the sort that rules out responsibility: it would be via weakly reasons-responsive mechanisms.

28   The response to the free will defense I have suggested says that God could have caused us to choose and act freely so that we always do the right thing via weakly reasons-responsive mechanisms. Alternatively, one might suppose that God does *not* causally determine our behavior, but rather sets up life as a sequence of Frankfurt-type situations (or analogues of such situations) in which intervention would be triggered by the inclination to choose and do evil things (or evil things of a certain magnitude). I am indebted to Andrew Eshleman for bringing this possibility to my attention.

29   Feinberg (1980), p. 36.

30   Feinberg (1980), p. 38.

31   Feinberg (1980), p. 38.

32   I am assuming here that nothing unusual or special characterizes the actual sequence that issues in Chuzzlewit's behavior.

33   Feinberg (1980), p. 36.

34   Swinburne (1989), p. 5.

35   The same is clearly true in van Inwagen's hypothesis (M). According to this hypothesis, when any human being is born, the Martians implant in his brain a tiny device – one that is undetectable by any observational technique we have at our disposal – which contains a 'program' for that

person's entire life: this program issues in a process which *causes* the agent to decide as he actually decides at any decision point.

36 If it would not be a particularly bad thing if we lacked alternative possibilities, what then is the interest in liberty? I believe that Feinberg's main interest is in the question of why we should have political institutions that protect certain sorts of behavior; he is concerned to understand why we wish to have a system of institutions that specify certain political liberties. Although a full and adequate answer would require more space, I believe that such an answer does not require the presupposition of the value of alternative possibilities. Presumably, we want institutions that ensure basic political liberty because such institutions will in some sense optimize our opportunities to act freely (i.e., to exercise guidance control of our behavior).

37 Dennett (1984), p. 8.

38 Dennett (1984), pp. 7–8.

39 John Locke, *Essay Concerning Human Understanding*, ed. Alexander Campbell Fraser (Oxford: Clarendon Press, 1690/1894), pp. 315–18.

40 Isaiah Berlin, *Historical Inevitability* (London: Oxford University Press, 1954), p. 68.

Chapter 9 *Putting it Together*

1 Keith Lehrer, "Self Profile," in Radu J. Bogdan, ed., *Profiles: Keith Lehrer* (Dordrecht: D. Reidel, 1981), p. 31.

2 Surely, an enormous gorge that separates your path from the path on the other side constitutes an obstacle (a present obstacle) which rules out your ability to take the other path. The Shadow Theorist embraces this claim. But why not consider the lack of connection with the actual past an analogous obstacle? Pictorially, there is an exact analogy between the space between the line representing the actual past and some putative past (associated with some allegedly possible action) and the space occupied by the gorge; why should the temporal gap be treated differently from the spatial gap?

3 Craig (1989), pp. 236, 237.

4 Hasker (1985), p. 135.

5 J. L. Borges, "The Analytical Language of John Wilkins," in *Other Inquisitions 1937–1952*, R. Sims trans. (Austin: University of Texas Press, 1964), p. 103. For this quotation, I am indebted to David Dolinko, "Three Mistakes of Retributivism," *UCLA Law Review* 39 (1992), p. 1639.

6 Nelson Pike, "A Latter-Day Look at the Foreknowledge Problem," *International Journal for Philosophy of Religion*, 33 (1993), pp. 129–64.

7 See John Turk Saunders, "Of God and Freedom," *Philosophical Review* 75

248 NOTES

(1966), pp. 219–25; also Saunders (1968).
8 Adams (1967). For a critical discussion, see Fischer (1983a).
9 Pike (1993), pp. 135–6.
10 Pike (1993), p. 136.
11 Pike (1993), p. 159.
12 Contrast van Inwagen's claim (presented in chapter three) that all three of his formulations of the Consequence Argument (the argument for incompatibilism) in *An Essay On Free Will* should "stand or fall together." ("I am quite sure that any specific and detailed objection to one of the arguments can be fairly easily translated into specific and detailed objections to the others; and I think that any objection to one of the arguments will be a good objection to *that* argument if and only if the corresponding objections to the others are good objections to *them*" (van Inwagen [1983], p. 57).)

My arguments have at least established a strong prima facie case that the various versions of the argument I have presented are not equivalent. I thus believe the onus is on the theorist who denies this to establish that, despite the appearances, the arguments are actually equivalent. Such a theorist might argue that all the versions of the argument I have presented – and perhaps all other versions – implicitly rely at a deep level upon some sort of modal principle. But I do not think such an argument is promising.

Some philosophers have focused their attention solely upon one version of the argument for incompatibilism. They have in some instances taken issue with one apparently crucial element of the selected version of the argument. This may be the Transfer Principle or the Conditional Version of the Principle of the Fixity of the Past. (Anthony Kenny has argued in personal correspondence that, even if my arguments against Scotism were valid, the Conditional Version of the Principle of the Fixity of the Past is unacceptable, and thus incompatibilism can be resisted. He argues on the basis of the sorts of examples I discussed in chapters four and five in which it appears that both a can-claim and a relevant backtracking counterfactual are true.) Also, various philosophers note that certain versions of the incompatibilist's argument make use of the locutions such as "bringing it about that p." Further, these versions of the argument seem to suppose that if an agent has it in his power to bring it about that p, and if p entails q, then the agent has it in his power to bring it about that q. For a development of this sort of "power entailment principle," see Hasker (1985), esp. pp. 142–4. But this sort of principle has been called into question by various philosophers; see, for example, Philip L. Quinn, "Plantinga on Foreknowledge and Freedom," in James E. Tomberlin and Peter van Inwagen, eds, *Profiles: Alvin Plantinga* (Dordrecht: D. Reidel, 1985), pp. 271–87; and Thomas B. Talbott, "On Divine Foreknowledge and Bringing about the Past," *Philosophy and Phenomenological Research* 46 (1986), pp. 455–69. For similar worries, see

Joshua Hoffman and Gary Rosenkrantz, "On Divine Foreknowledge and Human Freedom," *Philosophical Studies* 37 (1980), pp. 289–96 [cf. William L. Rowe, "On Divine Foreknowledge and Human Freedom: A Reply," *Philosophical Studies* 37 (1980), pp. 429–30]; and William Lane Craig (1989), and (1991), esp. pp. 88–90 [cf. John Martin Fischer, "Soft Facts and Harsh Realities: A Reply to William Craig," *Religious Studies* 27 (1991b), pp. 523–39].

Of course, it can be extremely helpful to see precisely why a particular version of the argument is problematic. But it is important to remember that there may be other, closely related versions of the argument which are not vulnerable to similar objections. Thus, the thrust of the incompatibilist's argument *cannot* be blunted by these objections – unless of course the critic can argue that the objections can be generalized. In a certain way, then, these objections can be seen to be relatively superficial.

13   For tentative and preliminary work toward a more general theory of moral responsibility which connects responsibility with control, see John Martin Fischer, "Responsibility and Failure," *Proceedings of the Aristotelian Society* 86 (1985/1986), pp. 251–70; "Responsibility and Inevitability," with Mark Ravizza, *Ethics* 101 (1991), pp. 258–78; "The Inevitable," with Mark Ravizza, *Australasian Journal of Philosophy* 70 (1992b), pp. 388–404; and "Responsibility for Consequences," with Mark Ravizza, in Jules Coleman and Allen Buchanan, eds, *In Harm's Way: Essays in Honor of Joel Feinberg* (Cambridge: Cambridge University Press, forthcoming 1994); also in Fischer and Ravizza, eds, 1993.

14   Fischer, "Responsiveness and Moral Responsibility," in Schoeman, ed., 1987, esp. pp. 103–5.

15   Frankfurt (1971), esp. p. 15.

16   Harry Frankfurt, "Identification and Externality," in A. O. Rorty, ed., *The Identities of Persons* (Berkeley: University of California Press, 1976), pp. 239–51, and "Identification and Wholeheartedness," in F. Schoeman, ed. (1987), pp. 27–45. The latter is reprinted in Fischer and Ravizza, eds, 1993.

17   For a more extended discussion of Frankfurt's refined approach, see John Martin Fischer and Mark Ravizza, "Responsibility and History," forthcoming in Peter A. French, Theodore E. Uehling, Jr., and Howard K. Wettstein, eds, *Midwest Studies in Philosophy XIX: Naturalism* (Notre Dame: University of Notre Dame Press, 1994). Also, see John Christman, "Autonomy and Personal History," *Canadian Journal of Philosophy* 21 (1991), pp. 1–24.

In his well-known critique of Frankfurt's early formulation of his mesh theory, Gary Watson argued that simply adding higher levels in the hierarchy of preferences does not provide enough to ground the claim that an agent is acting freely. (Gary Watson, "Free Agency," *Journal of Philosophy* 72 [1975], pp. 205–20.) Roughly, the point is that if acting on a first-order desire is not itself sufficient for moral responsibility because of considerations pertinent to the second level, then surely acting in accordance with a second-order desire of a certain sort is not itself sufficient for moral responsibility because of considerations pertinent to the third level, and so forth. This might be called the "logical" problem with the simple mesh view, and Frankfurt's new view seems to address the logical problem nicely (by positing the resonance condition). But the logical problem is clearly different from the "source" problem – the problem that the mesh can be induced in responsibility-undermining ways. (This problem for the simple mesh theory was presented by Michael Slote in his paper, "Understanding Free Will," *Journal of Philosophy* 77 [1980], pp. 136–51; reprinted in Fischer, ed., 1986.) Thus, it might be said that Frankfurt's new view addresses Watson's critique, but not Slote's – it addresses the logical problem, but not the source problem. Thus, the new view, even if it is successful in addressing the logical problem, does not in any way diminish the plausibility of the insight that responsibility is essentially historical.

18   The argument in the text indicates why Frankfurt's selected mesh cannot be a sufficient condition for moral responsibility. He has also argued that the mesh is a *necessary* condition for personhood and moral responsibility (Frankfurt [1971]). On Frankfurt's view, an individual who has no second-order volitions has not identified himself with any particular first-order preference; thus, the issue of whether there is a conformity between the preference he acts on and the one he identifies with obviously cannot arise. Frankfurt says:

> I shall use the term 'wanton' to refer to agents who have first-order desires but who are not persons because, whether or not they have desires of the second order, they have no second-order volitions. The essential characteristic of a wanton is that he does not care about his will. His desires move him to do certain things, without its being true of him either that he wants to be moved by those desires or that he prefers to be moved by other desires. The class of wantons includes all nonhuman animals that have desires and all very young children. Perhaps it also includes some adult human beings . . .
>   . . . It is only because a person has volitions of the second order that he is capable both of enjoying and of lacking freedom of the will. The concept of a person is not only the concept of a type of entity that has both first-order desires and volitions of the second order. It can also be construed as the concept of a type of entity for whom the freedom of its will may be a problem. This concept excludes all wantons, both infrahuman and human, since they fail to satisfy an essential condition for the enjoyment of freedom of the will. (Frankfurt [1971], pp. 11, 14)

Quite apart from issues pertaining to the analysis of the concept of a person, I have argued (following Frankfurt!) that a person need not possess freedom of the will. But must a person be the sort of "creature for whom freedom of its will may be a problem?"

I am not sure exactly how to understand this notion of a "creature for whom freedom of its will may be a problem." Clearly, Frankfurt interprets it in such a way as to require that the individual *actually* possess second-order volitions. But this seems too strong to me. I can imagine a human being who has first-order preferences but no second-order preferences (and who is thus a "wanton") but of whom it is nevertheless true that he *should* have second-order volitions. That is, intuitively it would seem that there could be such individuals who would be appropriately subject to criticism precisely for *not* forming suitable second-order volitions. If so, Frankfurt's requirement is too strong.

And if Frankfurt says that an individual who has the *power* to form the relevant higher-order volitions but actually does not is also an individual for whom freedom of its will may be a problem, then it would appear to follow that such an individual would be subject to the reactive attitudes on the basis of an unactualized putative power. But then evidently Frankfurt must give up the idea that moral responsibility does not require alternative possibilities. That is, Frankfurt's view (on this interpretation) would be in conflict with his general view that moral responsibility does not require alternative possibilities (which is crucial to the Frankfurt-type strategy for seeking to avoid the thrust of the argument for incompatibilism).

The view that a person must actually have second-order volitions is attractive for precisely the same reason as the mesh approach: they are both appealing in part because they fit well with an "actual-sequence" model of moral responsibility (according to which regulative control is not necessary for moral responsibility). But it is better to seek a different way of developing such a model of moral responsibility – one which attends to more than mere structural features of an agent's mental economy.

19 Watson (1975).
20 "Incoherentist" positions are developed in Galen Strawson (1986); and Richard Double, *The Non-Reality of Free Will* (New York: Oxford University Press, 1991). For considerable skepticism about the possibility of explaining the notion of free will so as to capture all its features, see Thomas Nagel, *The View from Nowhere* (New York: Oxford University Press, 1986). Nagel says:

> I change my mind about the problem of free will every time I think about it, and therefore cannot offer any view with even moderate confidence; but my present opinion is that nothing that might be a solution has yet been described. This is not a case where there are several possible candidate solutions and we don't know which is correct. It is a case where nothing believable has (to my knowledge) been proposed by anyone in the extensive public discussion of the subject. (p. 112)

21 Double (1991), p. 58.

er Strawson (1962).

eter Strawson (1962), p. 190.

Herbert Morris, "Persons and Punishment," in Jeffrie G. Murphy, ed., *Punishment and Rehabilitation* (Belmont, Ca.: Wadsworth Publishing Co., 1973, p. 44). As Morris points out, various theorists have explicitly adopted the "therapy model." Consider:

> When a man is suffering from an infectious disease, he is a danger to the community, and it is necessary to restrict his liberty of movement. But no one associates any idea of guilt with such a situation. On the contrary, he is an object of commiseration to his friends. Such steps as science recommends are taken to cure him of his disease, and he submits as a rule without reluctance to the curtailment of liberty involved meanwhile. The same method in spirit ought to be shown in the treatment of what is called 'crime.' (Bertrand Russell, *Roads to Freedom: Socialism, Anarchism, and Syndicalism* [London: George Allen and Unwin Ltd., 1918, p. 135])

> We do not hold people responsible for their reflexes – for example, for coughing in church. We hold them responsible for their operant behavior – for example, for whispering in church or remaining in church while coughing. But there are variables which are responsible for whispering as well as coughing, and these may be just as inexorable. When we recognize this, we are likely to drop the notion of responsibility altogether and with it the doctrine of free will as an inner causal agent. (B. F. Skinner, *Science and Human Behavior* [New York: Macmillan, 1953], pp. 115–16)

(I am indebted to Morris' classic article for these passages.) For examples of versions of a "purely instrumental" view of punishment (against which Strawson was reacting), see, for example, R. E. Hobart, "Free Will as Involving Determinism and Inconceivable Without It," *Mind* 43 (1934), pp. 1–27; Moritz Schlick, "When is a Man Responsible?" in *Problems of Ethics*, translated by David Rynin (New York: Prentice-Hall, 1939), pp. 143–56; and J. J. C. Smart, "Free-will, Praise and Blame," *Mind* 70 (1961), pp. 291–306.

25 Watson (1987b), p. 258.

26 Galen Strawson (1986), "Appendix C: The Brain in the Vat as Free Agent," pp. 320–3.

27 Galen Strawson (1986), p. 320. Strawson points out that something like this version is employed at certain points in Jonathan Glover's *What Sort of People Should There Be?* (Harmondsworth, Middlesex, England: Penguin, 1984), pp. 96, 101, 108.

28 Galen Strawson (1986), pp. 320–1.

29 Galen Strawson (1986), p. 321.

30 Borges (1974), p. 91.

31 This is a temporal analogue of David Lewis' view that all possible worlds

are equally concrete and real: David Lewis, *On the Plurality of Worlds* (Oxford: Basil Blackwell, 1986).

32 Speaking of different "ways" of taking the one path may seem to re-introduce alternative possibilities. But the arguments I presented against the Flicker of Freedom Strategy also apply here: the alternatives, even if somehow present, do not play the appropriate role in grounding our moral responsibility. Suppose I walk down the path of life in a certain way. Notice, as with the contexts in which it was alleged that there are flickers of freedom, that I may *not* be able to deliberate and then choose some *other way of taking the path* and then freely proceed in this alternative manner. And yet I may still walk freely.

Fischer Bibliography

The following list includes my published papers (and certain reviews) relevant to the topics of the book. I have not explicitly referred to all of them, but they all represent parts of the development of the overall approach presented here. The entries prefixed by an asterisk are pieces on which I have relied especially heavily. For each year there is first a sequence of pieces I have written, followed by a sequence of co-authored pieces or edited works.

1979. "Lehrer's New Move: 'Can' in Theory and Practice." *Theoria* 45, pp. 49–62.

1982. "Responsibility and Control." *Journal of Philosophy* 79, pp. 24–40. Reprinted in Fischer, ed., 1986.

1983a. "Freedom and Foreknowledge." *Philosophical Review* 92, pp. 67–79. Reprinted in Fischer, ed., 1989. Also reprinted in Baruch Brody, ed., *Readings in the Philosophy of Religion*. Englewood Cliffs, N.J.: Prentice-Hall, 1992.

1983b. "Incompatibilism." *Philosophical Studies* 43, pp. 127–37.

*1984. "Power Over the Past." *Pacific Philosophical Quarterly* 65, pp. 335–50.

1985a. "Ockhamism." *Philosophical Review* 94, pp. 81–100.

1985b. "Scotism." *Mind* 94, pp. 231–43.

1985/86. "Responsibility and Failure." *Proceedings of the Aristotelian Society* 86, pp. 251–70. Reprinted in Peter French, ed., *The Spectrum of Responsibility*. New York: St Martin's Press, 1991.

1986a. "Hard-Type Soft Facts." *Philosophical Review* 95, pp. 591–601.

1986b. "Pike's Ockhamism." *Analysis* 46, pp. 57–63.

*1986c. "Power Necessity." *Philosophical Topics* 14, pp. 77–91.

1986d. "Van Inwagen on Free Will." *Philosophical Quarterly* 36, pp. 252–60. Reprinted in L. Stevenson, R. Squires, and J. Haldane, eds, *Mind, Causation, and Action*. New York: Basil Blackwell, 1986.

1986, ed. *Moral Responsibility*. Ithaca: Cornell University Press.

*1987. "Responsiveness and Moral Responsibility." In Ferdinand Schoeman, ed., *Responsibility, Character, and the Emotions: New Essays on Moral Psychology*. Cambridge: Cambridge University Press (1987), pp. 81–106.

1988a. "Freedom and Actuality." In Thomas Morris, ed., *Divine and Human Action: Essays in the Metaphysics of Theism*. Ithaca: Cornell University Press (1988), pp. 236–54.

1988b. "Freedom and Miracles." *Noûs* 22, pp. 235–52.

1989, ed. *God, Foreknowledge, and Freedom*. Stanford: Stanford University Press.

1991a. "Snapshot Ockhamism." In James E. Tomberlin, ed., *Philosophical Perspectives V: Philosophy of Religion*. Atascadero, Ca.: Ridgeview Publishing Co. (1991), pp. 355–71.

1991b. "Soft Facts and Harsh Realities: A Reply to William Craig." *Religious Studies* 27, pp. 523–39.

1991. (with Mark Ravizza.) "Responsibility and Inevitability." *Ethics* 101, pp. 258–78.

1992a. "Critical Notice: William Lane Craig's *Divine Foreknowledge and Human Freedom*." *Religious Studies* 28, pp. 269–74.

1992b. "Recent Work on God and Freedom." *American Philosophical Quarterly* 29, pp. 91–109.

1992c. "Fate and Fatalism." In Lawrence C. Becker, ed., *The Encyclopedia of Ethics*. New York: Garland Publishing (1992), pp. 359–61.

1992d. "Freedom and Determinism." In L. Becker, ed., 1992, pp. 385–8.

1992a. (with Mark Ravizza.) "Responsibility, Freedom, and Reason." Review, *Freedom Within Reason* by Susan Wolf. *Ethics* 102, pp. 368–89.

1992b. (with Mark Ravizza.) "The Inevitable." *Australasian Journal of Philosophy* 70, pp. 388–404.

*1992c. (with Mark Ravizza.) "When the Will is Free." In James E. Tomberlin, ed., *Philosophical Perspectives VI: Ethics*. Atascadero, Ca.: Ridgeview Publishing Co. (1992), pp. 423–51.

1993a. "Hard Properties." *Faith and Philosophy* 10, pp. 161–9.

1993b. "Review of Rowe's *Thomas Reid on Freedom and Morality*." *Faith and Philosophy* 10, pp. 266–71.

1993, ed. *The Metaphysics of Death*. Stanford: Stanford University Press.

1993, ed. (with Mark Ravizza.) *Perspectives on Moral Responsibility*. Ithaca: Cornell University Press.

1994a (forthcoming). (with Mark Ravizza.) "Responsibility for Consequences." In Jules Coleman and Allen Buchanan, eds, *In Harm's Way: Essays in Honor of Joel Feinberg*. Cambridge: Cambridge University Press.

1994b (forthcoming). (with Mark Ravizza.) "Responsibility and History." In Peter A. French, Theodore E. Uehling, Jr., and Howard K. Wettstein, eds, *Midwest Studies in Philosophy XIX: Naturalism*. Notre Dame, In.: University of Notre Dame Press.

Bibliography

Abrahamson, Alan. 1993. "Lyle Menendez Admits Lies, Insists He Killed in Fear." *Los Angeles Times*, September 22, pp. A1, 18–19.

Adams, Marilyn McCord. 1967. "Is the Existence of God a 'Hard' Fact?" *Philosophical Review* 76, pp. 492–503. Reprinted in Fischer, ed., 1989.

Albritton, Rogers. 1985. "Freedom of the Will and Freedom of Action." Presidential Address, *Proceedings and Addresses of the American Philosophical Association* 59, pp. 239–51.

Alexander of Aphrodisias. 1983. In R. W. Sharples, ed. and trans., *Alexander of Aphrodisias on Fate*. London: Duckworth, 1983.

Alston, William P. 1985. "Divine Foreknowledge and Alternative Conceptions of Human Freedom." *International Journal for Philosophy of Religion* 18, pp. 19–32. Reprinted in Fischer, ed., 1989.

Audi, Robert. 1978. "Avoidability and Possible Worlds." *Philosophical Studies* 33, pp. 413–21.

—— 1980. "Defeated Knowledge, Reliability, and Justification." In P. French et al., eds, 1980, pp. 75–95.

—— 1983. "Foundationalism, Epistemic Dependence, and Defeasibility." *Synthese* 55, pp. 119–38.

Augustine, St 400/1961. *Confessions*. Trans. by R. S. Pine-Coffin. Baltimore: Penguin Books.

Beckett, Samuel. 1954. *Waiting for Godot: tragicomedy in 2 acts*. New York: Grove Press.

Bennett, Jonathan. 1984. "Counterfactuals and Temporal Direction." *Philosophical Review* 93, pp. 57–91.

Berlin, Isaiah. 1954. *Historical Inevitability*. London: Oxford University Press.

Berofsky, Bernard. 1987. *Freedom from Necessity: The Metaphysical Basis of Responsibility*. New York: Routledge and Kegan Paul.

Blumenfeld, David. 1971. "The Principle of Alternate Possibilities." *Journal of Philosophy* 67, pp. 339–44.

Bogdan, Radu J., ed. 1981. *Profiles: Keith Lehrer*. Dordrecht: D. Reidel.

Borges, Jorge Luis. 1964. *Other Inquisitions 1937–1952*. Trans. by Ruth Sims. Austin: University of Texas Press.

—— 1974. *Fictions*. Ed. by Anthony Kerrign. London: Calder and Boyars.

Brady, M. and Brand, M., eds 1980. *Bowling Green Studies in Applied Philosophy* 2. Bowling Green, Oh.: Bowling Green State University Press.

Brand, Myles and Walton, Douglas, eds 1976. *Action Theory: Proceedings of the Winnipeg Conference on Human Action*. Dordrecht: D. Reidel.

Brueckner, Anthony. 1985. "Skepticism and Epistemic Closure." *Philosophical Topics* 13, pp. 89–118.

Burge, Tyler. 1979. "Individualism and the Mental." In P. French et al., eds, 1979, pp. 73–121.

—— 1982. "Two Thought Experiments Reviewed." *Notre Dame Journal of Formal Logic* 23, pp. 284–93.

Campbell, Richmond and Sowden, Lanning, eds 1985. *Paradoxes of Rationality and Cooperation: Prisoner's Dilemma and Newcomb's Problem*. Vancouver: University of British Columbia Press.

Christensen, Scott M. and Turner, Dale R., eds 1993. *Folk Psychology and the Philosophy of Mind*. Hillsdale, N.J.: Lawrence Erlbaum Associates.

Christman, John. 1991. "Autonomy and Personal History." *Canadian Journal of Philosophy* 21, pp. 1–24.

Clarke, Karen. 1990. "Life on Death Row." *Connecticut Magazine* 53, pp. 51–5; 63–7.

Craig, William Lane. 1987a. "Divine Foreknowledge and Newcomb's Paradox." *Philosophia* 17, pp. 331–50.

—— 1987b. *The Only Wise God: The Compatibility of Divine Foreknowledge and Human Freedom*. Grand Rapids, Mich.: Baker Book House.

—— 1989. "'Nice Soft Facts': Fischer on Foreknowledge." *Religious Studies* 25, pp. 235–46.

—— 1991. *Divine Foreknowledge and Human Freedom: The Coherence of Theism: Omniscience*. Leiden: E. J. Brill.

Davies, Martin. 1983. "Boethius and Others on Divine Foreknowledge." *Pacific Philosophical Quarterly* 64, pp. 313–29. Reprinted in Fischer, ed., 1989.

Davis, Lawrence. 1979. *Theory of Action*. Englewood Cliffs, N.J.: Prentice-Hall.

Delillo, Don. 1986. *White Noise*. New York: Penguin Books.

De Molina, Luis. 1988. *On Divine Foreknowledge* (Part IV of the *Concordia*). Trans. by Alfred J. Freddoso. Ithaca: Cornell University Press.

Dennett, Daniel C. 1973. "Mechanism and Responsibility." In T. Honderich, ed., 1973, pp. 157–84.

—— 1984. *Elbow Room: The Varieties of Free Will Worth Wanting*. Cambridge, Mass.: MIT Press.

Dolinko, David. 1992. "Three Mistakes of Retributivism." *UCLA Law Review* 39, pp. 1623–57.

Dostoevsky, Feodor. 1866/1980. *Crime and Punishment*. Trans. by Jessie Coulson. Oxford: Oxford University Press.

Double, Richard. 1991. *The Non-Reality of Free Will*. New York: Oxford University Press.

Dretske, Fred. 1970. "Epistemic Operators." *Journal of Philosophy* 67, pp. 1007–23.

—— 1971. "Conclusive Reasons." *Australasian Journal of Philosophy* 49, pp. 1–22.

Duggan, Timothy and Gert, Bernard. 1979. "Free Will as the Ability to Will." *Noûs* 13, pp. 197–217. Reprinted in Fischer, ed., 1986.

Feinberg, Joel. 1980. *Rights, Justice, and the Bounds of Liberty: Essays in Social Philosophy*. Princeton: Princeton University Press.

Fine, Kit. 1975. "Critical Notice: *Counterfactuals*." *Mind* 84, pp. 451–8.

Fingarette, Herbert. 1972. *The Meaning of Criminal Insanity*. Berkeley: University of California Press.

Fodor, J. A. 1980. "Methodological Solipsism Considered as a Research Strategy in Cognitive Psychology." *Behavioral and Brain Sciences* 3, pp. 63–109.

—— 1982. "Cognitive Science and the Twin-Earth Problem." *Notre Dame Journal of Formal Logic* 23, pp. 98–118.

Foley, Richard. 1985. "What's Wrong with Reliabilism?" *The Monist* 68, pp. 188–202.

Frankfurt, Harry G. 1969. "Alternate Possibilities and Moral Responsibility." *Journal of Philosophy* 66, pp. 829–39. Reprinted in Fischer, ed., 1986.

—— 1971. "Freedom of the Will and the Concept of a Person." *Journal of Philosophy* 68, pp. 5–20. Reprinted in Fischer, ed., 1986.

—— 1976. "Identification and Externality." In A. O. Rorty, ed., 1976, pp. 239–51.

—— 1987. "Identification and Wholeheartedness." In F. Schoeman, ed., 1987, pp. 27–45. Reprinted in Fischer and Ravizza, eds, 1993.

—— 1988. *The Importance of What We Care About: Philosophical Essays*. New York: Cambridge University Press.

Freddoso, Alfred J. 1988. "Introduction." In Luis De Molina, *On Divine Foreknowledge* (Part IV of the *Concordia*). Trans. by A. Freddoso. Ithaca: Cornell University Press.

French, Peter A., Uehling, Theodore E., Jr., and Wettstein, Howard K., eds 1979. *Midwest Studies in Philosophy IV: Studies in Metaphysics*. Minneapolis: University of Minnesota Press.

—— eds 1980. *Midwest Studies in Philosophy V: Studies in Epistemology*. Minneapolis: University of Minnesota Press.

—— eds 1985. *Midwest Studies in Philosophy X: Studies in the Philosophy of Mind*. Minneapolis: University of Minnesota Press.

Gibbard, Alan. "Decision Matrices and Instrumental Expected Utility." (Unpublished paper presented at the University of Pittsburgh.)

Gibbard, Alan and Harper, W. L. 1978. "Counterfactuals and Two Kinds of Expected Utility." In C. A. Hooker et al., 1978, pp. 125–62.

Gibson, Mary, ed. 1983. *To Breathe Freely*. Totowa, N.J.: Rowman and Allanheld.

Ginet, Carl. 1966. "Might We Have No Choice?" In Keith Lehrer, ed., 1966, pp. 87–104.

—— 1980. "The Conditional Analysis of Freedom." In Peter van Inwagen, ed., 1980, pp. 171–86.

—— 1983. "In Defense of Incompatibilism." *Philosophical Studies* 44, pp. 391–400.

—— 1990. *On Action*. Cambridge: Cambridge University Press.

Glover, Jonathan. 1970. *Responsibility*. New York: Humanities Press.

—— 1984. *What Sort of People Should There Be?* Harmondsworth, UK: Penguin.

Goldman, Alvin. 1970. *A Theory of Human Action*. Englewood Cliffs, N.J.: Prentice-Hall.

—— 1976. "Discrimination and Perceptual Knowledge." *Journal of Philosophy* 73, pp. 771–91.

Harper, William L., Stalnaker, Robert, and Pearce, Glenn, eds 1981. *Ifs*. Dordrecht: D. Reidel.

Hasker, William. 1985. "Foreknowledge and Necessity." *Faith and Philosophy* 2, pp. 121–57.

—— 1989. *God, Time, and Knowledge*. Ithaca: Cornell University Press.

Herman, Barbara. 1981. "On the Value of Acting from the Motive of Duty." *Philosophical Review* 90, pp. 359–82.

Hobart, M. E. 1934. "Free Will as Involving Determinism and Inconceivable Without It." *Mind* 43, pp. 1–27.

Hoffman, Joshua, and Rosenkrantz, Gary. 1980. "On Divine Foreknowledge and Human Freedom." *Philosophical Studies* 37, pp. 289–96.

—— 1984. "Hard and Soft Facts." *Philosophical Review* 93, pp. 433–42. Reprinted in Fischer, ed., 1989.

Hoffman, Paul. "Freedom and Strength of Will: Descartes and Albritton." (Unpublished Manuscript, University of California, Riverside.)

Honderich, Ted, ed. 1973. *Essays on Freedom of Action*. Boston: Routledge and Kegan Paul.

Hooker, C. A., Leach, J. J., and McClennan, E. F., eds 1978. *Foundations and Applications of Decision Theory*. Dordrecht: D. Reidel.

Horgan, Terence. 1977. "Lehrer on 'Could'-Statements." *Philosophical Studies* 32, pp. 403–11.

—— 1979. "Could', Possible Worlds, and Moral Responsibility." *Southern Journal of Philosophy* 17, pp. 345–58.

—— 1981. "Counterfactuals and Newcomb's Problem." *Journal of Philosophy* 78, pp. 331–56.

—— 1985. "Newcomb's Problem: A Stalemate." In R. Campbell and L. Sowden, eds, 1985, pp. 223–34.

Jackson, Frank. 1977. "A Causal Theory of Counterfactuals." *Australasian Journal of Philosophy* 55, pp. 3–21.

Johnson, Oliver A. 1991. "'Is' and 'Ought': A Different Connection." *Journal of Value Inquiry* 25, pp. 147–60.

Joyce, James. 1961. *Ulysses*. New York: Random House.

Kavka, Gregory S. 1980. "What is Newcomb's Problem About?" *American Philosophical Quarterly* 17, pp. 271–80.

Kenny, Anthony. 1973. "Freedom, Spontaneity, and Indifference." In T. Honderich, ed., 1973, pp. 87–104.

—— 1975. *Will, Freedom, and Power*. Oxford: Basil Blackwell.

—— 1979. *The God of the Philosophers*. Oxford: Clarendon Press.

Kretzmann, Norman. 1983. "Goodness, Knowledge, and Indeterminacy in the Philosophy of Thomas Aquinas." *Journal of Philosophy* 80, pp. 631–49.

Kvanvig, Jonathan L. 1986. *The Possibility of an All-Knowing God*. New York: St Martin's Press.

Lehrer, Keith, ed. 1966. *Freedom and Determinism*. New York: Random House.

—— 1968. "Cans Without Ifs." *Analysis* 29, pp. 29–32.

—— 1976. "'Can' in Theory and Practice: A Possible Worlds Analysis." In M. Brand and D. Walton, eds, 1976, pp. 241–70.

—— 1981. "Self Profile." In R. J. Bogdan, ed., 1981, pp. 3–104.

Levi, Isaac. 1975. "Newcomb's Many Problems." *Theory and Decision* 6, pp. 161–75.

Levin, Michael. 1979. *Metaphysics and the Mind–Body Problem*. Oxford: Clarendon Press.

Lewis, David. 1973. *Counterfactuals*. Cambridge, Mass.: Harvard University Press.

—— 1979a. "Counterfactual Dependence and Time's Arrow." *Noûs* 13, pp. 455–76.

—— 1979b. "Prisoner's Dilemma is a Newcomb Problem." *Philosophy and Public Affairs* 8, pp. 235–40.

—— 1981a. "Are We Free to Break the Laws?" *Theoria* 47, pp. 113–21.

—— 1981b. "Why Ain'cha Rich?" *Noûs* 15, pp. 377–80.

—— 1983. "New Work for a Theory of Universals." *Australasian Journal of Philosophy* 61, pp. 343–77.

—— 1986. *On the Plurality of Worlds*. Oxford: Basil Blackwell.

Locke, John. 1690/1894. *Essay Concerning Human Understanding*. Ed. by Alexander Campbell Fraser. Oxford: Clarendon Press.

MacIntyre, Alasdair. 1957. "Determinism." *Mind* 66, pp. 28–41.

Marcus, Ruth Barcan. 1980. "Moral Dilemmas and Consistency." *Journal of Philosophy* 77, pp. 121–36.

Morris, Herbert. 1973. "Persons and Punishment." In Jeffrie G. Murphy, ed., 1973, pp. 40–64.

Murphy, Jeffrie G., ed. 1973. *Punishment and Rehabilitation*. Belmont, Ca.: Wadsworth Publishing Co.

Murphy, Jeffrie G. and Hampton, Jean. 1988. *Forgiveness and Mercy*. New York: Cambridge University Press.

Nagel, Thomas. 1986. *The View from Nowhere*. New York: Oxford University Press.

Naylor, Margery Bedford. 1984. "Frankfurt on the Principle of Alternate Possibilities." *Philosophical Studies* 46, pp. 249–58.

Neely, Wright. 1974. "Freedom and Desire." *Philosophical Review* 83, pp. 32–54.

Nozick, Robert. 1969. "Newcomb's Problem and Two Principles of Choice." In N. Rescher, ed., 1969, pp. 114–46.

—— 1981. *Philosophical Explanations*. Cambridge, Mass.: Harvard University Press.

Ockham, William of. 1969. *Predestination. God's Foreknowledge, and Future Contingents*. Trans. by Marilyn McCord Adams and Norman Kretzmann. New York: Appleton-Century-Crofts.

O'Connor, Timothy. 1993. "On the Transfer of Necessity." *Noûs* 27, pp. 204–18.

O'Shaugnessy, Brian. 1980. *The Will: A Dual Aspect Theory*. Cambridge: Cambridge University Press.

Pike, Nelson. 1965. "Divine Omniscience and Voluntary Action." *Philosophical Review* 74, pp. 27–46. Reprinted in Fischer, ed., 1989.

—— 1966. "Of God and Freedom: A Rejoinder." *Philosophical Review* 75, pp. 369–79.

—— 1984. "Fischer on Freedom and Foreknowledge." *Philosophical Review* 93, pp. 599–614.

—— 1993. "A Latter-Day Look at the Foreknowledge Problem." *International Journal for Philosophy of Religion* 33, pp. 129–64.

Plantinga, Alvin. 1986. "On Ockham's Way Out." *Faith and Philosophy* 3, pp. 235–69. Reprinted in Fischer, ed., 1989.

Pollock, John. 1976. *Subjunctive Reasoning*. Dordrecht: D. Reidel.

Putnam, Hilary. 1975. *Mind, Language, and Reality*. Cambridge: Cambridge University Press.

Quinn, Philip L. 1985. "Plantinga on Foreknowledge and Freedom." In J. Tomberlin and P. van Inwagen, eds, 1985, pp. 271–87.

Railton, Peter. 1984. "Alienation, Consequentialism, and the Demands of Morality." *Philosophy and Public Affairs* 13, pp. 134–71.

Ravizza, Mark. 1991. *Moral Responsibility and Control: An Actual-Sequence Approach*. Doctoral Dissertation, Yale University.

—— (forthcoming). "Semicompatibilism and the Transfer of Non-responsibility." *Philosophical Studies*.

—— "Is Responsiveness Sufficient for Moral Responsibility?" (Unpublished Manuscript.)

Rawls, John. 1973. *A Theory of Justice*. Cambridge, Mass.: Harvard University Press.

Rescher, Nicholas, ed. 1968. *Studies in Logical Theory*. Oxford: Basil Blackwell.

—— ed. 1980. *Essays in Honor of Carl G. Hempel*. Dordrecht: D. Reidel.

Rorty, Amelie O., ed. 1976. *The Identities of Persons*. Berkeley: University of California Press.

Roth. M. D. and Ross, G., eds 1990. *Doubting: Contemporary Perspectives on Skepticism*. Norwell: Kluwer.

Rowe, William. 1980. "On Divine Foreknowledge and Human Freedom: A Reply." *Philosophical Studies* 37, pp. 429–30.

—— 1991. *Thomas Reid on Freedom and Morality*. Ithaca: Cornell University Press.

Russell, Bertrand. 1918. *Roads to Freedom: Socialism, Anarchism, and Syndicalism*. London: George Allen and Unwin Ltd.

Saunders, John Turk. 1966. "Of God and Freedom." *Philosophical Review* 75, pp. 219–25.

—— 1968. "The Temptations of 'Powerlessness'." *American Philosophical Quarterly* 5, pp. 100–8.

Schlick, Moritz. 1939. "When is a Man Responsible?" In *Problems of Ethics*. Trans. by David Rynin, pp. 143–56. New York: Prentice-Hall.

Schoeman, F., ed. 1987. *Responsibility, Character, and the Emotions: New Essays on Moral Psychology*. Cambridge: Cambridge University Press.

Sharples, R. W., ed. 1983. *Alexander of Aphrodisias on Fate*. London: Duckworth.

Shatz, David. 1985. "Free Will and the Structure of Motivation." In P. French et al., eds, 1985, pp. 451–82.

—— 1988. "Compatibilism, Values, and 'Could Have Done Otherwise'." *Philosophical Topics* 16, pp. 151–200.

Shope, Robert. 1984. "Cognitive Abilities, Conditionals, and Knowledge: A Response to Nozick." *Journal of Philosophy* 81, pp. 29–48.

Skinner, B. F. 1953. *Science and Human Behavior*. New York: Macmillan.

Slote, Michael. 1980. "Understanding Free Will." *Journal of Philosophy* 77, pp. 136–51. Reprinted in Fischer, ed., 1986.

—— 1982. "Selective Necessity and the Free-Will Problem." *Journal of Philosophy* 79, pp. 5–24.

—— 1985. "Review of Peter van Inwagen's *An Essay on Free Will*." *Journal of Philosophy* 82, pp. 327–30.

Smart, J. J. C. 1961. "Free-will, Praise and Blame." *Mind* 70, pp. 291–306.

Stalnaker, Robert. 1968. "A Theory of Conditionals." In N. Rescher, ed., 1968, pp. 98–112.

—— 1981. "A Letter to David Lewis." In W. L. Harper et al., eds, 1981, pp. 151–2.

—— 1984. *Inquiry*. Cambridge, Mass.: MIT Press.

Strawson, Galen. 1986. *Freedom and Belief*. Oxford: Clarendon Press.

Strawson, Peter. F. 1962. "Freedom and Resentment." *Proceedings of the British Academy* 48, pp. 1–25. Reprinted in Fischer and Ravizza, eds, 1993.

Swanton, Christine. 1992. *Freedom: A Coherence Theory*. Indianapolis: Hackett

Publishing Company, Inc.

Swinburne, Richard. 1989. *Responsibility and Atonement*. Oxford: Clarendon Press.

Talbott, Thomas B. 1986. "On Divine Foreknowledge and Bringing About the Past." *Philosophy and Phenomenological Research* 46, pp. 455–69.

Thomson, Judith Jarvis. 1983. "Imposing Risks." In M. Gibson, ed., 1983, pp. 124–40.

Thorp, John. 1980. *Free Will: A Defence Against Neurophysiological Determinism*. London: Routledge and Kegan Paul.

Tomberlin, James E., ed. 1990. *Philosophical Perspectives IV: Action Theory and Philosophy of Mind*. Atascadero, Ca.: Ridgeview Publishing Company.

—— 1991. *Philosophical Perspectives V: Philosophy of Religion*. Atascadero, Ca.: Ridgeview Publishing Company.

—— 1992. *Philosophical Perspectives VI: Ethics*. Atascadero, Ca.: Ridgeview Publishing Company.

Tomberlin, James E. and van Inwagen, Peter, eds 1985. *Profiles: Alvin Plantinga*. Dordrecht: D. Reidel.

Van Inwagen, Peter. 1975. "The Incompatibility of Free Will and Determinism." *Philosophical Studies* 27, pp. 185–99.

—— 1979. "Laws and Counterfactuals." *Noûs* 13, pp. 439–53.

—— 1980. "The Incompatibility of Responsibility and Determinism." In M. Brady and M. Brand, eds, 1980, pp. 30–7. Reprinted in Fischer, ed., 1986.

—— ed. 1980. *Time and Cause: Essays Presented to Richard Taylor*. Dordrecht: D. Reidel.

—— 1983. *An Essay on Free Will*. Oxford: Clarendon Press.

—— 1990. "When is the Will Free?" In J. Tomberlin, ed., 1990, pp. 399–422.

—— (forthcoming). "When the Will is Not Free." *Philosophical Studies*.

Vogel, Jonathan. 1990. "Are There Counterexamples to the Closure Principle?" In M. D. Roth and G. Ross, eds, 1990, pp. 13–27.

Watson, Gary. 1975. "Free Agency." *Journal of Philosophy* 72, pp. 205–20. Reprinted in Fischer, ed., 1986.

—— 1987a. "Free Action and Free Will." *Mind* 96, pp. 145–72.

—— 1987b. "Responsibility and the Limits of Evil." In F. Schoeman, ed., 1987, pp. 256–86. Reprinted in Fischer and Ravizza, eds, 1993.

Widerker, David. 1987. "On an Argument for Incompatibilism." *Analysis* 47, pp. 37–41.

—— 1989a. "Two Fallacious Objections to Adams' Hard/Soft Fact Distinction." *Philosophical Studies* 57, pp. 103–7.

—— 1989b. "Two Forms of Fatalism." In Fischer, ed., 1989, pp. 97–110.

—— 1990. "Troubles with Ockhamism." *Journal of Philosophy* 87, pp. 462–80.

Wierenga, Edward. 1989. *The Nature of God: An Inquiry into Divine Attributes*. Ithaca: Cornell University Press.

Wiggins, David. 1973. "Towards a Reasonable Libertarianism." In

T. Honderich, ed., 1973, pp. 31–62.

Wolf, Susan. 1980. "Asymmetrical Freedom." *Journal of Philosophy* 77, pp. 151–66. Reprinted in Fischer, ed., 1986.

—— 1990. *Freedom Within Reason.* New York: Oxford University Press.

Zemach, Eddy and Widerker, David. 1988. "Facts, Freedom, and Foreknowledge." *Religious Studies* 23, pp. 19–28. Reprinted in Fischer, ed., 1989.

Zimmerman, Michael J. 1988. *An Essay on Moral Responsibility.* Totowa, N.J.: Roman and Littlefield.

Index